To M, from J ;

G000137495

The Home Book
of
Vegetarian Cookery

The Home Book of
VEGETARIAN COOKERY

N. BERRY HIGHTON
and
ROSEMARY B. HIGHTON

FABER AND FABER

3 Queen Square

London

First published in 1964
by Faber and Faber Limited
3 Queen Square London W.C.1
Second impression November 1964
Third impression 1971
Printed in Great Britain by
Latimer Trend & Co Ltd Whitstable

ISBN 0 571 05910 4

TO
OUR PARENTS

The line drawings are by Yvonne Skargon

Contents

Authors' Introduction

During a programme on B.B.C. Television Lord Reith was asked: 'What have you enjoyed most about your life and work?' or words to this effect, and his reply was one to remember, because he said he had been happiest when 'extended' to his greatest capacity, so that all his gifts had been employed and used to their utmost. We feel that this book has 'extended' us, and in consequence it has been a wonderful experience (although sometimes, with a young family, hectic!). It has made us realize how much we know and how much more there is to learn; it has reaffirmed and strengthened our beliefs about food and living in general, which can often be so buried in everyday life that one tends to forget and take them for granted. It has been so rewarding for us that we hope a little of this feeling has spilled over into the book itself. It may thus the more help you who read it and turn to it for advice.

When we were asked by the publishers to write this book we were at first very pleased—this was quickly followed by a certain amount of apprehension; there are many good vegetarian cookery books on the market, and others which, although they may not be written by or for vegetarians, can be used by them. In the end it was the title, *The Home Book of Vegetarian Cookery*, which gave us our lead. Nobody, we felt, had written a book about vegetarian cookery which presupposed that both cookery and vegetarianism were completely new to the reader. We have tried to do this in so far as it is possible for a book to fulfil this need, but we would stress that if you are quite new to cooking, any book of this nature has its

11

Introduction

limitations and nothing can equal *seeing* someone cooking, whether it is a demonstration in public or a friend cooking in his or her own home. We have therefore concentrated on basic recipes and proportions; giving the ingredients which can be used to vary the basic recipe. This is interesting, for you can now begin to see how to add variety to cooking for yourself, and most exciting as it is creative. If you know the basic recipe and the reasons for the method, then you can begin to experiment, judge other recipes and their possibilities and, if one can use the expression, 'know when you can break the rules'! In many books the beginner is confronted with page after page of recipes, none of which seem quite alike, whereas in actual fact many of them are derived from one simple recipe and method—it is so much easier to begin with the simple 'root' and then branch out. It is also easier to remember and understand if you know the reason for certain methods. We hope that those of you who are trained and experienced will bear with all the detail and even find something new among the recipes.

There are many reasons for being a vegetarian; but all of them mean that at some time or another one questions the generally accepted eating habits of one's country. Then we must arrive at a conclusion that satisfies us, if possible on all three planes of existence; remembering to keep an open mind, if we can, so that new ideas and findings may be considered and acted upon if they are convincing. Obviously this is a lonely process in so far as we each have to decide for ourselves what we feel is the best course to adopt, and, since we are individuals, our answers are unlikely to be the same. We have written from our own standpoint of lacto-vegetarianism with strong convictions regarding food reform and soil fertility, but we know that some of you will hold differing views.

If your opinions differ a lot from ours then we hope you will adapt the recipes herein to suit your own convictions and tastes. We should all enjoy our food if we are to get the best out of it and we can only enjoy it fundamentally if we are eating what we consider to be right. It is very interesting that once one begins to question, one thing leads to another, so in all charity let us just

Introduction

say that some of us may have questioned more, and some less, than others.

Now we must thank, with warmest gratitude, those people without whom this book would have been much more difficult to write. First, all the people who looked after the family so that we could write, especially 'D', Mrs. Cooper, Hilary and many more. Second, those who read and corrected the manuscript, Mummy and Pa. Last but not least, all the people who have written about vegetarianism, food reform, soil fertility and natural methods of healing; they have given us and many others 'furiously to think'.

Guildford,
March 1963

I

The Kitchen

For a woman who is a housewife, the kitchen is not only her workshop, but the place where she spends about a third of her day and it is the hub of the household during this time.

Thus the kitchen should be well planned both for comfort and for cooking. It should be a cheerful, pleasant room where one is happy to be. Most of our kitchens are already built, so we have to make the best of them; this can be an exciting challenge. Some of us are lucky enough to be able to plan and build exactly what we want. We should like to write a little about kitchen planning and what is generally referred to as 'time and motion' study. It is most important to save energy and time; and so leave one less frustrated with the chores and with more time to devote to the family, creative cookery, one's job, or whatever other interests there may be. We wish to indicate the main points and awaken your interest to study this subject by means of books and kitchen displays.

To explain everything fully would be outside the scope of this book and experts have already dealt very fully with these subjects.

KITCHEN PLANNING

If possible this should run like this: back door—food storage—work space—sink—work space—cooking stove, refrigerator—more work space if you want it and have room. Whether all this is along one, two or three walls depends on the size and shape of the kitchen. We feel that large kitchens are very pleasing but the cooking and preparation areas may be situated too far apart, thus

15

increasing the running about. Many people prefer to site the kitchen table in the centre of the kitchen, but we feel that we are always walking round it! On the other hand a very small kitchen, if it is used a great deal, can be very restricting, awkward and make storage difficult.

Food storage

This usually comprises a larder or ventilated cupboard (which should face north if possible), cupboards for storing dry foodstuffs, racks for fruit and vegetables and sometimes a refrigerator. If at all possible site these near the back door for ease when unloading the shopping, or try to group them together. There should also be a cupboard near the stove for the dry stores in constant use.

Working space

This should be a flat, hard-wearing surface of easily cleaned material. Today this usually means utilizing the tops of cupboards which stand against the walls and are at working height. The standard height is 3 feet and nearly all kitchen units and cookers are made to this specification. It is very pleasing to enter a kitchen and see a clean unbroken working surface. However it is better to arrange a lower surface for such tasks as beating, and creaming and chopping. We are 5 ft. 7 in. and 5 ft. 10 in. respectively and the 3-foot level suits us for most but not all preparation.

Sinks

The material of which they are made is a matter of personal choice; we were lucky enough to start with a double stainless steel sink and we would not change it for anything else, but there are very good and less expensive materials on the market. If you can afford it, and have the room, a double sink is a great blessing. Where, and how many draining-boards depends on the size of the kitchen; they can also be used as working surfaces in a small kitchen.

Lighting

This is of major importance; ideally there should be a light over the sink and cooker, as well as a general light, especially in a large kitchen. The sink is usually placed under the window for obvious reasons, but one tends to forget the winter evenings when artificial light is necessary. While on the subject of lighting we should mention power points. When we were altering our kitchen we had eight power points put in (including the mains switch for an electric cooker which incorporates a power point) much to the amusement of all concerned, but we insisted and we have uses for all of them.

Flooring

This is a matter of personal choice. There is no ideal kitchen flooring. It is a case of balancing the disadvantages against the advantages in each case.

Cupboards

All cupboards should be finished so that they are easily cleaned. When planning cupboard space it is wise to allow for more than immediate requirements. Try to arrange that the china cupboard and cutlery drawer are near the sink unit. The cooking-tins, dishes and saucepans should be stored near the cooker or sink; the dry stores and cookery equipment should be near the working surfaces between sink and stove or wherever most of the cookery preparation is done.

Adjustable shelving is a great help and we have a small gadget to hold all the small bottles and jars of spices and flavourings, etc., which is very useful. It looks rather like a small staircase and enables us to see clearly what varieties and quantities are there. For larger jars one step is enough; it is a mistake to have large jars more than two deep as they are difficult to get at and one cannot see what is there without time-wasting movement.

The cooker

We left this until the last as it is so important. What kind of cooker you have—gas, electric or solid fuel—depends on personal preference and the type of supply available. Careful and prolonged consideration should be given to the choice of cooker; first: look at the showrooms; second: try to find someone who has practical experience of the one you have in mind and ask their opinion; they may even allow you to try it; third: do be quite certain you have seen all the models available. If you live near London we suggest you visit the Design Centre. There are also model kitchens in all the big stores and last but not least there is the mine of information given by the Consumers' Association. The latter can also help a great deal with the kitchen as a whole and if you are starting from scratch and doing your own planning the Building Centre in London is a great help.

Today, all cookers are thermostatically controlled and much easier to clean; many have eye-level grills. There is a growing tendency to place ovens at eye-level as well. If you are choosing manufactured fitted cupboards for your kitchen you will find that most modern cookers will pleasingly accord with them.

Guide to oven temperatures

In this book we have followed the system:

Electric ° F.	Gas thermostat marking
200	½ very cool
225	1 slow oven
250	
275	2 slow oven
300	
325	3 moderate
350	4 moderate
375	5 moderate
400	6 moderate—hot
425	7 hot
450	8 very hot

This is an approximate but convenient system. Each make of gas-cooker has its own system of thermostat marking (although many now follow the B.S.I. scale); electric-cookers are usually marked in ° F. However, each individual cooker has its own variations (usually very slight) and the user gets to know them by experience.

If you are following our recipes using a new cooker, we would suggest you compare this simplified scale with the manufacturers' instructions and follow their advice. We have tried to give a simple description of the appearance of the finished dish when cooked and this is one of the best guides. It is very difficult to give an exact cooking time for the various dishes; so much depends on the size of the dish and where it is placed in the oven. Some dishes are very tolerant and may be cooked fairly slowly at a slow to medium heat or more quickly in an hot oven; it is really a matter of experience and common sense. An economy is effected if you plan your meal so that most of it is cooked in the oven, or it is all cooked on the top of the stove. It can be quite expensive to heat the oven for one dish.

General decoration

Colour schemes are a matter of personal taste, but try to have everything easily cleaned without being too clinical, i.e. white tiles. A kitchen should be a cheerful place, not one you are glad to leave. Try to have something beautiful to look at. If you are lucky this can be the view from the window, or plants on the window-sill, an interesting calendar or a small indoor herb garden; there are a number of such amenities. The kitchen is, however, really a workshop. We have a convenient corner for cookery books, a file in which we collect favourite recipes and new recipes, a book in which we make notes of the meals we have provided for visitors (this saves us the ghastly feeling, on a third or fourth visitation, of having given our friends a similar meal last time they came!) and a small desk or table on which to write and plan either meals or the household budget. An adjustable stool is useful— 'never stand when you can sit' is a good piece of advice for the busy housewife who can otherwise be on her feet all day.

Time and Motion study

We are both lucky in that we had a strict training in cookery methods. No matter how much one may resent this when young, habits are formed which one uses later without realizing, such as using a knife correctly and so on.

The first essential is to plan the kitchen in such a way that

The Kitchen

walking is reduced to a minimum—we have already indicated a basic plan for the essential fittings and mentioned that utensils and food should be kept near the place where they will be used.

The second item is to check that at the commencement of a cookery or preparation process you have the various pots, bowls, plates, etc. in a position which enables the work to flow easily. The easiest way to explain this is by examples:

1. *Preparing apples for purée*

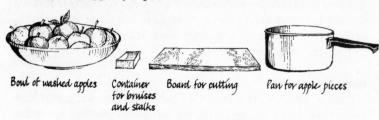

Bowl of washed apples   Container for bruises and stalks   Board for cutting   Pan for apple pieces

If you are left-handed reverse the order.

If the container for the bruised pieces and stalks is small, this can be placed in front of the bowl for the washed apples. This is a very simple example and many people will have already worked this out, nevertheless, it is amazing how many people would put the apples in the middle, travel to the left for the stalks, bits and chopping, and then return to the right for the saucepan; thus increasing the work by 50 per cent.

2. *Egg and breadcrumbing for deep fat frying*

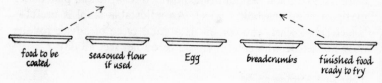

food to be coated   seasoned flour if used   Egg   breadcrumbs   finished food ready to fry

Most people feel that this process is long, lengthy and messy— it can be! If, however, you prepare everything as shown in the diagram and work methodically you will be surprised at the speed with which this can be accomplished. If the amounts of food are

20

The Kitchen

small, or working space is limited, rearrange the dishes as shown by the dotted lines.

Thirdly, take some time in planning your meals—both as to what you will be eating and then some sort of work plan for each meal so that each dish is ready at the right time. If you are new to cooking it is a good idea to write all this down, very roughly, until the system is fixed in your mind. It is then quite simple to do it in your head; although for a dinner-party we still jot down the menu and make a work plan. There are two points that should be mentioned for beginners:

1. Do start heating the oven so that it will be hot in time for the dish to be placed in it.

2. Try to collect everything you will need before you actually start preparation and work. If you have a mixing machine do another job whilst the machine is working; if you have not it is good to do all weighing of ingredients and greasing of pans before you start cooking.

Vegetarian and Food Reform Store Cupboard

The following foods can normally be obtained from the local health food store—if you have no health food store in your district you can try to get these foods by post or from a high-class grocer or delicatessen. If there is sufficient demand from the public for some foods on health food lines you will find the ordinary grocer will keep in stock some of the items; it is up to us to ask and make a good-humoured, polite but earnest request if necessary.

In our local town we have found a baker who bakes Allinson's Wholemeal bread (large and small) each day, another shop which has Prewett's loaves on Tuesdays and Fridays (large and small) and also have a large selection of health foods and herbal remedies, and a large combine store where we get yoghourt, cottage cheese and cultured cream if we have insufficient time to make our own. All this without having to make a fuss (thanks to others before us) and we are sure you will be able to trace or encourage a supplier locally if you try. The nearest vegetarian society help with information. Any reader who is a vegetarian and not Food Reform

21

need pay no heed to the brown flour, brown sugar, etc. Try not to buy too much at a time—it is much better to buy in small quantities (in particular little-used foodstuffs such as cereals or flavourings which lose their aroma) and replace with fresh when needed. This is only a sample list intended as a guide and you may have favourites which we have not mentioned.

Beverages

Tea: a stimulant which should be made as weak as possible and not allowed to stand, otherwise the tannin is extracted. There are many forms of herbal teas or tisanes which are beneficial to health, e.g. lime, peppermint and camomile. China tea (varieties) is better than the stronger Indian or Ceylon. Keep in an airtight tin or jar in a cool place.

Coffee: even more of a stimulant than tea—do not allow it to become habit-forming. Try the decaffeinated type particularly at night. It is better to buy the beans freshly roasted and grind them yourself than use the tinned types. Must be kept in an airtight and cool container or the aroma will be lost.

Instant postum: Keep jar tightly closed and cool.

Tinned fruits and vegetable juices: These are very much better freshly prepared—but are useful in emergencies. Keep cool, but chill if necessary.

Bottles of fruit juices: There are some excellent grape and apple juices on the market which have no added sugar. Grape juice in particular is good as the grapes are sun-ripened. Keep in a dark and cool place. Chill if necessary.

Cereals

Flour—try to obtain the compost-grown and freshly ground flours. The following kinds are available: 100 per cent wholemeal —plain or self-raising, either can be milled coarsely or fine; 81 per cent wholemeal (bran only sifted out)—plain or self-raising. You will find the 81 per cent can be substituted in most cases for the white flour and is so much better dietetically. Keep in the cool and dark. Use and replace regularly.

Pearl barley and whole barley flakes: used in soups and milk puddings. Store in an airtight container in the dark and in a cool place.

Wholemeal macaroni: keep in a dark and cool place.

Oatmeal: can be obtained compost-grown either medium or coarse. Buy in small amounts and replace regularly. Store in an airtight tin or jar in a dark and cool place.

Rice: buy only natural rice—it can be used for all purposes. Store in an airtight container, cool and dark.

There are other whole-grain cereals available, e.g., barley flakes, crushed wheat, and these should be stored as above.

Raising agents for flour

Yeast—this is the best and most natural. Either buy fresh yeast from the baker (this will last 4–5 days kept cool in the refrigerator) or if this is difficult buy dried yeast which works just as well. Keep the tin in a cool place.

Baking powder: use as little as possible—buy in small amounts and keep in an airtight tin in a cool place.

Bicarbonate of soda and cream of tartar: again use as little as possible but it is preferable to baking powder. Chemists stock the chemically purest form.

Dried Fruits

If stored in a dark cool place these keep well, but if they are left in the warm they tend to shrivel; in a damp place they may ferment after a month or two. It is better therefore to buy them as required, in very small amounts. The best kinds of dried fruit are those which have been sun-dried and not treated with sulphur at all—these have a very poor appearance and look inferior in quality to the sulphured fruits but they are much better for us. They can be obtained from health food stores but not, generally, elsewhere. If the dried fruit has a whitish incrustation this is natural sugar, not mould. If you are unable to obtain the sun-dried fruit, pour boiling water over the sulphured fruit and then dry it slowly in a warm place. Use immediately. The following dried fruits are usually obtainable:

currants	raisins with or	apple rings (home-made best)
bananas	without stones	apricots
prunes	pears	dried fruit salad (it is an
figs	dates	economy to mix own)
peaches	sultanas	

We do not recommend either glacé cherries, as they are bleached, dyed and then preserved in a heavy white sugar syrup; or candied peel as this is also coated with a heavy white sugar syrup.

There are some very good fruitarian cakes made which are usually a mixture of dried fruits and nuts and can be used as substitutes for sweets.

Flavourings

Today, most people use artificial flavourings without question. Where cooking is regarded as an art this is looked upon with horror; anybody with a good palate can taste how inferior these artificial flavourings are.

May we suggest the following:

Almond: it is very difficult to find real almond essence, we have only found it in good chemists, and this was some time ago. It is better to use almond cream or ground almonds.

Chocolate: use the raw sugar chocolate (either milk or plain). This can be chopped, grated or melted and is better than anything else. If you want cocoa, be sure to buy the unsweetened kind and buy the best quality available. There should be a list of the contents on the tin or packet—avoid any with added flavouring or colouring.

Coffee: this is easily made from powdered coffee decaffeinated or not as desired; just mix a teaspoonful or so with a little boiling water.

Dried herbs: these should be kept in small amounts in airtight containers, preferably in the dark and definitely in the cool. Keep only those in regular use and remember, if you have a garden, that fresh herbs are best. Dried herbs should be used sparingly as they are more pungent than fresh herbs:

bay leaves	marjoram	sage
chervil	mint	savoury
celery seed	parsley	thyme (and lemon
mace	mixed herbs	thyme)

are the usual herbs.

Special dried herbs for curry: see Curry section.

Orange and lemon: it is far better to use the grated rind (zest) of the lemon or orange fruit or to infuse slivers of the zest in liquid. However, one ought to be sure that the skin has not been dyed or treated chemically in any way—this is not easy to ascertain.

Vanilla: vanilla pods are easily obtainable these days and nothing is better for vanilla flavouring. These pods are from an orchid which originated in Mexico but is now grown freely in the tropics. The pods are gathered before they are ripe, dried in the shade and wrapped in oiled cloths or oiled paper to prevent them opening. The best are those which have fine white crystals on the surface, this proves they are fresh. The pods look like long thin black twigs and can be stored in an airtight jar on their own or better still in a jar packed with brown sugar. After a week or so the sugar will become vanilla sugar and can be used accordingly. To flavour milk the pod or piece of pod is infused in the milk for 10–20 minutes then dried and returned to the sugar jar. The pod is exhausted when there is no more flavour or smell and this depends on how often it has been used.

Real vanilla essence can be bought but one has to search high and low for it—a good chemist or a really high-class grocer or delicatessen will usually have it in stock. In some continental countries powdered vanilla is sold (we are not sure if this is available here). Use this as you would powdered spice.

Nuts

If shelled they should be stored in a cool dark place in airtight containers. If you have the time, buy nuts in the shell and shell them as required; they keep better thus and the flavour is far superior. This, however, approaches a counsel of perfection! Nuts in shell need only to be kept in a cool airy place.

The Kitchen

Nuts have a high oil content and tend to become bitter and rancid if they are kept too long. Buy as and when required, keeping only a small amount in hand:

whole almonds	ground almonds	hazelnuts
brazil nuts	pistachio nuts	cashew nuts
walnuts	fresh cococut	desiccated coconut

Nut butters: are good for use with bread, in a savoury, or eaten with cooked vegetables.

Nut creams: can be bought at health food stores and can be used as they are, or diluted. They make a good substitute for custard or ordinary cream, and keep well without loss of food value; but if you can make your own they have a better flavour.

almond   cashew

Fruitarian cakes (see Dried Fruits)

Oils

Are good to use as they are natural unhardened fats which are easily digested. Olive oil is the best oil for deep fat frying (in our opinion) but some other oils are good, e.g.

deodorized peanut oil   sunflower seed oil

Preserves

Generally made with a large percentage of white sugar and should be used sparingly or avoided. If you like the flavour, some jams can be made at home using a mixture of brown sugar and honey. The only natural preserve is honey which contains wonderful health-giving properties and can be used as a sweetener in place of sugar. It has a natural activation not found in any other source of sweetness.

Pulses

The common types are as follows:

butter beans	haricot beans	lentils
dried peas	split dried peas	

The Kitchen

There are some very interesting dried beans available in delicatessen and health food stores which are great fun to use and with which one can experiment.

Seasonings

These must be used with great care because they can blunt the palate and so lead us to use more and more. We feel that they are useful to add variety to cooking for healthy people, but if there is any digestive trouble it is probably better not to use hot seasoning, i.e. hot peppers and mustard, as they can cause irritation of the digestive tract.

Aromatic seasonings require to be stored in the same way as spices.

curry paste	curry powder	continental or
pepper cayenne (very hot)	peppercorns	French
pepper paprika (mild)	white or black	mustard

Peppercorns should be freshly ground in a wooden mill; use sparingly as they are very pungent.

Salt—this should definitely be sea salt as it contains valuable trace elements, in particular iodine. If you would rather have finer salt, buy a wooden salt mill and grind it down. Vesop, marmite, yeastrel, vecon, etc. are all useful for seasoning, flavouring and adding food value to the diet.

Setting agents

Carrageen or Irish Moss. This is a small seaweed which is dried when gathered. It is very valuable because of the trace elements which it provides. It can be bought in powder form or under the trade name of Gelazone or as the dried seaweed. This is used for milk jellies or creamy sweets as it does not make such a clear jelly as agar-agar; it is also very good for thickening soups and sauces. It should be kept dry and stored in a cool place.

Agar-agar is also derived from seaweed but gives a clear jelly; it is therefore more useful for jellied vegetable stocks and pure fruit juices. Store in an airtight container in a dry, cool place.

The Kitchen

Spices

Special curry spices are mentioned in the section on Curries. These should be stored in the same way as seasonings, that is, in small amounts in airtight containers preferably kept in the dark and cool. The most commonly used spices are:

caraway seeds	cinnamon, ground or stick
cloves, whole or ground	ginger, ground
mixed spice	

Sugars and syrups

For those who believe in food reform we recommend only the unrefined dark brown, soft sugar and black treacle; also honey (listed under preserves). For very occasional use or for those vegetarians not interested in food reform there are the following:

caster sugar	granulated sugar	icing sugar
fine white sugar	coarse white sugar	powdered white sugar
golden syrup		

Tinned foods

If possible these should be used for emergencies only, as they will have lost some of their food value in preservation and will lose more if they are heated again. Always buy the best quality as the lacquer inside the tin will be good. Only buy foods tinned, which you cannot obtain frozen. Freezing is a better form of preservation. We do not recommend tinned fruits in syrup as the white sugar content is high. Tomatoes are said by most authorities to 'tin well' as they lose less food value than other fruits or vegetables.

If you 'can' your own surplus fruit this is very good and is a better method than bottling as the food is kept in the dark.

There are some pure tinned fruit juices on the market without added sugar, which may be better than the fresh juice. This is because the juice is canned immediately from sun-ripened fruit, whereas imported fruit has been picked green and ripened in the dark.

There is a very useful booklet obtainable through the London

Vegetarian Society which tells you what tinned foods are vegetarian.

The following are some of the tinned foods available:

vegetable soups

butter beans

double or triple concentrated tomato purée

fruits or vegetables

mixed vegetable juices

baked haricot and soya beans

spaghetti in tomato sauce

fruit juices

tomato juice

a large variety of nut savouries in various forms

Vinegar

We prefer to use lemon juice whenever possible. If you wish to use vinegar, use sparingly and use either apple vinegar or a good French wine vinegar.

The herb and garlic vinegars are useful for flavouring.

Larder and refrigerator

The larder can be a ventilated cupboard or a small room with its own door and window. It should be finished so that the walls and shelves are easily cleaned, for any place where food is kept should be scrupulously clean. The window should open for summer ventilation and coolness but it should be covered with a fine mesh screen which keeps out insects—flies and wasps in particular! If the larder is the coolest place, the fruit and vegetables can be kept there, and there are many good, easily cleaned vegetable racks on the market which allow air to circulate freely.

A refrigerator is extremely useful, especially in summer-time, but it is not essential. There are methods of keeping milk, butter, eggs, etc. cool, without one. If you feel that home-made ice cream is much better for health, or you are not able to cut your own fresh vegetables then a refrigerator really helps. Ideally, one should shop for fruit and vegetables every day but this is not always possible and fruit and vegetables lose less food value if kept very cool. Modern refrigerators have special drawers or containers for keeping salads, vegetables and fruit. If you have

The Kitchen

no refrigerator a covered container with a very little water in the bottom and a tight-fitting lid (a saucepan makes a good container) is the best way of keeping salad plants.

Refrigerators are really cool cabinets in which bacterial action practically ceases and there is hardly any loss of food value; it must be remembered that once food is taken out of the refrigerator and returns to normal room temperature, deterioration continues as before.

The freezing section (where the ice cubes are formed) may be used for making ice cream, and maintaining frozen foods. If you are keen to do your own 'home freezing' it is better to buy a separate 'deep freeze'.

It is necessary to clean the refrigerator regularly and defrost as needed. You should look in the refrigerator every day to make sure that foods are used up. Make sure that the temperature setting is right, foods being kept cool but not frozen. Slow freezing has a bad effect on fruits and vegetables. We find the refrigerator very useful for storing dairy produce, especially in the summer, but you must remember to take out fats and eggs prior to baking. Cheese can be kept in the larder during cold weather but keeps well in the less cool part of the refrigerator in the summer. If you haven't a refrigerator and want to keep milk and butter cool in the summer either purchase a cooler or stand them in a little cold water and cover with damp butter muslin, the ends of which are immersed in the water. Cheese can be hung in a bag of butter muslin so that air can circulate freely. We must admit it would be rather difficult to manage without a refrigerator especially as we now have a young family and no larder in our kitchen.

USEFUL KITCHEN EQUIPMENT

This is not a comprehensive list but a few simple things which we have found useful in our own kitchen and of which you may know very little. It is essential to have the correct tool for the job, well made and not just a gadget; collecting gadgets is fascinating but not worth the time or money.

The Kitchen

Machines

These are not essential but can be a great help. The most important in our experience is the juice extractor. It saves a great deal of time and is in constant use. Ours is a Gayelord Hauser which is good and easy to use.

If you make all your own cakes, biscuits, bread, soups, etc. an electric mixer is also invaluable. There are good large and small models available, but we would recommend you choose one which also has a liquidizer. This makes light work of soups, mayonnaise, french dressing and fruit purées, etc. The larger models have many more accessories. Vegetarians find the one for grating very useful.

Tools for cutting, grating and chopping

First and foremost you must have a good working surface on which to perform these tasks—formica is good but tends to damage the edge of the knives and also wears. We have a large board 19 in. × 14 in. and 1 in. deep made from well-seasoned beech. Seasoned wood is essential, otherwise the board warps badly when subjected to warmth and/or damp. One side of the board should be marked 'savoury' and the other, 'sweet'. We use each for the purpose described, rolling pastry on the one side, using the other for chopping.

Knives: today, stainless steel knives can be purchased with a very keen cutting edge.

The following are necessary:

1 vegetable knife	1 grapefruit knife
1 small French cook's knife	1 large French cook's knife
1 steel or good knife-sharpener	

Knives should be kept very sharp and if possible in a knife-rack hung on the wall out of the reach of children; this also prevents the edge from being blunted. Time is saved and work halved when knives are kept really sharp and used correctly. To watch a chef use a knife is an eye-opener and a carver in a kitchen looks after his knives like all true craftsmen who care for their tools.

The Kitchen

Graters

There are good stainless steel graters on the market costing less than £1, but if you have much grating to do it would be better to invest in a 'mill' with different-sized grating plates. A 'mill' looks like a mincer. There are a number of very useful hand graters made by French manufacturers which do fine grating. We use one for nuts and sometimes for cheese used to 'top' a dish.

Choppers

The best choppers we know are those which are enclosed. One simply pushes the handle down and the chopping blade rotates, inside a drum which houses it on three sides. The blade moves round a little each push of the handle. There is a large one for onions and vegetables. A chopped salad makes a pleasant change from a grated one. A smaller one is used for nuts, dried fruits and sweet things. The food must be prepared and cut into pieces of medium size before using the chopper. If the handle is pushed down just a few times the result is a coarse chopping, but the more one continues the finer is the end product.

Parsley, mint and herbs in general, are required in small amounts. We use a Mouli Parsmint and would not be without it; it is simple, easy to use and costs only a few shillings.

Chopping can be done with a French cook's knife by holding the point firmly on the chopping-board with the left hand (vice versa if you are left-handed) and then moving the handle of the knife fan-wise across the food to be chopped. Chop vigorously and when a semicircular section has been completed the food should be piled again and the operation repeated until the requisite fineness is achieved.

Saucepans

There is nothing to compare with stainless steel and it is heartening to see this metal gaining popularity, mainly through Scandinavian influence, so we hope the prices may soon be reduced!

We were fortunate to start our home with some stainless steel saucepans as a result of our stay in Norway. We were thus able to obtain the type we felt had the best features, namely:

The Kitchen

1. They are very attractive to look at, having copper bases for quick heat conduction.

2. They are made in many sizes.

3. For each size of saucepan two parts are obtainable as extras, a bowl-shaped part with two handles which transforms the pan into a double saucepan (the bowl can be lifted out and wiped and used as a serving dish). The other section has holes in the base, so that the saucepan can be used as a steamer.

4. There is an indentation in the rim in order that the lid shall fit well, and when the vegetables are almost cooked the heat can be turned off. The lid seals the saucepan with the condensed steam in this small rim, so that the vegetables cook in their own heat for 5–10 minutes longer. Frying-pans are also made in numerous sizes and with lids. We strongly recommend this type of pan to everyone and especially the young home makers, as the pans last a lifetime!

You will also need a deep fat pan and wire basket (if you do any frying) and a girdle is useful for making scones and some Eastern types of bread.

Tools for purées and sieving

If a mixture does not have to be sieved the liquidizer of an electric food mixer is very good, or failing that a 'Moulin-Legume' is the answer.

These can be bought in four or five sizes from the very tiny ones for babies' food to the largest size for hotels and guest houses. This machine, having a rotary paddle, eliminates sieving by hand, which saves time and effort. There are at least three different plates provided, with small, medium and large holes.

If you need to sieve very finely use a hair or nylon sieve and either the back of a wooden spoon or a 'mushroom'—this is a wooden presser shaped like a mushroom and saves time if you have much sieving to do.

Baking tins

A minimum list would read something like this:

The Kitchen

1 set of bun tins	2 sponge tins
1–2 baking sheets	2 bread tins
1 wire rack for cooling	2 cake tins (small and medium)

Many other shapes and sizes can be bought. We find the heat-proof glass dishes very good. They look good and are easy to clean, but like so many other good things in life they are expensive.

Baking will necessitate the following also:

A set of baking-bowls (those with a pouring lip, a graduated measure on the side and fireproof are ideal).

A pastry-board (we use our large chopping-board on the 'sweet' side).

Rolling-pin.

Cutters for biscuits, pastry and scones. Sets of both fluted and plain are desirable.

Kitchen scales (preferably balance, and not 'spring').

This is not a comprehensive list, but for the beginner is a 'basic necessities' indication.

Other important utensils

We have a set of stainless steel kitchen tools with rosewood handles which are very well made and consist of the following:

Soup ladle, a large server spoon with holes and one without potato-masher, omelette-turner, palette-knife, rotary whisk and a long-handled turner for shallow frying.

Smaller ladles are useful for serving sweet and savoury sauces

Wire whisks are better than the rotary type for beating sauces and cream. They may also be used instead of a rotary whisk for other items.

A colander for straining with a container beneath for keeping the stock. If possible find a container with a lid; we use the saucepan part of the double stainless steel saucepan and the saucepan lid; it is then easy to keep in the refrigerator or in a cool place.

Mincing machine—not essential, but it can give variety of

34

texture to a nut or vegetable savoury and it is very good for making breadcrumbs from dried bread.

A measure or set of measures; heat-proof glass if possible.

Glass lemon-squeezer.

A salad shaker—we have a French type which collapses to store flat, the cost was less than 10s. and if stood on its handles, drops down to form a basket in which the salad is placed.

Pair of kitchen scissors.

A continental peeler—takes off a very thin peel.

An ordinary peeler—good for orange- or lemon-rind.

Tin opener—a good wall fixture is probably the best but is more expensive.

Corkscrew.

Bottle opener.

Metal knives, forks and spoons.

Wooden spoons—the square ended are best for saucepan work. Mark the 'sweet' from the 'savoury' lest you have an egg custard tasting of onions! Round spoons are used for creaming and beating.

Sugar thermometer—this is useful for home-made sweets and measuring the temperature in the deep fat pan.

Baking dishes: we try to use dishes we can bake in and take straight to the table as this saves time and looks most decorative. There are many well-designed glass, porcelain, stoneware heat-proof dishes available in most stores nowadays. They may also be used for serving fruit, salads or cold sweets.

2

Cookery Terms and Processes

Au gratin

Originally this meant that the top of the dish was browned under the grill or in the oven, the white sauce was either sprinkled with breadcrumbs or grated cheese. Today it often means the food is coated with a cheese sauce as well.

Baking blind

A method used for baking empty flan cases. The pastry is covered with greaseproof paper and filled with crusts, beans, rice, etc. always kept for this purpose. When the flan is nearly cooked the paper and 'filling' are removed and the flan case is returned to the oven to complete the baking.

Blanching

Food is placed in cold water, brought to the boil and then drained. Some authorities recommend this method for vegetables (spinach and sprouts) before cooking, but we feel that it removes food value. Useful for removing almond skins and a modified method is used for peeling chestnuts.

Basting (see Roasting)

Blending

To blend is really to mix. A term generally used when a flour of any kind is mixed with a cold liquid prior to cooking.

Cookery Terms and Processes

Boiling

To boil is to cook in a boiling liquid, usually water, milk or stock. Sometimes the food should be cooked with the liquid boiling as fast as is possible, but usually the food is cooked with the liquid boiling steadily.

Braising

Originally braising was cooking with both top and bottom heat, nowadays it means first sautéing and then cooking with flavouring vegetables in stock.

Breadcrumbs

These are used either fresh or dried. Fresh breadcrumbs are made by crumbing bread with hands, grating it or if required very fine, rubbing the bread through a sieve. They are used in various forms of cookery and should be used immediately as they do not keep.

Dried breadcrumbs are used mainly as a coating for deep fat frying or sprinkled on top of au gratin dishes. To make them, cut some bread into pieces of even size (this is a good way to use stale pieces of bread) and dry in a cool oven until crisp and hard. Crush them with a rolling-pin, then put them through a mincer or grind them in a liquidizer. To keep well, put in an airtight jar in a cool place. They are sometimes called raspings.

Bouchées

Small round pastry cases which are filled with a variety of savoury or sweet fillings.

Bouquet garni

A bundle of herbs tied together with thread or clean string or in a small muslin bag (to facilitate later removal). The herbs are then used for flavouring soups, stews, gravies, etc. The classic bouquet garni is parsley stalks, sprig of thyme and a bay leaf, but one can also use a stick of celery, basil, mint, etc., depending on the flavouring required.

Cookery Terms and Processes

Caramel

Sugar boiled until at the 'toffee' stage (thick and syrupy) and used for flavouring.

Clarify

To clarify butter or margarine, melt the fat and heat very gently until it stops bubbling (which means all the water is driven off). Remove from the heat, skim if necessary and allow to stand for a few minutes. Then strain the fat through a sieve lined with butter muslin, into a jar, taking care not to disturb any sediment at the bottom. Cover the jar and keep in a cool place. This improves butter and margarine for frying purposes.

Coating

To coat something is to cover it with either a coating sauce, coating batter, egg and breadcrumbs, etc. It is important that the coating, if it is liquid, is of the correct consistency; if too thick it is really unpalatable; if too thin, it will not coat.

Creaming

To cream, means to work the ingredients together and then beat them so that an emulsion is formed and air is incorporated. This term is usually applied to the mixing of fats and sugars in cake-making but it is sometimes used for other ingredients.

Croquettes

Cork or cylindrical shapes of savoury foods, usually bread-crumbed and deep fat fried.

Croûtons

Literally little crusts. Small cubes of toasted or fried bread, usually served with soups.

Cutting and folding

This is done with a metal spoon and is used to add flour, egg-whites, cream, etc. to the main mixture. The idea is to add and incorporate another ingredient without losing too much of the air already beaten in. First add the ingredient then with the side of the spoon cut through the mixture several times towards you, then drawing the spoon across the bottom of the bowl, carefully turn the bottom on to the top. Repeat until the ingredients are mixed enough or completely.

Darioles

Small bucket-shaped metal moulds, used for individual sweets, cakes or savouries.

Dough

A mixture of flour and other ingredients, used mainly for bread, cake, biscuits and pastry-making. There are different textures of dough:

Firm—the dough can be handled and leaves the fingers and bowl clean, e.g. pastry.

Fairly soft—can still be handled but does not leave the fingers and bowl, e.g. scones.

Dropping consistency—soft dough which shakes off the spoon, e.g. creamed mixtures.

Pouring consistency—so that the mixture can be poured from the bowl, e.g. gingerbread and some sponges.

Flan

A case made of pastry, cooked potato or sponge which is filled with a savoury or sweet filling.

Frying

This is cooking in hot fat. There are two types of frying:

1. Shallow fat frying. This usually means just enough fat to cover the bottom of the pan or sufficient to cover half-way up the food. The fat can be olive oil, vegetable oil, nutter or vegetable fat; butter may also be used, it produces a fine flavour but must be watched carefully as it burns so easily.

2. Deep fat frying. This is done in a special thick and deep pan which is kept for frying only and has a fitting wire basket with a handle. The best frying medium is olive oil, and although because

Cookery Terms and Processes

expensive this may seem extravagant when beginning a fat bath, it is more economical than shallow fat frying in the long run. The olive oil must be of good quality and purchased in one large tin; it is cheaper than buying in many bottles. If olive oil is too expensive try vegetable oil or deodorized peanut oil instead, these give good results and are better than the hard vegetable fats as they have not been hardened in the factory. Deep fat frying is a much better form of frying than shallow fat frying as the food is coated and fried so quickly that the oil does not penetrate and the flavour of the food does not escape into the oil. It can thereby be strained and used again and again.

Even so, good digestions are needed for fried foods, which should not be included in the diet more than once a week.

Coatings for deep fat frying Egg and dried breadcrumbs, coating batter, milk and seasoned flour. Pastry and crushed vermicelli are used only occasionally.

Temperatures for deep fat frying It is useful to have a thermometer which will register for both sugar and fat boiling; this will eliminate guesswork for anyone who does not use the fat bath often.

Food to be cooked	° F	Other methods of gauging the temperature
Choux paste and doughnuts	340–370 rising gradually	Drop in a small cube of bread and if it rises and just frizzles it is ready.
First frying of potatoes	340	As above.
Croquettes, rissoles and fritters	370–385	A pale blue haze rises from the surface and the cube of bread browns in 1 minute.
Second frying of potatoes, croûtons, small fritters and fried parsley	390	The haze is thicker; care must be taken to immerse the food quickly or the oil may burn.

Cookery Terms and Processes

Other points to note when deep fat frying:

1. The oil should be strained after use to remove pieces of food left behind; but allow it to cool before straining.

2. The oil should not be allowed to burn (go dark brown) or it will give a most unpleasant flavour to the food—the oil may brown a little gradually but this usually disappears when the pan is topped up with new oil.

3. The oil will need to be topped up after it has been used several times; never add more if the old oil is badly discoloured but start afresh. Never fill the pan more than two-thirds full; this will allow for bubbling when the food is first immersed.

4. Fry only small pieces of food, and only a few at a time—this ensures not more than a small drop in temperature.

5. Do not put wet food into the pan as the fat will rise too quickly and may spill over and catch fire. If this happens, do not panic, but have at hand a baking-sheet or a flat piece of metal and place it quickly over the burning oil; the oil cannot continue to burn without air.

6. Drain the food after frying, first in the basket or with a strainer spoon and then on a rack or crumpled kitchen paper.

7. If possible serve food immediately. If you are unable to do so, keep it warm in a cool oven in an uncovered dish. If you cover fried foods they will become soft and lose crispness.

8. When frying foods which are covered with batter, doughnuts, choux paste, etc., do not use the wire basket as the food will stick to the basket. These foods first sink to the bottom of the pan and then rise.

9. Cover the pan after straining and keep in a cool place.

Garnish

Is a very important part of cookery because it presents the food more attractively. Forms of garnishing are described in the various chapters or in the section on garnishing; two points may be stressed here, (a) the garnish indicates of what the dish is made, (b) it should be edible.

Cookery Terms and Processes

Glaze

Is to give a shiny surface. It is usually brushed on at the end of cooking or just before the end, and may be of egg, water and sugar or syrup; or it may be a cold glaze, such as jelly for flans.

Grilling

To cook under a grill or salamander. Only small portions of food can be cooked in this way and are usually served with a flavoured butter of some kind.

Hors-d'œuvre

Small savouries and salads, served at the beginning of the meal.

Infuse

Tea-making is an example of infusing.

Liaison

The addition of starch (usually to a soup) to keep particles of food in suspension in a liquid without thickening.

Macédoine

Fruit or vegetables cut into small cubes.

Marinade

To soak fruit or vegetables in a liquid with herbs and spices to give good flavour.

Menu

A French word which translated as 'Bill of Fare' is used much more often than the English translation. To be correct 'menu' should be used, with the food named in French; whilst 'Bill of Fare' for descriptions in English.

Panada

A very stiff sauce made from a roux and liquid, used as a base for soufflés and croquettes.

Cookery Terms and Processes

Piping

This gives a decorative finish to many vegetable and other dishes. It is effected by means of a piping bag (cloth for large pipes or greaseproof paper for small pipes) and pipes either large or small. Large pipes are used for biscuits, meringues, creamed potatoes and occasionally for whipped cream. Small pipes are used for cakes, sweets, whipped cream and for decorating small savouries. To make greaseproof-paper piping bag:

Cut a square and fold into a triangle, then make a fold C–D. Fold B to C and then A to C to make a cone. Fold ABC down once or twice so that they are held together securely.

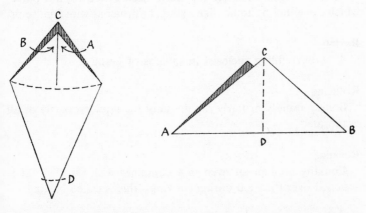

Cut off the tip at D so that the nozzle of the pipe is just clear of the paper. Fill half to two-thirds full with mixture to be piped. If a cloth piping bag is used twist the top and place the twisted part between the thumb and forefinger and against the palm; press the thumb towards the fingers so that the piping bag is caught securely. Fold over the fingers so that the mixture is squeezed out of the pipe, varying the pressure as required. If the mixture comes out of the top you have twisted the bag insufficiently at the top, or you are not gripping the bag between the thumb and forefinger sufficiently firmly. If a paper bag is used, fold over the top two or three times. Grip the fold with both hands (the pipe pointing away from you), the two forefingers forming a ledge

43

underneath and the thumb pressing on the top. Pipe as required; piping can be tremendous fun, and if you have not done any before, we suggest you practise on a baking-sheet with some creamed potato. You will be surprised to find how easy it is.

Poaching

Cooking in hot water which is just moving—the actual temperature is about 170–180° F., but one can tell by the movement of the water.

Purée

Fruit or vegetables after they have been sieved form a purée, which can either be liquid, like a soup, or firmer as with fruit fools.

Ravioli

A savoury filling enclosed in squares of pasta.

Reducing

Boiling rapidly or fairly rapidly until the liquid is partly or all evaporated.

Roasting

Cooking food in an oven in a container with fat. The fat is spooned over the food during cooking—this is called basting.

Roux

A mixture of melted fat with sufficient flour stirred in to make a soft paste. This is cooked gently for a few minutes for a white sauce, and for a brown sauce cooked gently until it browns; on no account allow it to burn.

Rubbing in

Generally means rubbing fat into flour. The fat is first cut into small pieces and then added to the sieved flour. The fat is gently rubbed into the flour with the *tips* of the fingers and thumbs; whilst carrying out this operation the hands are lifted out of the bowl allowing the mixture to fall back into the bowl. This is to keep the mixture as cool as possible; the cooler it is the better the final result.

Sautéing

Sauté literally means to jump. Either raw or cooked foods are tossed in melted fat (usually butter) until they are beginning to cook or until they are browned.

Seasoned flour

Flour with added seasoning, used to coat foods before frying.

Simmering

Cooking very slowly in water which is just below boiling point. The surface of the water is gently moving but only occasionally breaks into bubbles.

Skimming

Some soups and vegetables throw up a scum during the cooking process and this should be taken off with a spoon. Cream is skimmed from the top of milk which has been left to stand in a shallow bowl.

Steaming

Cooking food in steam from boiling water. It takes longer than other cooking methods. Steamed puddings are often partly steamed and partly boiled. They stand on a rack in boiling water to cook.

Stewing

Gentle slow cooking, in a suitable container, either on top of the stove or in the oven so that the pieces of food remain whole.

Stock

Liquid, usually water, in which vegetables have been cooked. Its use ensures that the natural salts dissolved in it are not wasted and it imparts flavour. It can be specially made, but is more usually the water in which vegetables or rice have been cooked.

Cookery Terms and Processes

Thermometer

Graduated to 400–450° F. or more. Very useful for deep fat frying and sugar boiling. When a new thermometer is bought 'prove' it by allowing it to stand in a saucepan of water which comes gradually to the boil, then allow it to cool in the water. Thermometers measure more accurately if brought to boiling-point in a saucepan of water and then placed in the hot fat, or syrup as it starts to boil. The thermometer should be returned to the pan of boiling water after use to reduce shock, and it helps to clean it.

Tutti-frutti

A mixture of many fruits.

Vol-au-vent

A 'puff of wind' by translation, but actually an oval case of flaky or puff pastry which is filled with a sweet or savoury filling; the case can be large or small.

To whip

This means to beat very well and quickly. Generally applied to egg-whites and cream, both of which become stiff with the added air. Whipping can be done with a rotary whisk or a wire whisk. To whip egg-whites: separate the whites from the yolks and place the whites in a dry scalded basin. Add a little sea-salt and whip with a dry scalded whisk until the egg-whites are stiff enough for the recipe. Whites whip badly if there is any grease present, and will never whisk really stiff if any yolk is present. The salt helps to drop the temperature slightly and so helps with the whisking.

To whip cream: this is best done with a wire whisk as the cream stiffens quickly and it can be over-beaten with the rotary type of whisk. Turn the cream into a basin; if it is stiff then add a little cream from the top of the milk or milk until it is runny but still thick-looking. Whisk well; it should thicken in 3–5 minutes if you have the knack of whisking in the air. If it thickens very quickly then add just a little more milk as whipped cream should be light

46

Cookery Terms and Processes

and fluffy. Be careful when taking cream to be whisked from the refrigerator as the cold appears to thicken the cream and you may add too much milk.

Zest

The thin coloured part of the rind of citrus fruits; the real essential oils are extracted from this part. The thick white part of the rind is the pith and as it is bitter should be avoided. The grated zest makes a good natural flavouring, unfortunately nowadays the skins are sometimes treated with chemicals which may be injurious. This creates a problem which each of us must resolve for ourselves—if you can be sure the zest has not been treated, no problem arises. If thin ribbons of zest are required for infusing, peel them off with an ordinary peeler.

MEASURING

Although, with experience, most people get a shrewd idea of the amount of an ingredient needed there are times when it is essential to weigh and measure accurately. The following tables may be of some help:

4 level teaspoons = 2 level dessertspoons = 1 level tablespoon
1 pint = 20 fluid oz.   1 gill = $\frac{1}{4}$ pint
$\frac{1}{2}$ pint = 10 fluid oz. $\frac{1}{2}$ gill = $\frac{1}{8}$ pint = 4 tablespoons
$\frac{1}{4}$ pint =   5 fluid oz. $\frac{1}{4}$ gill = $\frac{1}{16}$ pint = 2 tablespoons

An American pint is equal to 16 oz.
1 American cup for measuring is $\frac{1}{2}$ American pint =   8 fluid oz.
An English cup for measuring is $\frac{1}{2}$ English pint   = 10 fluid oz.
When buying scales choose a beam balance rather than a spring balance as these can become inaccurate with constant use. Also buy scales which measure to $\frac{1}{4}$ of an ounce. If you do much continental cookery it is good to invest in a pair of scale for weighing grams, decigrams and kilograms. If you can find a good pair of scales which are easily cleaned then you are very lucky!

47

Cookery Terms and Processes

When measuring teaspoons, dessertspoons and tablespoons, we find the level measure is more accurate. Many recipes use the following terms:

Rounded spoonfuls—this means as much above the bowl as below, so this is really 2 level teaspoons.

Heaped spoonfuls—as much as you can put on the spoon.

Cutlery does vary in size; if you want to be very accurate, buy a small set of plastic spoons which are made to B.S.I. standards.

To weigh syrup or honey: first weigh the pan or bowl in which it is going to be used, then increase the weights by the desired amount.

When a recipe states $\frac{1}{2}$ lb. of pastry, this is pastry made with $\frac{1}{2}$ lb. of flour. Likewise $\frac{1}{2}$ a pint of sauce, is made with $\frac{1}{2}$ a pint of liquid and so on.

A pinch is as much as can be held between thumb and forefinger.

A good pinch is as much as can be held between two or three fingers and thumb.

Amounts of food needed per person

This list is intended as a guide for those who may be cooking something for the first time and may not have much general cooking experience. It must be used with common sense, e.g. if you are only serving one vegetable with a savoury, you must allow more; if you are giving a dinner-party with several courses then less of each item will be required. Naturally, people have special likes and dislikes and these too, must be allowed for.

	Per person
Soup	$\frac{1}{4}$–$\frac{1}{3}$ pint
Sauces	$\frac{1}{8}$–$\frac{1}{4}$ pint
Rice ⎫	
Macaroni ⎬	1–2 oz.
Oatmeal ⎭	
Pulses	2–3 oz.
Cooked fruits	4–6 oz.

	Per person
Fresh fruits	about 2–3 fruits, e.g. apple, pear and peach
	¼ pineapple or melon
	¼–½ lb. grapes
	¼–½ lb. strawberries, cherries, raspberries
Puddings and pastry	1½–2 oz. flour
Junkets and milk sweets	¼–⅓ pint
Batters, pancakes and Yorkshire puddings	1–2 oz.
Lettuce, endive, batavian, cos	½ large or 1 small
Tomatoes	2
Watercress, mustard and cress	½ bundle or punnet
Cucumber	¼
Chicory	2 small or 1 large
Artichokes, globe	1
Artichokes, Jerusalem	4–6 oz.
Asparagus	8 oz.
Broad beans for shelling	¾ lb.
Broad beans, mange tout ⎫ French and Runner beans ⎭	6–8 oz.
Beetroot, cooked	4–6 oz.
Brussels sprouts	8 oz.
Cabbage ⎫ Turnip tops ⎪ Spring greens ⎬ Savoys ⎪ Curly kale ⎭	8 oz.
Carrots	6 oz.
Celeriac	6 oz.
Celery	½ large head or 1 small
Kohl rabi ⎫ Onions ⎬ Parsnips ⎭	6 oz.
Green peas	8 oz.

Cookery Terms and Processes

	Per person
Potatoes	6 oz.
Seakale	4 oz.
Spinach	12 oz.
Turnips and Swedes	6 oz.

3
Beginnings

This may seem an unusual chapter heading but we wanted a term which would cover all the foods which can be served at the beginning of a meal, thus turning a two-course meal into a three- or four-course meal. There are so many other terms for first courses, that even the experts seem to have difficulty in naming them. Some of these beginnings such as soups and salads can of course be meals in themselves and not necessarily initial items on dinner menus only. If one is planning a dinner with the main course as a hot savoury and cooked vegetables, it is a good plan to start the meal with something fresh. Whether this is fruit, salad or juices depends on the remainder of the meal and also on personal tastes. Here are some suggestions:

FRUIT AND VEGETABLE JUICES

When served at the beginning of lunch or dinner these are usually called fruit or vegetable cocktails and are served in medium to small wineglasses. But this is not the only use for these juices, they are the perfect answer to our over-refined and 'processed' food. They supply us with minerals and vitamins in an easily assimilated form—it is far easier to drink the juice from six carrots than to have to chew six carrots!

This does not mean that we should neglect salads and fruits. We need the roughage and nature's way of obtaining the juices is for these foods to be crushed by the teeth when eaten. How good and decay-avoiding it is for the teeth too! This means that

51

as soon as the cells are broken open and the juices released, digestion starts and oxidation which destroys some food value is prevented. It is on account of rapid oxidization that these juices should be freshly prepared. If they *have* to be kept, it is better to cover and place them in the refrigerator. They can be taken separately or mixed—some vegetable juices are very strong, e.g. parsley, spinach and watercress, and are more palatable when mixed with a milder juice.

If juices are prepared daily, or weekly, it is very well worth while to invest in a juice extractor. There are many models available and the Consumers' Association have already prepared a report on their merits and demerits. The alternative is preparation by grating or shredding the food as finely as possible and pressing the juice out with a hand-press or squeezing in butter muslin. It is most important that the juices should not come into contact with metals, unless of stainless steel, as these can hasten and increase oxidization.

There are so many combinations of juices it would be impossible to give a complete list but we hope the following will be helpful.

Preparation

The fruits and vegetables should be washed in cold running water and any bad parts removed, but do not remove the skins. Cut into pieces which will fit into the juicer. Juice immediately. The fruit and vegetables should be as fresh as possible; straight from the garden if you have one.

FRUIT COCKTAILS

Ripe apple juice, a little lemon juice, honey if necessary, mint, watercress or parsley juice to flavour. This combines well with other fruit and vegetable juices.

Ripe apple juice with equal quantities of orange juice, add a little lemon juice, if too sweet.

Green or black grapes.

Grapefruit juice—combines very well with apple and mint. Add a little honey if necessary.

Beginnings

Melon—this is best made in a liquidizer and strained afterwards, if necessary. Garnish with small pieces of strawberry or raspberry.

Orange juice—this combines well with other juices and is very good flavoured with mint.

Pineapple—makes a beautiful frothy juice and with a little green (watercress, parsley or mint) is good.

Rhubarb—this should be taken in small quantities combined with strawberry juice. It makes a lovely cocktail sweetened with a little honey. Garnish with borage.

VEGETABLE COCKTAILS

Beetroot—use young beetroots, which give a very good colour but should be combined with other juices. Beetroot, celery, watercress and parsley. Beetroot with yoghourt and a little lemon is very pleasant. It also mixes with pineapple juice.

Cabbage—makes a pleasant drink but is improved if flavoured with celery, carrot or tomato juice.

Carrot—this is a wonderful drink—combined with juice from green celery stalks and apples it gives practically all the needed vitamins and minerals. Garnish with mint. Combines well with strong-tasting juices. Garnish with cucumber.

Celery—mix with a little lemon, orange or grapefruit juice to prevent it turning dark. If it is too strong on its own, mix with a sweeter and blander juice.

Cucumber with orange, celery, pineapple or carrot juice. Garnish with borage.

Parsley, Spinach and Watercress—all these juices contain much cleansing and food value but they need to be mixed with other juices.

Tomato juice—with a little lemon juice, brown sugar and sea-salt. Try a suggestion of garlic! Garnish with watercress or parsley. Combines well with orange juice.

Mixed vegetable juice—this is a lovely drink, especially good with a little pimento and onion juice. If you are on a cleansing diet try putting your salad through a juicer. These juices are best freshly prepared, but they can be bought in tins and although some goodness will be lost these are very valuable. Try to buy fruit juices without added sugar and vegetable juices without much added salt.

Fruit, hors-d'œuvre or appetizers

These are always served in small amounts, beautifully prepared and garnished.

GRAPEFRUIT

1. Halve the grapefruit and allow one half for each person. Remove any pips. With a grapefruit-knife cut around the centre and remove it. The knife should be moved up and down with a sawing motion. Then cut around the outside edge just inside the pith. When the grapefruit is cut free from the rind, free each section from the skin and remove the skin if desired. Sprinkle the grapefuit with a little brown sugar, kirsch may also be added if desired. Chill the grapefruit. Put a half cherry in the centre.

2. Prepare the grapefruit as above and for two grapefruit allow: 3–4 oz. of brown sugar and 2 tablespoons of butter: mix and spread this mixture over the grapefruit. Sprinkle with sherry. Grill under a low heat for 15–20 minutes.

3. Prepare grapefruit as with number 1 and pour over a little brown sugar syrup, flavour with cinnamon and ginger. Chill the grapefruit.

4. Remove the grapefruit flesh and take away all the skin, leaving the sections. Add a few raspberries and pieces of pineapple and return all the fruit to the grapefruit cup. Garnish with mint leaves. Chill the mixture.

5. Prepare as number 4 above but mix the grapefruit with chopped mint and brown sugar. Chill the grapefruit.

The grapefruit may be served in a grapefruit glass or in a larger bowl, the space between the fruit and bowl being packed with ice.

The edge of the grapefruit can be serrated as illustrated:

The point of the knife must pierce the centre of the grapefruit on

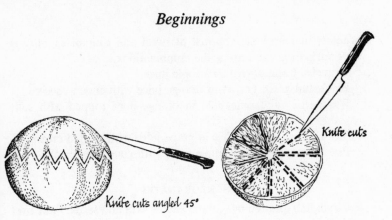

Knife cuts angled 45°

Knife cuts

each insertion otherwise the two halves will not break cleanly.
Finish the two halves as desired.

MELON

For types of melon see Fruit section.

1. Chill the melon and cut into wedge shapes. Remove the
seeds. Serve with powdered or chopped ginger and brown sugar.
Lemon wedges may be used to replace the ginger. Serve on cold
plates.

2. Cube the melon and serve as above but from small cut-glass
bowls or grapefruit dishes.

3. Cut a melon in half and remove the seeds. Fill each half with
a well-seasoned cream-cheese filling. A mixture of Roquefort and
cream cheese makes a good filling. Chill in the refrigerator until
the cheese is hard. Cut the melon into wedges and serve.

4. Cut the melon into cubes and place in glass bowls or stem-
glasses. Pour grapefruit or orange juice over it and garnish with
sour cream and mint leaves.

MIXED FRUIT COCKTAILS

These are mixtures of fruit with fruit juices, often served with
sour cream or a savoury cream. They are generally served in
chilled glasses and garnished with a complementary herb. If it is

properly managed the contrast of sweet and sour or savoury is very attractive. Here are some combinations:

Grapefruit and apricots in apple juice.

Black and green grapes in orange juice with cream cheese.

Raspberries and pineapple in orange juice topped with sour cream.

Strawberries and peaches in grape juice with minted cream.

Peaches and melon in apple juice with cucumber cream.

POMEGRANATES

Cut in half and remove all the yellow skin and seeds. Pour over whipped cream which has been sweetened with a little brown sugar and soured with a little lemon juice. Chill and serve.

VEGETABLE HORS-D'OEUVRE OR APPETIZERS

These can be attractively arranged on a large tray or plate, and handed round the table; or they can be prepared individually on small plates and garnished carefully.

It cannot be over-emphasized that all the portions should be very small and well flavoured (this does not mean over-seasoned) and that they should be freshly prepared. Too many cooks and writers of cookery books assume that this is an opportunity to use up bits and pieces.

COOKED VEGETABLES

Asparagus, seakale and globe artichokes are often served hot at the beginning of a meal. Their preparation and how to serve will be found in the Vegetable chapter.

COOKED, COLD VEGETABLES

The green vegetables should be slightly underdone so that when they are dressed (usually French dressing) they are fairly soft but still need to be chewed. Other vegetables which make good hors-d'œuvre are as follows:

Beetroot—French dressed	Mushrooms—French dressed
Potato—in mayonnaise	Globe artichokes—French
Peas—French dressed	dressed
Asparagus tips—French	Runner beans—French dressed
dressed	Carrots—in mayonnaise
Turnips—in mayonnaise	Cauliflower—French dressed

The root vegetables are better diced or sliced and the green vegetables cut or broken into pieces.

Various combinations of vegetables can be used for macedoine.

RAW VEGETABLES AND SALADS

The dressing for these can be found in the Salad section, but use smaller amounts and garnish more delicately. For example, Patrick's salad—line a stem-glass with curly, attractive small lettuce leaves and fill with a small amount of very finely grated carrot mayonnaise. Garnish with a $\frac{1}{4}$ of a hard-boiled egg and 1 small sprig of very green, curly parsley.

Other ingredients

Eggs—these can be hard-boiled and sliced or quartered. They may also be stuffed and the stuffing piped into each half, or they can be stuffed and joined again to form one whole egg, or coated with mayonnaise so that the stuffing is a surprise.

Nut Savouries—these are made in small shapes, cooked and used when cold. Or grated nuts can be moistened with dressing and mixed with finely grated vegetables for use as a filling.

Cheese—used for fillings or in the dressings. Finely grated.

Rice—brown rice cooked and drained. Moisten with curry flavoured mayonnaise. Add raisins, chopped pimento, peas and a little garlic.

Baked beans in tomato sauce—either home-made (see Vegetable section) or tinned.

Beginnings

Suggestions for hors-d'œuvre combinations

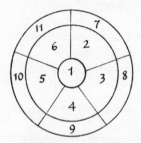

1. Stuffed eggs garnished with black olives.
2. Cucumber.
3. Cooked diced beetroot with chives.
4. Potato salad.
5. Tomato salad
6. Celery and apple salad.
7. Red cabbage and date salad.
8. White cabbage and green pimento salad.
9. Green olives and gherkins.
10. Vegetable mayonnaise.
11. Cherry or sliced orange salad.

1. Raw beetroot and horse-radish salad.
2. Cucumber with yoghourt dressing.
3. Cabbage and currant salad.
4. Tomato and chives.
5. Potato salad garnished with radish.
6. Carrot mayonnaise garnished with cucumber cones (See p. 60).
7. Stuffed eggs.
8. Pimento and rice salad.

Garnish between sections with parsley, watercress and mustard and cress.

Individual hors-d'œuvre

Tomato Ice

¼ pint of thick mayonnaise and a little whipped cream, ¼ pint of thick fresh tomato pulp (add a little concentrated tomato purée if the tomatoes lack colour and flavour), brown sugar, sea salt, lemon juice and grated orange rind to taste. Add the tomato to the mayonnaise, then add the seasoning and flavourings. Stir in the cream; it should be a thick creamy mixture. Pour into the 'freezing' tray of a refrigerator. Beat when the mixture is half frozen and then finish freezing. Serve in a stem-glass on a lettuce leaf and garnish with mint and watercress.

AVOCADO PEARS

The pears are ripe when the fruit is slightly soft to finger-pressure. If they are under-ripe when purchased, keep them in a warm room. Cut the pear in half from stem to base around the stone inside the pear (it is rather large) and twist the halves in opposite directions to separate. Remove the stone. Wash and lay each half on a bed of lettuce leaves on a small plate. Fill the hollow left by removing the stone, with a sharp French dressing. Allow one half-pear per person unless the pears are very tiny. The pear is eaten with a small spoon. Brown bread and butter may also be served with it. Avocados are often served chilled, but they should be placed in the refrigerator only an hour or two prior to serving. The flesh of the pear may also be removed from the skin (which is rather tough), mixed with a French dressing, and then returned to the skin.

CHERRY AND CHEESE SALAD

Wash, stalk and stone some red cherries, leaving them as whole as possible. Whip a ¼ pint of cream and fold in ½ lb. of cottage cheese. Add a little lemon juice or 1 small packet of St. Ivel cheese to give a pleasantly sharp flavour. (These quantities can be halved or doubled as required.) Arrange some crisp lettuce leaves on small plates, place a mound of the cheese in the centre and decorate generously with the cherries.

PEAR HORS-D'ŒUVRE

Wash some black and green grapes, halve them and remove the seeds. Wash some pears, halve them and scoop out the core with the tip of a teaspoon. Spread the skin of the pear with a sour-tasting cream cheese and place the half-pear with this covering

59

Beginnings

flat down on a small plate lined with lettuce leaves and mustard and cress. Press the grape halves into the cheese, arranging them so that the pear resembles a small bunch of grapes. Garnish with watercress or parsley. This dish is very attractive in appearance.

GRAPE HORS-D'ŒUVRE

Wash some large black grapes, slit them and remove the seeds. With a fine star pipe, pipe a creamy cheese mixture into the slit and dust the grapes with paprika pepper. Serve 6–8 on a small plate lined with lettuce leaves and garnish with watercress. Stilton, Roquefort or a Camembert cheese make good flavourings for the filling but do remember that the cheese mixture must be sieved, or the pipe may clog.

CUCUMBER HORS-D'ŒUVRE

Wash a large cucumber and slice it finely. Make a cut in each circle to the centre as shown in the diagram. Overlap the cucumber to form a cone and press where shown on the fold. Pipe the cones full with sour paprika cream and garnish with a minute sprig of parsley. Place 4–5 cones on a bed of lettuce and garnish with black olives and radish roses. The olives may be stoned.

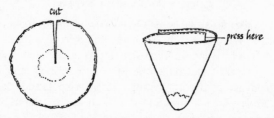

To make the radish roses Cut the radish after topping and tailing into eight sections allowing a small uncut piece of the radish at the base to hold these sections together, then with a very sharp knife, peel the red skin down each section to this base. With both the sections and peel held by the base, drop the radish into a bowl of ice-cold water and in a little while the radish swells and the whole will open out into a rosette.

Beginnings

SAVOURY CELERY

Wash some celery stems and cut in 2–3-inch lengths. Pipe into them a soft cream cheese and sprinkle the surface with chopped gherkins and red peppers. Serve on a bed of watercress on a small plate; 3–4 pieces to each portion. Garnish with the fine small celery leaves from the heart of the celery.

SOUPS AND BROTHS

Stock

The stock in common use is the water in which vegetables, rice, sweet corn, pulses, macaroni, etc. have been cooked and which is saved by the wise cook.

If the stock is to be kept it should be put into a container which can be easily cleaned and which has a lid. It should be placed in the refrigerator or in a cool place until required. It should be used within 24 hours, for cooking other vegetables, for hot savoury drinks, for sauces, soups, broths, etc. We sometimes have to make stock specially when we have used up all we had saved previously.

Special soups, broths and sauces may require different kinds of stock and these should be made with great care.

The flavour of the main ingredient should not be lost when using a stock. The temptation to make onion stock always, has to be firmly resisted! The ingredients are cut finely or grated and brought slowly to simmering point, to extract all the goodness and flavour possible. They are then simmered for a short time only to preserve as much food value as possible and so that the liquor will not become bitter through overcooking. Root vegetables will need longer.

When making a stock with a white vegetable try to keep the flavouring vegetables very light in colour too.

The general proportion of vegetables to water is 12 oz.–1 lb. vegetables to 1 quart of water, and 1–2 teaspoons of salt to 1 quart of water.

Beginnings

BROWN MIXED VEGETABLE STOCK

½ oz. butter
Equal amounts of carrot and onion or leek ⎫
2–3 sprigs cauliflower   ⎪ to make
1–2 stalks celery   ⎬ 1 lb. of
1–2 oz. mushrooms   ⎪ vegetables
2–3 tomatoes   ⎭
A small piece turnip or swede
Bouquet garni
1–2 teaspoons sea salt or Vesop, Marmite, etc.
    Parsley stalks, ½ bay leaf, ordinary or lemon—thyme,
    marjoram, balm, savoury or 1 teaspoon of mixed
    fresh herbs or dried
2 pints water, potato, rice or macaroni water

Wash and prepare the vegetables. Grate or chop them finely. Melt the butter, add the vegetables and cook gently until the butter is absorbed and the vegetables are a good brown colour. Add the water or stock, seasonings and bouquet garni. Simmer for ½–¾ of an hour, remove the bouquet garni, strain and use. (The cooked vegetables make good compost!) This stock can be varied by using 2–3 oz. of pulses and an extra pint of water. Lentils can be added after the vegetables are browned, but other pulses need to be soaked and nearly cooked before using (see Vegetable chapter); they can then be added with their cooking water to the browned vegetables.

WHITE ONION STOCK

12 oz. onions, leeks or shallots
1 clove garlic
A few button mushrooms if you have them
1–2 celery stalks or a piece of celeriac
1–2 sprigs cauliflower
A very small piece turnip or kohl rabi
Bouquet garni
1 teaspoon sea salt
2 pints water, potato, macaroni or rice water, etc.

Beginnings

Prepare the vegetables. Place all the ingredients in a saucepan and bring slowly to the boil. Simmer for 30 minutes or until the vegetables are cooked. Remove the bouquet garni. Strain and use.

Brown onion stock can be made by browning the vegetables in a little butter and continuing as for brown mixed vegetable stock. Carrot, tomato and Vesop, Marmite, etc., can also be used.

MUSHROOM STOCK

12 oz. mushroom stalks
2 oz. mushrooms
A very small piece of onion
½ a stick celery and 1 sprig cauliflower
1¾ pints water (mushrooms will give a little liquid)
1 teaspoon sea salt
A small bouquet garni

Make the stock as for white onion stock. Great care must be taken that the flavourings do not overpower the mushroom flavour. The mushrooms can be left whole for cooking the stock and then sliced, diced and added to the strained stock to garnish it.

CARROT STOCK

12 oz. carrots
1 small onion
2–3 sticks celery
1–2 sprigs cauliflower
3–4 button mushrooms
Bouquet garni
1 teaspoon sea salt
2 pints water, potato, rice or macaroni water

This can be made as a white or a brown stock, though it will not make a *very* light-coloured stock.

Broths

SIMPLE VEGETABLE BROTH

This is a quick and easy way to make broth, particularly when

Beginnings

potatoes and a green vegetable are being cooked for the second course. Drain most of the cooking liquid from the vegetables. Mix the liquids, taste and season them if necessary. Serve immediately with some fresh chopped herbs.

CLEAR BROTHS

These can be made from any of the special stocks or from the general household stock. Clear broths are not clear in the sense that water is clear, they are cloudy because of flavouring and nutritional substances which we feel it is a great pity to remove (although this is done in high-class cookery). They are generally served with various accompaniments or garnishes.

Accompaniments

1. Toasted or fried croûtons (dice) of bread.
2. Browned cheese on toast, cut into diced squares. These are called 'cheese croûtons'.
3. Fried potato dice or pommes allumettes (matchsticks).
4. Grated cheese.
5. Macaroni, noodles or pasta 'alphabetique'.

Garnishes

These are small amounts of cooked vegetables, etc. which are added to and served with the broth. Wherever possible the garnish shows the nature of the broth, i.e. asparagus broth is garnished with asparagus-tips, green-pea broth with a few cooked green peas.

Vegetable broth with diced or shredded mixed vegetables (carrots, potatoes, celery, peas and beans).

Mushroom broth with cooked mushrooms.

Onion broth with fried onion rings.

Apart from vegetable garnishes the following may also be used:

1. 1–2 oz. of cooked pearl barley—this takes 1½–2 hours to cook, it can be parboiled and the barley water added with the barley to the stock or it can be fully cooked and then added to the stock.

2. Small pieces of pasta, small pieces of spaghetti, shells, etc. or small ravioli made with an appropriate filling.

Beginnings

3. Small cubes of egg custard.
4. Small strips of fried pancakes.
5. Cooked rice.

Before leaving broths we must mention the broths which are served full of vegetables. In the country districts where they were evolved they are often served as the main course. The one which is best known and very popular is called 'Minestrone'. When it is purely vegetarian, it should be called 'Minestra'.

MINESTRA

1 tablespoon olive oil
4 peeled tomatoes
2–3 celery stalks or 1 celeriac
2–3 carrots
A small piece turnip, swede or kohl rabi
2–3 onions including leeks and shallots if available
1 clove garlic
Approximately 2 pints good vegetable stock
Sea salt to taste and a good pinch of brown sugar
Bouquet garni, including a few peppercorns, if liked
½–1 tablespoon concentrated tomato purée
2 tablespoons wholemeal macaroni
1 potato
½ small cabbage
6–8 French (or runner) beans or 6–7 brussels sprouts
6–8 small sprigs cauliflower
1–2 tablespoons chopped parsley
Grated cheese (Parmesan if possible) to serve separately
    with the 'Minestra'

Wash and prepare the vegetables. Cut them into small pieces and slice. Warm the oil and sauté the carrots, onions, celery and turnips until just browning, and until they have absorbed most of the oil. Add garlic crushed with the sea salt, tomato, tomato purée, brown sugar, bouquet garni and stock. Simmer for 30 minutes, then add the potato, cauliflower, macaroni and the green vegetables. Add a little more stock if necessary; the broth should

65

Beginnings

be full of vegetables and so, fairly thick; but remember the macaroni will absorb a little of the stock. Simmer for another 20–30 minutes, add the parsley and serve immediately, handing the cheese round separately so that each person may sprinkle a little over the broth.

Another good vegetable broth is Spring broth, but we think it should be called early Summer broth!

> 1 lb. of the following: new potatoes, new carrots, broad
>   beans, peas, runner or french beans
> $\frac{1}{2}$ oz. butter
> 1 chopped onion
> 5–6 button mushrooms
> 2 pints vegetable stock
> Sea salt or Vesop, Marmite, etc.
> Bouquet garni, including a sprig of mint, savoury or thyme
> 1 tablespoon chopped mixed fresh herbs

Wash and prepare the vegetables. Cut the potatoes, carrots and beans into dice. Slice the mushrooms. Heat the butter and gently sauté the vegetables for 10–15 minutes or until the butter is absorbed. Add the stock, seasoning and bouquet garni, simmer for 20–30 minutes. Remove the bouquet garni. Taste and adjust for seasoning. Sprinkle the fresh herbs and serve immediately.

FRENCH ONION SOUP
is really a form of onion broth

> $\frac{1}{2}$–$\frac{3}{4}$ lb. onions—3–4 Spanish onions make a good broth
> $1\frac{1}{2}$–2 oz. butter
> $\frac{1}{2}$ oz. 81 per cent extraction flour
> $1\frac{1}{2}$ pints boiling stock
> Sea salt and brown sugar to taste
> $\frac{1}{2}$ bay leaf
> 2 sliced wholemeal rolls or pieces of bread
> Freshly grated Gruyère cheese

Prepare and slice the onions finely in rings. Melt the butter and brown the onions slowly—this may take up to half an hour. Sprinkle with flour, stir it in, add the boiling stock, seasoning and bay leaf.

Simmer for 30–40 minutes. Taste and adjust for seasoning. Place the slices of bread or roll in a hot earthenware soup tureen. Pour on the soup and sprinkle the top thickly with the cheese. Place in a very hot oven 425–450° F., M7–8 until the cheese is browned. Serve immediately.

CHINESE BROTH

Cook sliced mushrooms and shredded lettuce leaves in a good stock and just before serving pour in spoonfuls of beaten egg.

THICKENED SOUPS

These can be divided into two main groups—puréed soups and cream soups, though cream added to a puréed soup improves it enormously and cream soups are very often sieved, so it can be a little confusing! The amounts given below are for soups of usual thickness, that is, thicker than milk but not as thick as porridge, of the consistency of a pouring cream. The consistency can be varied to suit individual tastes either by altering the proportion of the ingredients, i.e. add more vegetables and thickening (for a potage) or by the speed of cooking. Puréed soups are usually made with water and stock only; the sieved vegetable provides the thickness and a small amount of thickening agent, called liaison, is used to hold the puréed vegetables in suspension so that they do not settle on standing. Cream soups are made with milk and stock or water; sometimes the vegetables are puréed and sometimes they are strained out and a few pieces added as a garnish. When most of the vegetables are strained out, more liaison is required; cream and/or egg-yolks are always used as part of this liaison. At home we find that all our soups tend to become a mixture of these methods as we prefer to keep all the vegetables in the soup but at the same time enjoy a creamy texture.

The following recipes are mainly like this but they can be converted into either puréed or a cream soup by following the directions above.

Proportions of vegetables to liquid

Pulses—haricots, split peas, lentils, 6 oz. pulse to 2 pints liquid.
Other vegetables—1 lb. vegetables to 2 pints liquid.

Beginnings

Proportion of liaison for soups

    For 2 pints soup use—1 gill cream

                       2–4 egg-yolks

    For pulse soups use $\frac{1}{2}$ oz. roux ($\frac{1}{2}$ oz. fat and $\frac{1}{2}$ oz. flour)

    For tomato, green pea and carrot use $\frac{1}{2}$ oz. roux.

    For spinach and cucumber use 1 oz. roux

    Asparagus, etc. use 1 oz. roux

General method

Prepare the vegetables according to type and chop finely or grate coarsely if needed. *Either* sauté in butter, oil or vegetable fat until the fat is absorbed by the vegetables, add the liquid, bring to the boil, skim if necessary and simmer until tender; *or* place the vegetables straight into the liquid and cook as above. Add the seasonings and bouquet garni when the liquid is added. Sieve the ingredients (through a moulin legume if you have one), saving some of the vegetable as a garnish if required. Melt the fat in a saucepan, add the flour and then the sieved soup. Boil for a minute or two, remove from the heat and add the cream and egg-yolks if used, taste, add seasoning if needed, and adjust consistency. If cream and egg-yolks have been added, never reboil or the soup will curdle. Serve immediately with croûtons, chopped parsley or grated cheese, whichever is preferred or is suitable for the soup.

Here are some recipes with any additional notes needed for the method.

ASPARAGUS

    1 large bundle asparagus (about 1 lb.)

    1 quart white, not too highly flavoured, stock.

    Sea salt and brown sugar to taste

    1 oz. butter or margarine

    1 oz. 81 per cent extraction flour

    A little milk, if the soup needs thinning

    1 gill cream

Beginnings

Reserve some of the tips as a garnish to be added later on with the cream.

BRUSSELS SPROUTS OR CABBAGE

1–1½ lb. chopped cabbage or brussels sprouts
1 finely chopped onion
1 sliced potato
Seasonings
Bouquet garni, including a blade of mace
2 pints liquid stock or 1 pint stock and 1 pint milk
1 oz. butter
1 oz. 81 per cent extraction flour
¼ pint whipped cream or yoghourt
Chopped parsley mixed with a little finely grated cheese

The cream or yoghurt is placed in spoonfuls on the surface of the soup which is then sprinkled with parsley and cheese.

CARROT

1 tablespoon oil
1 lb. carrots
1 onion and a little crushed garlic
1 stick celery
1 potato
Small piece of turnip
2 pints stock or 1 pint milk and 1 pint stock
Bouquet garni and seasoning
1 oz. butter
1 oz. 81 per cent extraction flour
1 yolk egg and a little cream
Chopped parsley
Sauté the vegetables in the oil

Sprinkle the soup with a little chopped parsley; some diced cooked carrots may also be added. Serve with toasted croûtons.

Beginnings

CAULIFLOWER

1 tablespoon butter or oil
1 medium-sized cauliflower divided into sprigs
1 stick chopped celery and a small piece of celeriac
1 finely chopped onion
2 pints stock or 1 pint stock and 1 pint milk
Seasoning
Bouquet garni with a bay leaf and mace
1 oz. butter
1 oz. 81 per cent extraction flour
Herb or cheese dumplings

If the soup is to be made with milk do not add the milk with the stock as it may curdle; use it to make a thin sauce with the roux. To this add the puréed vegetables. Add the very small dumplings and simmer until these are cooked.

CELERY

As with the above soup there is a risk of the milk curdling if it is cooked with the vegetables, so use the same recipe and method but substitute 1 head of celery for the cauliflower or use 1 lb. of celeriac. This soup is improved by adding a little cream before serving and is very good accompanied by toasted cheese croûtons.

CUCUMBER

2 small diced cucumbers
½ a small onion finely chopped
A little spinach
2 pints white stock
Seasonings
1 oz. butter
1 oz. 81 per cent extraction flour
A little whipped cream or yoghourt flavoured delicately
with mint

Be very careful not to lose the cucumber flavour—if the stock is well flavoured leave out the onion. Spinach or parsley juice can be added to give colour if needed, but again be very careful with the flavouring. Serve the soup topped with yoghourt or cream.

LENTIL

2 tablespoons oil
6 oz. washed lentils
1 large chopped onion
2 chopped carrots
2 chopped celery stalks
Small piece turnip, swede or parsnip
Seasonings
Bouquet garni
2 pints brown stock
$\frac{1}{2}$ oz. butter
$\frac{1}{2}$ oz. 81 per cent extraction flour
2–3 tablespoons cream
Fried croûtons
Potatoes or tomatoes can be added to give variety

LETTUCE

1 lb. shredded lettuce
Seasonings
$\frac{1}{2}$–$\frac{3}{4}$ pint stock
1 oz. butter
1 oz. 81 per cent extraction flour
1 pint milk
1 egg-yolk and a little cream

The method is the same as for cauliflower but do not sauté the lettuce.

MUSHROOM

$\frac{1}{2}$ lb. mushrooms
$\frac{1}{2}$ lb. mushroom stalks
1 small chopped onion
$1\frac{1}{2}$ pints mushroom or vegetable stock
Seasoning with a little paprika pepper

Beginnings

1 oz. butter
1 oz. 81 per cent extraction flour
¼ pint cream
2 egg-yolks
Garnish with sliced mushrooms or quartered mushrooms and chopped parsley

Onion

1 lb. chopped onions
1 quart stock or 1 pint milk and 1 pint stock
Seasonings
Bouquet garni
1 oz. butter
1 oz. 81 per cent extraction flour
A little cream
Chopped parsley
Toasted cheese croûtons

If the onions are chopped finely this soup can be made in 15–20
minutes and need not be sieved.

Green Pea

1 tablespoon oil
1 lb. shelled peas
1 small chopped onion or a few spring onions or 2 leeks
(green part only)
1 small shredded lettuce
Seasoning
Bouquet garni including mint
2 pints pea stock (made from the pea pods)
1 oz. butter
1 oz. 81 per cent extraction flour
Some small cooked peas for garnishing

The colouring may be improved with a little spinach or parsley
juice.

Beginnings

DRIED PEA

Follow the recipe for lentil, but soak the washed peas overnight and use the soaking water in the soup.

POTATO

As this is a starchy vegetable the recipe and method are slightly different:

1½ oz. butter or oil
1 lb. sliced potatoes
1 finely chopped onion
Seasoning
A bay leaf
1½ pints milk or stock and milk
1 egg-yolk
A little cream
Croûtons and chopped parsley

No roux is needed for this soup, the egg and the cream are sufficient liaison and thickening. Potato soup has many variations —potato and leek or onion; potato and watercress; potato and herb; potato and carrot; potato and parsley; potato and cauliflower; potato and tomato; etc. Watercress, herb and parsley are cleaned and chopped finely and put into the soup 5 minutes before serving, to soften them. Potato is especially good when flavoured with curry, and is an excellent foundation for any vegetable soup.

SPINACH

1 lb. spinach
1 chopped onion
Seasoning and a little nutmeg
1½ pints stock
1 oz. butter
1 oz. 81 per cent extraction flour
A little cream
Sieved hard-boiled egg

The sieved egg is sprinkled on the soup just before serving. Spinach soup is also served with a little rice.

Beginnings

Tomato

1 oz. butter or oil
1 chopped onion
1 grated carrot
1 sliced celery stalk
1 lb. ripe red tomatoes
Bouquet garni, including a little mint, mace, bay leaf and peppercorns
Seasonings, brown sugar will be needed
1½ pints stock
1 oz. butter
1 oz. 81 per cent extraction flour
A little milk for thinning the soup if needed—must be added after the roux has thickened.
Whipped cream flavoured with chive or chopped basil.
Toasted cheese croûtons

The onion and celery are sautéd in the fat for 5–10 minutes before adding the tomatoes, bouqui garni and seasonings. Garnish with the whipped cream, or cream may be stirred into the soup before serving. In winter, tomato soup is always improved by adding some concentrated tomato purée.

Vegetable Soup

The 1 lb. of vegetables for this soup must be carefully made up, so that there is as much variety as possible without any particular flavour predominating. The soup may be made white or brown, in fact a white soup with the vegetables cut into dice and left in can be most attractive.

COLD SOUPS

Savoury

These can be made from broths or thickened soups but care must be taken with the flavour and thickening. Smaller amounts

Beginnings

of seasoning are usually necessary and the amount of thickening must be reduced a little. We find that agar-agar makes a good thickening, especially for tomato soup which can be served almost jellied with wedges of lemon.

The soups should be served chilled; if possible stand the bowls in a large serving-dish packed around with crushed ice. This looks very attractive if care has been taken with the garnishing. As they are served cold more cream may be used, which gives a richer and very lovely soup.

Mushroom, herb and cucumber soup are very good, as is a lightly curried soup.

At the 'Vega' we serve a cold Spanish soup *Gazpacho andaluz* which makes a meal in Spain when eaten with a roll. It is made of cucumber, tomato, breadcrumbs and a trace of garlic to taste.

Sweet or fruit soups

Originating on the Continent, these soups deserve greater recognition in Britain, particularly by those of us who grow our own fruit and may have a surplus.

The amount of fruit is 1 lb. to 1 quart of water or water with white or red wine added. We sometimes use water and fruit juices, such as grape juice, apple juice or juice left over from stewing fruit, provided the flavour blends with the fruit which is being used. If sweetening is needed use brown sugar or honey or a mixture of both but the fruit flavour rather than sweetness should predominate.

These soups are often served with whipped cream and unsweetened biscuits.

CHERRY SOUP

> 1 lb. red cherries (stoned)
> Brown sugar or honey to taste
> 2 pints liquid (water, fruit juice, 1 glass red wine optional)
> Grated zest and the strained juice of 1 orange
> Agar-agar

Gently cook the cherries in the liquid with the orange rind, then sieve. Measure the juice and use 1 level teaspoon of agar-agar per pint of juice. The consistency may be varied by using more or less agar-agar.

Dissolve the agar-agar in some of the hot juice over a gentle heat, add the orange juice, then chill. Taste and add honey or brown sugar, dissolved in hot water, if necessary. Serve with a little whipped cream and biscuits if preferred.

More suggestions for cold soups

Apple and lemon (apple is rather like potato in that it is a useful foundation for most flavourings).

Apple and strawberry.

Gooseberry—good served with small oat crunchies or flapjacks.

Plum.

Pear—serve with pieces of pear in the clear juice and do not thicken.

Melon and ginger.

Use of the liquidizer

This electric mixer attachment simplifies many of the foregoing operations and saves time and effort. A smooth creamy liquid obtainable by no other means is obtained.

Another great advantage is that it liquifies raw foods just as easily as cooked. Cold soups made from raw fruits and vegetables have a marvellous flavour and greater food value.

As a change in really hot weather, these raw fruit and vegetable purées can be half frozen in the ice-box. The use of less fruit and vegetables and more juice will result in some really exciting fruit and vegetable cocktails.

Follow the makers' instructions on (or with) the machine for the manner of use, as these may vary from one machine to another. The liquidizer is so useful for other general operations, e.g. making salad dressings (see Salad chapter) that we consider it a piece of kitchen equipment of primary importance.

4

Salads

Salads are a most important part of our diet and we should serve one each day, either as a complete course or to accompany a savoury dish. It is easy when preparing a daily salad to get into a rut, losing sight of how refreshing variety can be. We hope what follows will help to make 'ringing the changes' easy.

PREPARATION OF SALAD MATERIALS

Green salads

All lettuce, endive, chicory, watercress, dandelion, lamb's lettuce, sorrel, etc.

If possible pick green salad items just before using, or when buying, use the same day. If salad greens are bought, store them, after removing the damaged or dead leaves, either in the special storage compartments of the refrigerator (usually at the bottom as lockers or drawers), or in a covered saucepan with a very small amount of water at the bottom. Stand the saucepan in a cool place. Watercress should be stood in a bowl of water. All large green-leaved salad plants should be washed, just before use, in cold running water and shaken in a salad basket or tea-towel. Do be careful to remove as much water as possible from the salad greens without bruising or the salad when served will be swimming in diluted dressing.

The exceptions are all small-leaved plants, cresses, particularly

Salads

watercress, which have a tendency to harbour small minute fresh-water creatures. They should be left to soak for 5–10 minutes, in salted water, rinsed in clean water, then shaken free from surplus water.

If mustard and cress is used as a garnish, either wash in small bundles and pat dry on a clean tea-towel or wash like spinach until the water is clear; then collect and shake in a round sieve. The black, empty seeds float to the top of the water and will float away when the bowl is gently tipped.

Lamb's lettuce and dandelion leaves are also washed like spinach.

Root and other vegetables

These should be prepared as for cooking. Peeling depends very much upon the state of the skin, age of the vegetable and whether or not the vegetable was grown in compost, or was sprayed, etc.

Dressings

As soon as a plant cell is broken, either by cutting or breaking, oxidization begins which results in a steady loss of vitamins. Ideally salads should consist of whole leaves, fruits and roots as no oxidization and vitamin loss can occur during the natural chewing and salivory processes in the mouth. The general inclination, however, is to prefer salad chopped and grated. Dressings not only add flavour and variety but the intermingled acid and oil of which they are in the main composed, prevent oxidization and vitamin loss. They also aid digestive assimilation and are of considerable dietetic value.

There are two main types of salad dressings:

1. French Dressing

1 part vinegar
2–3 parts oil and seasoning to taste

This is made from the best olive oil and wine vinegar. The

vinegar may be replaced with apple vinegar or lemon juice. The dressing can be seasoned with sea salt, brown sugar, pepper (black or white or paprika) or French mustard if desired.

Mix and dissolve the seasonings in the vinegar, add the oil a little at a time and beat it in with a fork or basket whisk until the dressing thickens and enough oil is added to taste. Use immediately or beat again before using, as the oil and vinegar separate on standing.

Other methods are: (1) put the ingredients in a screw-top bottle or jar and shake until they are well mixed; or (2) easily the best result is obtained by using a liquidizer.

If this dressing is used often, make it in large quantities and store in the refrigerator.

Additions and variations

1. Cream dressing. Use cream in place of oil and lemon juice in place of vinegar, otherwise the seasonings and method of making are the same.

2. Use grapefruit, pineapple or orange juice to replace some of the vinegar or lemon juice.

3. Fluid honey can be used to make a sweet/sour dressing, but the pepper should be omitted.

4. Grated cheese or chopped hard-boiled eggs.

5. Chopped onion, crushed garlic with or without fresh chopped herbs.

6. Red and green sweet peppers.

7. Chopped green and black olives, gherkins, pickled cucumber or capers.

8. Sour cream or yoghourt.

9. A little grated horseradish.

10. Chopped mint, parsley, basil, thyme, savoury, chives, dill, etc., either mixed or separate.

11. Ginger, curry powder and various spices may be used in small quantities.

Salads

2. MAYONNAISE

2 yolks of eggs
Sea salt and brown sugar to taste
A little French mustard, paprika or cayenne pepper if
liked
Up to $\frac{1}{2}$ pint of best quality olive oil (other oils can be
substituted)
Vinegar or lemon juice to taste
A little cream to thin the mayonnaise if necessary

Mayonnaise is an emulsion consisting of minute droplets of oil
or fat suspended in a watery fluid. When mayonnaise curdles, the
fat globules coalesce and become blobs floating in the mother
liquid. To prevent this:

1. Leave all the ingredients in a warm kitchen for a little while
so that they will be of an even temperature.

2. Always stir the mayonnaise in the *same* direction, whether
clockwise or anti-clockwise is immaterial.

3. Add the oil drop by drop until the mixture becomes stiff
when a little vinegar or lemon juice is added to thin it, after which
it can be added a little more freely. When making large quantities,
a little vinegar or lemon juice may be added to the yolks before
starting to add the oil, this will minimize the risk of curdling.

Place the yolks and seasonings in a bowl. Stand the bowl on a
damp cloth, or twist the cloth around the bottom so that the bowl
will not move. The lemon juice or vinegar should be to hand.

The cork of the bottle containing the oil should be
fitted with a notched cork (see diagram), this ensures that the oil will come out in drops easily. Stir
the yolks with a wooden spoon until they are well
mixed, then add the oil drop by drop until the
mixture becomes thick and creamy. Add a little
lemon juice or vinegar to thin and continue adding
the oil a little faster, until all the oil is in. Add vinegar or lemon
juice to taste. If the mixture is stiff a little thin cream or top of
the milk can be added to thin it down. A small wire whisk may

be used instead of the wooden spoon. A liquidizer makes this dressing to perfection and takes much less time. We make as much as possible each time and store it in the refrigerator.

Additions and variations

1. Use either hard-boiled egg-yolks or a baked sieved potato in place of the egg-yolks.

2. If the mayonnaise is too rich, try adding some cold smooth white, or béchamel sauce. This makes a smooth dressing. The seasonings may need to be adjusted.

3. Honey can replace brown sugar.

4. Just before serving fold in a stiffly beaten egg-white.

5. Add any chopped fresh herbs singly or as a mixture, with or without onion, chives, garlic, etc.

6. Chopped red and green peppers.

7. For a piquante dressing use chopped capers, green or black olives, gherkins or pickled cucumber.

8. Fruit dressings use lemon, orange or pineapple juice in the mayonnaise, also chopped ginger or a little nutmeg or cinnamon.

9. Whipped cream is also good.

10. Crumbled, cubed or grated cheese.

11. Chopped hard-boiled eggs.

12. Add some grated horseradish, this is especially good with beetroot.

13. For a crisp mayonnaise add some finely diced or chopped raw celery and cucumber.

Apart from French dressing and mayonnaise, very good salad dressings can be made using sour cream, sour milk, cottage cheese or yoghourt. These need to be seasoned and usually sweetened a little.

Dressings should be used in moderation, excess is both wasteful and unappetizing.

COOKED SALADS

These may be made from any cooked vegetables. The vegetables should be specially cooked so that they are slightly underdone and

Salads

are firm and have a 'bite', not soft and soggy. They may be served separately, usually on lettuce leaves and garnished with cress or they can be served with raw salads. Many people prefer cooked salads but they do not equal raw salads in food value.

Here are some of the more usual cooked salads:

ASPARAGUS

Serve on lettuce leaves, use a little French dressing and sprinkle with chopped chervil or parsley. Mayonnaise may be handed separately; if delicately flavoured with tangerine or orange zest it makes a pleasant change.

BEANS

French, broad or runner beans. Serve on lettuce leaves with mayonnaise. Sprinkle with chopped savoury or thyme and garnish with chopped hard-boiled eggs.

Haricot, brown or butter beans. Mix with mayonnaise flavoured with spring onions, shallot, leek, onion or garlic and a little fresh or concentrated tomato purée. Serve on lettuce leaves garnished with watercress.

Baked bean salad. Take equal quantities of baked beans and cabbage or brussels sprouts. Shred the greens and mix with the baked beans, using a little mayonnaise to moisten. Serve on endive leaves and garnish with tomato slices. This is a good winter salad.

BEETROOT

Cook and cool. Slice very finely or dice and allow to soak in lemon juice or French dressing for about 30 minutes. Serve chilled if desired. Beetroot is very useful because the colour provides a good contrast. A drawback is that the colour tends to run into the mayonnaise or the other vegetables if they are too close.

BROCCOLI

One of the finest cold salads. Dress with French dressing or a creamy mayonnaise and garnish with paprika pepper.

Salads

CAULIFLOWER

Cook in sprigs, taking care not to overcook. Dress with a cheese mayonnaise to which is added some chopped gherkins and capers. Place on lettuce leaves and surround with sliced tomatoes or beetroot. They may also be served with a Mint French dressing.

MUSHROOMS

Fry the mushrooms quickly in butter for 2–3 minutes. Marinade in French dressing and serve as a garnish on lettuce leaves with tomatoes. (They can also be used raw, finely chopped, in a mixed salad.)

PEAS

Serve on lettuce leaves and garnish with chopped mint. If they are well cooked they need almost no dressing. If cooked, young carrots are mixed with them and a pleasing colour contrast results.

POTATO

Use new potatoes and cut into slices or dice while they are hot. Sprinkle well with French dressing and leave until cold. Dress with mayonnaise; the following may be added: chopped mint, parsley, spring onion, gherkins, pickled cucumber, red peppers.

If you have old potatoes mash them with French dressing or mayonnaise and flavour as before. This may be served either hot or cold.

Mixed cooked salads

Varieties of these are well-nigh endless, but here are some of those in general use:

MACÉDOINE
(or mixed vegetable salad)

Mix together cooked peas, diced potatoes, carrots, French or runner beans and a little diced red pepper. Mix with mayonnaise; a little chopped onion and parsley to flavour may be added.

Salads

RUSSIAN SALAD

This should be sharp in taste. Mix together cooked peas, small sprigs of cauliflower, potatoes, beetroot, French beans, carrots and celeriac. Add chopped gherkins, capers, cucumber, olives, etc. to give piquancy, and dress with French dressing. Just before serving coat with a mayonnaise and sprinkle with chopped chervil, tarragon, chives, mint or parsley.

RICE SALAD

Cook the rice in sea-salted water and allow to cool. Add any of the following:

> chopped chives or onion
> sliced cooked mushrooms
> small quartered tomatoes
> chopped red and green peppers
> some washed sultanas
> diced apple
> diced cucumber
> diced celeriac
> chopped celery

Dress with French dressing or mayonnaise flavoured with mango chutney and a little curry paste.

MACARONI SALAD

1. Mix cooked macaroni with diced beetroot, raw chopped onion and French dressing. Leave to stand a little while before serving with chopped mint, parsley or a mixture of herbs.
2. Mix some macaroni into the mixed vegetable salad.
3. Mince some onion and green pepper and dice some tomatoes. Mix with the macaroni and dress with mayonnaise.

RAW SALADS

These are important for general health and one raw salad should be eaten daily, even in winter.

Salads

One of the best ways of using a raw salad as a main course is to make a combined salad of leaves, roots and fruit. This gives variety and is therefore more likely to be enjoyed and to provide all the trace elements, vitamins, etc. needed. It also combines the various plant proteins; but in the main, salads provide minerals and vitamins which is why they should be freshly prepared if possible.

Here under the various headings are some suggestions for raw salads; you will find that stem and flower vegetables usually come under leaf salads but they may be used as an alternative to roots if desired.

Fruit salads

WALDORF SALAD

Mix together apples, bananas, walnuts, dates and celery with a little mayonnaise and brown sugar. Celeriac may be used in the place of celery, but should be shredded.

BLACK-EYED SUSAN

Peel some oranges and cut into transverse slices, fairly thickly. Mince or chop some dates, apples, raisins and currants. Make this mixture into small balls and coat with grated nuts. Place one of these savoury-sweet rolls in the centre of each slice of orange.

AMERICAN FRUIT SALAD

Dice some peeled orange and grapefruit. Add some sliced apple and diced tomatoes. Dress with a sweet French dressing or honey. Small pieces of pear and cherries can be added. Garnish with whipped fresh cream or sour cream.

JAPANESE SALAD

An American fruit salad topped with cottage cheese and finished with a sprinkling of mint.

Salads

BANANA AND GRAPE

Prepare some French dressing or honey dissolved in lemon juice. Into this slice the bananas and turn them in the liquid to prevent discoloration. Add halved black and green grapes, remove the pips if you wish. Serve with cinnamon cream if desired.

PLUM, APPLE AND ORANGE

Prepare the dressing as above and add the diced fruits.

APPLE, ORANGE AND DATE SALAD

As above.

TOMATO SALAD

Slice or dice the tomatoes. Dress with French dressing; a little chopped onion and basil make this a wonderful salad.

CUCUMBER SALAD

Wash and dice the cucumber. Dress with a sharp French dressing as cucumber is a watery fruit and the dressing becomes diluted. Yoghourt dressing is very good.

TOMATO AND CUCUMBER SALAD

Dress with French dressing, chopped spring onions and a little mint. Top with cottage cheese.

LEEK, TOMATO AND APPLE

Dice the tomatoes and slice the leeks finely. Place in a French dressing and add the apples just before serving.

GRAPEFRUIT, AVOCADO PEAR, GRAPE AND ORANGE SALAD

Pulp the avocado pear, mix in the grapes and cubes of grapefruit and orange. Coat with mayonnaise, then sprinkle with chopped nuts and serve.

Salads

MELON AND GINGER SALAD

Cube the melon and serve with creamy ginger mayonnaise.

STUFFED APPLES

Cut medium to large dessert apples in half horizontally. Remove the core and scoop out the remainder of the flesh leaving an empty shell. Mix the apple with the celery, nuts, red and green peppers and mayonnaise. Pile the mixture back in the halves. Sprinkle with chopped chives.

STUFFED TOMATOES

Remove the lids and take out the inside, keep the juice and pulp but not the centre piece. Fill with cream cheese, chives, diced cucumber, currants and the tomato pulp or any other filling you may prefer.

MELON SUPRÊME

Cut the melon in half horizontally, take off the outside skin and scoop out the seeds. Cut a thin slice off the base so that the melon stands upright. Fill the centre with diced fresh fruits, cover with honey or brown sugar. Serve chilled.

Root Salads

BEETROOT

Wash and prepare the beetroot. Shred finely and dress with lemon juice and sea salt.

(1) Add grated horseradish if liked. Serve with apple mayonnaise.

(2) Grate with apple and mix with lemon juice, chopped mint and currants.

Young beetroots are very good on their own.

Salads

CARROT

Wash and prepare the carrots. Shred and dress with:

(1) Mayonnaise and chopped parsley.

(2) Finely shred the carrots, add ground almonds and enough mayonnaise to give a stiff mixture.

(3) Dress with French dressing and serve with a piquante mayonnaise.

(4) Add some chopped celery to the carrots and mix with apple mayonnaise.

(5) Grate the carrots and dress with French dressing or mayonnaise. Sprinkle with mint.

(6) Carrot combines well with cheese, either grated, mixed with the carrot, or cream cheese used as a dressing.

CELERIAC

Wash and peel the celeriac. Grate and dress immediately with mayonnaise. Sprinkle with cheese and/or chopped parsley. A little onion grated with the celeriac improves the flavour.

CELERY

This is not really a root but a blanched stem and may also be used as a leaf salad. Wash well and slice across the stems. Dress with mayonnaise or with cheese mayonnaise. Celery combines well with fruits, i.e. tomatoes and apple. See also Waldorf salad in the first section.

CAULIFLOWER

This is not a root either but a flower in bud. It makes a good salad, but needs more dressing than most salads as it tends to be dry. Wash and grate the cauliflower, add some grated walnuts and mix with plenty of mayonnaise.

KOHL RABI

Prepare and grate the kohl rabi. Dress with French dressing or mayonnaise.

Salads

MIXED ROOT

Grate a little of all the roots available, but use only a little of the strongly flavoured ones such as turnip and only a little beetroot or the varying colour effects will be lost. Use any dressing you prefer and sprinkle with chopped herbs.

RADISH

These make a good grated salad, particularly if the radishes are large. Grate and dress with cream cheese, mint, chives, brown sugar and a little lemon juice.

SWEDE

This is a strong-tasting root and is better in a mixed root salad. Young swedes may be used alone if desired. We prefer swede salad with French dressing and chives but it may be coated with mayonnaise.

TURNIP

Young tender turnips make a very good salad. Grate and mix with a piquante mayonnaise.

Leaf Salads

CABBAGE

1. Red. Wash and grate the cabbage. Dress with apple mayonnaise and top with whipped cream flavoured with a little mixed spice and cinnamon.
2. White. Wash and finely slice the cabbage. Dress with French dressing, onion and sultanas or currants or with mayonnaise, a little grated carrot and chopped sweet peppers. (Cole Slaw salad.)
3. Green cabbage. Wash and slice the cabbage finely. Mix with French dressing or mayonnaise as preferred. A little chopped onion, chopped tomatoes or grated cheese all make good additions. If you like carraway seeds try yoghourt dressing with a few of these sprinkled in.

Salads

CHICORY

Wash the chicory well and slice lengthwise in quarters. This leaf combines well with fruits, e.g. tomatoes and oranges or since it is bitter it can be used with a dried fruit such as sultanas or currants. Chicory and currants with chopped chives for example. If you wish to use a mayonnaise, try dressing the salad with one to which you have added finely chopped tomatoes, watercress and gherkins.

CORN SALAD

Sometimes known as lamb's lettuce. This makes a very good garnish. Children like to eat it with their fingers, dipping the salad into small jars of French dressing or mayonnaise.

DANDELION

The young leaves may be added to a green salad or they may be used to garnish a salad. Dandelion has a pleasant, rather bitter taste.

ENDIVE

Wash and shred the endive. This is a fine salad when dressed with French dressing and a little chopped onion with tomato added. Endive garnishes a salad very well when the sprigs are left whole or it can be shredded and dressed with a cheese or nut mayonnaise.

LETTUCE

1. Round lettuce is the basis of most salads and green salad in particular. It is not normally dressed but the leaves simply washed thoroughly, dried and left whole.
2. Cos is a coarse and crisp lettuce with a sweet flavour. An excellent 'first' lettuce for children. Cut into short pieces with a sharp stainless steel knife and toss in a French dressing. Combines

Salads

well with eggs, or cheese, nuts, tomatoes, onions, oranges. It may be served with a piquante mayonnaise.

3. Batavian. Very similar to endive in taste but the leaves are much broader. Use as for endive or cos lettuce.

MUSTARD AND CRESS

Used generally as a garnish.

NASTURTIUM

The leaves of the nasturtium have a pleasantly hot flavour and hence make a good addition to a salad. They should be washed thoroughly. Dress with a mayonnaise and garnish with 3–4 edible nasturtium flowers.

SEAKALE

This is a wonderful raw salad—crisp and nutty in flavour. Use French dressing or creamy mayonnaise after washing and chopping or slicing the seakale. It combines well with tomatoes, oranges and apples.

SORREL

There are really two types. The wild sorrel has a very sharp taste but the cultivated kind is milder. The leaves make a good addition to any green salad or a few can be mixed in with a spinach salad. Wash carefully before adding.

SPINACH

Wash very well. The young leaves may be eaten like lettuce leaves and may be used to garnish a salad in exactly the same manner, or they may be shredded and dressed with French dressing or mayonnaise. Spinach and egg are a good combination served either garnished with sliced egg or the salad coated with an egg mayonnaise.

Salads

SPROUTS

A good winter salad (when greens are scarce) can be made from shredded brussels sprouts; they are nice dressed in any of the ways for cabbage. A favourite of ours is cold baked beans with shredded sprouts and chopped tomatoes moistened with a little mayonnaise.

WATERCRESS

A wonderful plant which contains many minerals (particularly iron) and vitamins; it is used in green salads and as a garnish.

MIXED GREEN SALAD

This can be used with other salads but it is often used to accompany hot savouries in place of the customary green vegetable. Any of the following may be used when available: lettuce, Cos lettuce, Batavian lettuce, endive and chicory, dandelion leaves, sorrel, nasturtium leaves, spinach leaves, lambs lettuce, watercress and mustard and cress.

Wash the green leaves and drain very carefully. Prepare a French dressing. Rub round the inside of the salad bowl with a cut clove of garlic, if liked. Break the large leaves into small pieces and add the small leaves (watercress, lambs lettuce, etc.). Mix well together. Add a little of the French dressing and toss the salad well, using the salad servers, add more dressing if necessary. There should be just enough dressing to coat the leaves without a pool being formed in the bottom of the bowl. Serve immediately. You may prefer to dress the salad at the table. This salad is very nice garnished with the leaves of mixed herbs, e.g. all varieties of mint, thyme, basil, savoury, chervil, etc. Do not include the strong herbs such as rosemary and sage.

Accompaniments
When salads are served as the main course they are frequently

accompanied by special breads, scones, potatoes and various forms of protein. Here are a few suggestions:

1. Potatoes. Boiled or baked in their jackets. Serve with butter and chopped parsley. Or serve cheese-baked potatoes. Bake the potatoes, remove the cooked potato and mash with some grated cheese, season and add fried onions to taste. Return to the potato skins and brown in the oven. Dust with sea salt.

2. Bread. Make savoury or cheese bread (see Yeast section). Cut some wholemeal loaves in half and take out the centres. Spread the shells with garlic or mustard butter and bake in a moderate to hot oven until crisp. Fill with a cheese mixture, or scrambled eggs, or creamed asparagus tips.

3. Scones. Make some cheese scones and serve hot with butter or spread with cream cheese and chives.

4. Iced cheese. Press some of your favourite soft cheese through a sieve. Add some soft beaten butter and enough cream to make a soft mixture of dropping consistency. Add herbs and seasonings to taste. Smooth into a small oiled flan-ring and chill in the refrigerator until firm. Remove from the flan-ring and coat with very finely grated dry cheese or paprika or chopped parsley. Serve in wedges. We like this very much, especially made with Camembert or Brie.

5. Any cold nut meats or savouries can be sliced and served with salads, as can wedges of savoury flans.

6. Stuffed eggs. Hard-boil some eggs and cut in half. Remove the yolks. Cut a small slice from the base to form a stand. Sieve the yolks and mix with any one of the following:

   (a) Tartex, a little tomato purée and mayonnaise to moisten. Garnish with gherkins.
   (b) Cream and paprika. Garnish with parsley.
   (c) French mustard and mayonnaise. Garnish with black olives or stuffed olives.
   (d) Softened butter, mayonnaise and enough parsley and thyme to give a good green colour. Garnish with a small piece of walnut.
   (e) Either pipe the mixture into the whites or pile it on the plates in rough heaps, using a fork.

Salads

7. Nut savouries. Mince and grate some nuts of your own choice with a little onion, skinned tomato and sweet peppers. Add chopped herbs and seasonings. Add a little mayonnaise to bind the mixture and shape into balls or drums. Roll in chopped nuts and serve.

5

Savouries

NUT SAVOURIES

Practically all nut savouries can be made from a basic recipe, variety being introduced by using different nuts. The 'backing' for the nuts will vary with the method of cooking. The exception is the chestnut; we will give some recipes for this separately.

Basic recipe

4–6 oz. nuts—almonds, Brazils, cashews, hazel, pea, pine kernels and walnuts are all suitable.

6–8 oz. 'backing'—mashed potato, cooked brown rice, fresh wholemeal breadcrumbs, wholemeal bread soaked in stock and squeezed dry, and cooked vegetables.

Seasoning. Sea salt and a pinch of brown sugar. Vesop, Marmite, etc. Pepper if liked. Paprika or cayenne. French mustard.

Flavourings. Fried onion and/or garlic. Leek or shallot. Herbs and chives. Curry paste, concentrated tomato purée. Mushrooms.

Liquid to mix. This may not be necessary. Beaten eggs, milk, sauce or stock.

Basic method

Chop the onions, etc. and fry them in nut fat, oil or butter until brown and soft. While they are cooking prepare the 'backing' and the nuts. 'Backing' is used because nuts are very rich concentrated food and need 'building out'; also because nuts cooked by themselves tend to be rather dry unless there is some moisture-holding substance. The nuts can be milled very finely or chopped coarsely, depending on personal taste, they may be skinned or not as preferred and they can be browned in the oven before chopping to bring out the flavour (the latter operation is especially good for nut savouries which are not being oven cooked). When everything is prepared mix all the ingredients together and use as required. Here are some recipes to show what can be done with this basic recipe and we hope that you will be able to create many more to your own liking. A point worth remembering is that although mixing the various types of nuts is nice for a change—there are so many different *kinds* of nuts that more variety can be introduced by using them separately and bringing out the individual flavours. We have omitted any recipes using walnuts because we prefer them in sweet dishes, but they *can* be used in savouries if you like the flavour.

Baked Hazel and Tomato Savoury

6 oz. chopped hazel nuts
½ lb. mashed potato
1 oz. fat or oil
1 onion
1 clove garlic
1 lb. skinned tomatoes
1 tablespoon chopped parsley with a little basil if available or if not lemon or ordinary thyme
A little concentrated tomato purée
A little grated lemon rind
A little potato water if required
Seasonings.

Method. Grease a shallow fire-proof dish and heat the oven to 350–375° F., M4–5. Prepare the potatoes and the nuts. Chop the onion and garlic and brown in the fat or oil, add the chopped skinned tomatoes and cook quickly with the lid off the pan until the tomato mixture has reduced. Add the tomato purée if needed for colour and flavouring. Add the seasonings and other flavourings, mix with the potatoes and nuts to make a creamy mixture. Put this in the greased dish and spread evenly. Sprinkle the top with some chopped hazel nuts and cook in the oven for 30–40 minutes. Serve with onion or brown sauce, salad or a green vegetable.

N.B. When baking savouries make sure they are moist when placed in the oven or they will dry out when cooking.

ROAST CASHEW NUT AND MUSHROOM SAVOURY

8 oz. stale wholemeal bread, soaked in stock and squeezed dry

2 oz. oil or suenut or nutter

1–2 onions

1 oz. butter

½ lb. mushrooms or 4 oz. mushrooms and 4 oz. stalks

6 oz. milled cashew nuts

1 teaspoon chopped parsley and a squeeze of lemon juice

Seasoning, including a little paprika

1 beaten egg

A little cold sauce or milk

Method. Break the bread into small pieces and soak them in the stock. Heat the oven to 375–400° F., M5–6. When hot put in a roasting-tin containing the fat and the onions cut into halves or quarters. The onion flavours the roasting fat; herbs and garlic may also be used for this. (You may wish to finish cooking accompanying vegetables around the dish, e.g. potatoes, carrots, parsnips, artichokes, etc.; if so, please allow enough room on the tin.) Melt the butter in a frying-pan and cook the sliced mushrooms quickly, reducing all the excess liquid. Squeeze the bread and crumble into a bowl, add the cashew nuts, the mushrooms and herbs with the seasonings. Bind to a fairly firm dough with the egg and sauce or milk (it must retain its shape during cooking but should not be too dry in the centre when cooked) and shape into an oblong, or a roll, or a cake. Place carefully in the hot fat, using two slices or palette-knives. Decorate the top with nuts and baste well with the hot fat.

Savouries

Roast for ¾–1 hour, basting every now and then so that a rich brown crisp savoury crust is formed. Serve on a hot dish with apple sauce and brown or tomato sauce.

This type of savoury is very nice when stuffed—the stuffing adds flavour and tends to keep the savoury moist. See the section on Stuffings for recipes.

FRIED BRAZIL RICE

1 large finely chopped or grated onion.
½ oz. butter
8 oz. cooked brown rice
4 oz. browned milled Brazil nuts
Seasoning and a little chopped sage
1–2 eggs
Dried breadcrumbs
Butter or oil for frying

Method. Fry the onions until light brown and cooked. Add to the rice, Brazil nuts and seasoning. Beat one egg and mix well, all together—if the mixture is a little dry add more beaten egg. Shape into flat cakes ½–¾ inch thick and 1½–2 inches wide and coat these with dried breadcrumbs. Press on the dried breadcrumbs and leave to cool and set. Heat the fat (there should be enough to come half-way up the cakes) and fry them on both sides until golden brown. Butter gives the best flavour but tends to burn easily. Serve immediately with tomato or herb sauce.

SCOTCH EGGS

Method. Hard-boil eggs in the proportion of one for each two persons. Make a nut savoury mixture (using potato or bread crumbs as a 'backing'). When the eggs are cold, coat with the savoury ½–¾ inch in thickness so that the egg is within a fat cylinder. Dip and coat these in beaten egg, then breadcrumbs. Fry in deep fat until a golden brown. Slice in half so that the egg shows and stand on end. Serve hot with vegetables and sauce or cold with a salad.

Savouries

CROQUETTES OR RISSOLES

Using a savoury nut mixture form into cylinders or round cakes.

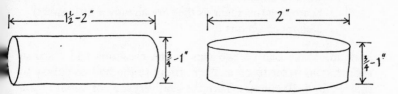

Coat with beaten egg and then with dried wholemeal bread-crumbs. Leave to set, then fry in deep fat or oil until a golden brown. Serve immediately or allow to cool and serve with a salad.

CROQUETTES OR RISSOLES EN SURPRISE

Place a small amount of stuffing in the centre of each croquette or rissole. This takes longer but makes a more interesting dish.

STEAMED ALMOND PUDDING

8 oz. finely grated blanched almonds
8 oz. fine breadcrumbs made from bread made with 81 per cent extraction flour
1 oz. butter
2 chopped onions
Seasonings
1 beaten egg
Milk or stock to mix

Method. Mix all the ingredients, using enough liquid to produce a dropping consistency. Put into a greased pudding basin, cover with greased greaseproof paper and a pudding-cloth. Stand on a rack in a pan of boiling water and cook for 1 hour. Turn out and serve with parsley or tomato sauce.

Colour and variety may be enhanced by the addition of cooked peas and diced carrots to the mixture.

Savouries

CHESTNUT SAVOURY

1–2 lb. chestnuts
Milk or stock
Seasoning (no sugar as they are already a little sweet)
2 chopped onions.

Method. Make one or two cuts in the chestnuts and place in enough cold water to cover them. Bring to the boil and allow to simmer for 5–10 minutes. Turn the heat very low, or remove from the heat and take out a spoonful of chestnuts at a time, reheating on each occasion. The two skins are removed, this is much easier when the chestnuts are hot! Rubber gloves are useful for this job. Cover the peeled chestnuts with milk or stock, add the chopped onion and seasoning. Simmer gently for 30–45 minutes or until the chestnuts are quite soft. Mash well with a potato-masher and use as follows:

1. Add 1–2 beaten eggs, allow to cool and shape. Egg and breadcrumb the shapes and fry. The mixture should be quite stiff for this.

2. Make a fairly moist mixture and use it for a stuffing.

3. Add breadcrumbs or mashed carrots or mushrooms or other vegetables and bake in the oven.

To keep chestnuts whole either cook for 45 minutes—1 hour in simmering water and remove the skins, or remove the skins first and cook as above for 10 minutes, then remove the second skin. Whole chestnuts are very good in vegetable stews or fried with onions.

Chestnuts are complementary to, and combine excellently with, brussels sprouts.

NUT SAVOURIES WITH PASTRY

Care must be taken to ensure that these are not too stodgy. It is important to remember that the nut savoury does NOT have to 'stand up' on its own. These savouries are better if mixed with vegetables.

100

Savouries

SAVOURY TRICORNES

Make some nut savoury (fairly moist mixture) and some short-crust or flaky type of pastry. Roll out the pastry and cut into 3–4-inch rounds (let the size depend on your estimate of the appetites!). Turn the rounds over and damp the edges. Place a spoonful of mixture in the centre of each round and fold the edges to form a tricorne (see diagram).

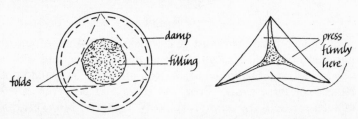

Press the pastry firmly at the corners, the centre can be left open a little to show the filling. Glaze with a beaten egg and bake in an oven suitable to the pastry. These can then be served hot or cold.

SAVOURY PASTIES

Make as above but shape as follows:

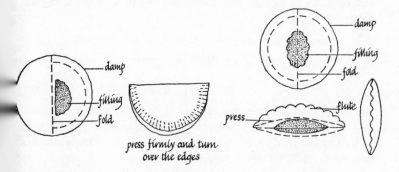

NUT FLANS

Prepare a good shortcrust pastry and with it line a shallow

oblong tin or a flan-ring. Bake this 'blind' for 10–15 minutes. Fill with a soft nut savoury mixture and continue baking for 20 minutes. Serve either hot or cold.

The nut savoury may be placed over a layer of lightly cooked vegetable, e.g. chestnut savoury over sprouts or celery, hazel-nut savoury over carrots, Brazil or cashew-nut savoury over onions and/or tomatoes. All these flans are very nice served with apple sauce.

Nut Rolls

1. Make a good shortcrust pastry including 2–4 oz. of grated nuts per 8 oz. of flour. Roll out to an oblong and spread with a vegetable filling. Damp the edges. Roll up very loosely (and not more than three turns). Press the edges and bake for 30–40 minutes (or until the centre is cooked) at 400° F., M6. This can be made with self-raising flour which gives a lighter centre.

2. Make some suet pastry and roll out thinly to an oblong. Fill with a nut and vegetable mixture. Roll up and wrap in greased greaseproof paper. Steam for 1–1½ hours. Unwrap and serve on a hot dish with brown onion sauce and a green vegetable or salad.

3. Make a savoury shortcrust (flavoured with curry powder is good) and make a roll, using a nut filling. This can be baked as a roll or it can be formed into a ring, cut and twisted as for the tea-ring in the yeast section.

EGGS

Boiled Eggs

Use eggs as fresh as possible. If in the refrigerator, take out and allow to resume normal temperature. Carefully put the eggs in boiling water (if they should crack, a little salt in the water will help to prevent the white from escaping). Cook as follows:

Soft-boiled eggs—4–5 minutes (white only just set).

Medium-boiled eggs—5–7 minutes (yolk just beginning to firm).

Hard-boiled eggs—10–15 minutes.

Savouries

If they are to be served as boiled eggs, lift them out of the water at once and place in the egg-cup—tap the end to crack and serve immediately. If they are to be shelled, pour out the boiling water and fill the saucepan with cold water. Tap the eggs very gently against the side and leave to stand until wanted.

Medium-boiled eggs make a very good savoury as they stand being heated again, but they must be shelled very carefully. Try them on cooked tomatoes or covered with a white mint sauce, or on savoury rice covered with cheese sauce and browned in the oven. They are also very good heated through in a curry sauce (see Curry section). Hard-boiled eggs may be treated in the same way or halved, stuffed, placed together again and covered with a sauce. This is known as *Oeuf en surprise* and is capable of many variations. Our favourite is the eggs stuffed with tomato filling, placed on spinach and covered with a mock hollandaise sauce.

POACHED EGGS

In the original method water is used, but there are pans on the market called 'poachers' which answer the same purpose. Actually these steam the eggs, and as they give a dryer, neater finish, many people prefer this method. The small containers of the poacher should be greased before cooking, otherwise the eggs will stick.

Water method

Fill a deep frying-pan or wide saucepan with enough water to cover the eggs and put a pinch of sea salt in the water. Bring the water just to boiling point. Break the eggs into a teacup or into a large spoon and slide the eggs one by one into the water. The water should be allowed to return just to boiling point before adding another egg. If the white of the egg does not quite enclose the yolk, help it to do so with a spoon. The eggs take about 3–4 minutes to set. Lift them out (when cooked to your liking) with a strainer spoon. Drain the eggs and place on buttered toast, buttered spinach, or mashed potato and serve immediately.

There is another method of poaching with water—half fill a small saucepan with sea-salted water. When just on boiling point, stir the water vigorously with a spoon so that a small whirlpool

Savouries

is formed. Drop the egg into the whirlpool and the action of the water gives a good shape; only one egg at a time can be cooked by this method.

'Poacher' method

Grease each little mould with butter or oil and put them in their tray over the pan filled with water, put the lid on and bring to the boil. When the water boils, remove the lid. Crack each egg into a teacup and slide it into the mould. Sprinkle each egg with a little sea salt and pepper if desired. Replace the lid and cook until sufficiently firm. Serve as before. If the eggs tend to stick in the mould help them out with a round-ended knife.

SCRAMBLED OR BUTTERED EGGS

Generally scrambled eggs contain a little milk but buttered eggs are made with eggs and butter only. Allow 2–3 eggs per person and 1–2 tablespoons of milk for each egg. Beat the eggs, milk (if used) and seasonings together. Melt 1–2 oz. of butter in a saucepan or frying-pan and allow it to become hot without browning. Pour in the egg mixture. Leave for a while until the bottom is set and then stir slowly, allowing the liquid to run underneath. When the mixture is nearly solid, remove from the heat and continue stirring gently; the heat from the pan is usually sufficient to complete the cooking. If the eggs are overcooked the curd becomes hard and tough and a watery liquid escapes, this is due to hardening and shrinking of the protein.

Scrambled eggs are usually served on buttered toast but there are other ways of cooking and serving:

1. Allow the butter to become nicely brown before adding the eggs and just before the eggs are cooked sprinkle in chopped parsley or chives or mint, etc.

2. Top large grilled tomatoes with scrambled egg and garnish with mint or parsley. Serve the tomatoes on spinach or potato.

3. Fry some chopped onion until golden brown and remove from the frying-pan. Now sauté some cooked potato until golden brown, add the cooked onion, pour in some scrambled egg and

cook until the egg is firm. Serve with peas, beans, spinach or any other green vegetable.

4. Sauté mushrooms or tomatoes, add scrambled egg and cook the eggs. A cooked vegetable such as peas, or diced carrots can be added to the beaten egg mixture and all cooked together.

FRIED EGGS

In shallow fat or oil Heat the oil or fat and slip the shelled egg in from a saucer. Baste the top of the egg with the hot fat, when cooked to your liking lift out with a slice and drain. The eggs may be cooked on both sides by turning with a slice when half-cooked. They can be served with fried bread, toast or vegetables.

In deep fat These can be fried in the deep fat bath if it is being used, or they can be fried one at a time in a small deep saucepan $\frac{1}{2}-\frac{3}{4}$ full of oil or fat. The fat should be heated until it is just smoking. Break the egg into a cup and gently slide it into the fat. If necessary use a spoon to bring the white around the yolk. Cook until the egg is firm and lift it out, drain well and serve with aubergines, pimentoes and garlic (if liked), tomatoes, or chipped potatoes and spinach.

SCOTCH EGGS
(*See Nut savoury section*)

STUFFED EGGS

Stuff some halved hard-boiled eggs and place the two halves together again. Flour the eggs, coat with beaten egg and finally with dried breadcrumbs. Leave to set and then fry in deep fat. Serve with vegetables and sauce.

BAKED EGGS

These can be baked in ramekin dishes (*en cocotte*) or on small fire-proof plates or flat dishes (*sur le plat*). The simplest way of baking is to put the dishes in a moderate to hot oven 375–400° F., M5–6 with a small pat of butter or a little oil in the

Savouries

bottom. Leave for 4–5 minutes, then remove from the oven, crack and drop in the eggs. Sprinkle the top with seasoning. Return to the oven for 8–10 minutes.

Variations

1. A little cream spooned over the top of the egg.

2. A little grated cheese, both under or over the egg.

3. A slice of tomato over the egg, sprinkled with grated cheese.

4. A base consisting of pimento, fried onions, tomato and sauté potato. When this is hot the egg is cracked and dropped on the top. Pour over some cream and bake until the egg is set. This must be done on a flat dish.

5. Chop some mushrooms and place in the previously warmed dishes, leave in the oven until the mushrooms are cooking nicely.

6. Place some asparagus tips in the bottom and warm through. Break in the egg and pour some cream over. Bake until the eggs are cooked.

Eggs can also be baked in nests of mashed potatoes. The nests can either be piped with a large star pipe individually; or the mashed potato can be put in an entrée dish and depressions made for the eggs. If the potato is brushed with a little beaten egg, the potato browns as the eggs bake. The result is most attractive in appearance.

Omelettes

There are two types of savoury omelettes: plain and soufflé. The plain kind are usually savoury and the soufflé sweet, but they may be made the other way round.

To make an omelette it is essential to have a proper pan (this may also be used for pancakes—see Batter section). It should be 6–8 inches in diameter and must be of really good quality with a thick heavy base and a smooth finish on the inside.

Stainless steel with a heavy base finished with copper is best, but iron, copper and aluminium pans are also available. These pans should never be washed unless unavoidable and be used only

106

Savouries

for omelettes and pancakes. Wipe a new pan free from dust, fill it with oil and let it stand for 12–24 hours. Then pour off the oil, heat the pan until the residual oil smokes. Remove from the heat and when it has cooled a little, wipe around with clean absorbent kitchen paper. It is then ready for use. Food may still stick a few times until the surface is 'proved' or 'seasoned'. The pan should always be left with a slightly oily and greasy surface so it should be stored in a plastic or paper bag to prevent dust collecting on it. It must always be wiped with a well-rung-out cloth or crumpled absorbent kitchen paper before using. After use it should be wiped again and put away when cool—if food sticks to the pan try to remove this carefully with a round-ended knife; failing this, scour the pan with sea salt and a well-rung-out cloth. After this treatment the pan should be 're-seasoned'.

Plain Omelette

Allow 1–3 eggs per person
Seasoning
1 dessertspoon–1 tablespoon water

Omelettes are better when made individually and eaten immediately, but if it is necessary to serve them all at the same time have a serving-dish ready in a warm oven. Cook the first ones lightly (they will cook a little in the oven whilst waiting for the others) and keep them warm in the oven while the others are being made; or one really large omelette can be made and divided at the table. This does not look nearly so attractive and it also presents cooking problems.

Method. Heat the omelette pan on a medium heat with a tablespoon or 1 oz. unsalted (if possible) butter in it. (Butter gives the best flavour, but if it contains salt, it tends to stick.) Oil gives a very good finish to the omelette. Beat the eggs with the water and seasoning until the yolks and whites are just mixed—do not beat until they are frothy. Some experts advocate using cream or milk, but we find this tends to produce a somewhat scrambled-egg texture. The water helps to lighten the omelette.

107

Savouries

When the pan and fat are hot, pour in the egg mixture, stir slowly with a fork to allow the liquid to run on to the bottom and set. When the top is nearly set, but still quite moist, stop stirring and cook quickly until the underside is nicely browned. With a palette-knife roll the omelette and gently press the roll to the side of the pan, so that when it is turned out the omelette will fit the curve of the plate. With a flick of the wrist turn the omelette on to a plate, add vegetables or garnish with grilled mushrooms, tomatoes and parsley or watercress. Serve.

The omelette should be cooked as quickly as possible so that the egg does not become tough and leathery; the centre should be slightly moist and creamy, a pleasant contrast to the firm outside.

Variations

1. Fines herbes. The classical 'fines herbes' consists of chopped parsley, chives, chervil and tarragon in equal parts, but any mixture can be used so long as no one flavour predominates. Parsley, mint, thyme or basil omelettes can also be made.

2. Cheese. While the omelette is cooking, but after it has set, sprinkle some finely grated cheese all over the surface, fold and turn out.

3. Tomato. Skin some tomatoes and chop them coarsely. Heat some butter and cook in it some garlic and chopped onion. Whilst hot add the tomatoes with a little seasoning. Cook until the mixture is fairly thick. Keep warm and spoon over the omelette just before rolling. A little chopped basil in the omelette gives a pleasant flavour.

4. Mushrooms. Slice some mushrooms and cook as above until nearly dry. Use the mushrooms as above mixture.

5. Spinach. Have some warm moist spinach purée ready and fill the omelette with it before rolling.

6. Sweet corn. Add 2–3 tablespoons of cooked sweet corn to the egg mixture before cooking and make the omelette in the usual way.

7. Onion. Prepare some spring onions or leek and add to the omelette before rolling. Garnish with plenty of onion rings (Spanish if possible).

Savouries

SOUFFLÉ OMELETTE

3 eggs
Seasoning
1–2 tablespoons water
1 oz. butter

Method. Separate the yolks from the whites of the eggs. Put the butter in the pan and heat. Beat the yolks with the seasoning and the water until all are creamy. Add the stiffly beaten egg-whites and mix fairly well together with a fork or the side of a metal spoon. Pour on to the hot butter and cook gently until the bottom is set and light brown. Then either place in a warm oven at 300–350° F., M2–4, until the omelette is set, or place under a medium grill and cook until the top is nicely browned. With a knife make a cut across the middle of the omelette (easier to fold) and fold in half. Turn out on to a warm plate and serve. These omelettes are usually stuffed with mixtures similar to the plain omelette; they are very good stuffed, coated with cheese or mornay sauce, then quickly browned under the grill.

SPANISH OMELETTES OR TORTILLAS

For these omelettes the above methods do NOT apply. They are a much more substantial dish than the plain omelette and are served as a meal in themselves. The ingredients vary according to the particular Spanish locality in which the tortillas are being made.

Method. Pour into a large frying-pan some good olive oil to at least ¼-inch deep. Heat until the oil is just smoking, then remove from the heat, add some chopped onions and 1–2 crushed cloves of garlic. Cook until nearly tender but not brown. Add ½ lb. of cooked potatoes finely sliced. About 10 minutes before they are done add 1 chopped red sweet pepper and some peas. When all the vegetables are cooked pour off any surplus oil (more oil should be added if the vegetables absorb it all), season the mixture well and pour on enough beaten eggs to cover the vegetables, this will probably require 4–5 eggs. The quantities depend on the size

Savouries

of the pan; when the vegetables are cooked they should not be more than 2 inches deep. Cook the omelette until the bottom is set and nicely browned, turn carefully with two slices or palette knives or turn into a pan of the same size and cook the other side in the same way. Serve immediately cut into wedges, or leave to cool and serve with a green salad (marvellous).

SOUFFLÉS

See Egg and Cheese section If you prefer not to mix proteins plain soufflés flavoured with vegetables can easily be made.

CURRIED EGGS
(*See Curry section*, p. 229)

Eggs with pastry

EGG VOL-AU-VENTS

Method. Make some small or one large vol-au-vents and fill with chopped hard-boiled eggs moistened with a creamy béchamel sauce. Chopped mint, mushrooms, peas and pimentoes can be added singly or together.

EGG PIE

Make some flaky type pastry, roll out to a large square and

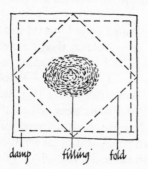

damp   filling   fold

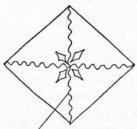

press fluted edges together
and decorate if desired

damp the edges. Place the filling (as above) in the centre; or use egg and mushrooms, or egg and mixed vegetables mixed with a little thick creamy béchamel sauce. Bring the corners together to form an envelope (see diagram).

Press the edges very firmly together and flute with the fingers. Leave a small opening in the centre to allow the steam to escape and decorate with pastry leaves. Brush with beaten egg and cook in a very hot oven 450° F., M8 for 15–20 minutes until the pastry is cooked. Serve with vegetables or cold with salad.

EGG AND MUSHROOM ROLL

Method. Make some rich shortcrust savoury pastry and roll out to an oblong. Damp the edges. Spread with a well-seasoned mixture of chopped, medium-boiled eggs and raw, finely chopped mushrooms. Add fresh chopped herbs if desired. Roll up loosely with not too many rounds of pastry—otherwise the centre may be heavy (to avoid this, self-raising flour may be used in the pastry, but it does not give a real pastry texture to the finished savoury). Bake in a hot oven 400–425° F., M6–7 until cooked, about 30–40 minutes. If the pastry tends to brown too much on top, cover with a greased paper. Serve with a sauce (tomato, parsley, béchamel, etc.) and vegetables.

VEGETABLE PATTIES OR FLANS FILLED WITH A SAVOURY EGG CUSTARD

Method. Make some shortcrust pastry and line some patty (or bun) tins or a flan case. Bake blind for 10–15 minutes and then fill with a warm savoury egg custard (see below). Bake in a slower oven until the custard is set and brown on top.

Variations to add to the egg custard
   1. Chopped fresh herbs and chopped cooked onion or leek.
   2. Sliced raw mushrooms.
   3. Skinned tomatoes, garlic and green pimento. A little cooked rice is good added to this.
   4. Spinach purée mixed with the custard.

5. Mashed carrots mixed with the custard.
6. Cooked peas and beans (broad, French or runner).

SAVOURY EGG CUSTARD

Basic recipe for 1 pint liquid.

Up to ¼ pint thin cream ⎤
Milk   ⎬
Up to ½ pint stock   ⎦
2–4 eggs or 2 eggs and 2 yolks
Flavourings as desired
Seasonings

Warm the liquid to about 120° F. and pour on to the eggs previously beaten with the seasonings. Pour into a greased fire-proof dish. Stand the dish in a tin of near-boiling water and bake in a moderate oven 350° F., M4, until it is set in the middle. Test by piercing the middle with a sharp pointed knife, no liquid should well out from the cut. This custard is occasionally made plain, but is usually flavoured as given above.

CHEESE

'Au gratin' dishes

Although this term is now closely associated with a browned cheese sauce, originally it meant no more than a coating with a white sauce and sprinkled with browned breadcrumbs or browned under the grill.

The food is usually cooked and placed in a shallow fire-proof dish, coated with a thick cheese sauce and sprinkled with grated cheese or a mixture of grated cheese and breadcrumbs. It is then browned under a medium-hot grill and served immediately or placed in the top of a hot oven to brown; when time is short it can be grilled a little first and then browned in the oven. A shallow dish is used so that proportionally more brown crust which is the best part, is formed. Practically any vegetables or mixture of vegetables can be treated in this way but here is a list from which new ideas may come:

Aubergine, potatoes and tomatoes

Beetroot and onions

Sprouting broccoli, broccoli or cauliflower

Brussels sprouts

Carrots and onions or leeks

Leeks, onions and shallots

Carrot and celery

Sweet corn, tomato and pimento

Carrot and spinach

Potato and spinach

Potato and carrot

Potato and celery

Potato, mushroom and peas

Parsnip, turnip and swedes

Potato, carrot and peas or any of the green bean family

Any of these mixtures can also be put into a half-baked flan case or patty cases of rich shortcrust or savoury pastry.

It is best to brown these flans or patties in the oven as the grill tends to catch the edge of the pastry.

CHEESE PUFFS

Method. Heat the oven to 400° F., M6. Make some choux paste (see Pastry section) and either pipe with a large plain pipe into éclair lengths or place in spoonfuls on a greased baking sheet. Bake until risen and golden brown. This generally takes about 25–30 minutes.

Prepare some thick white, béchamel or onion sauce and add any of the following:

1. Crumbled farmhouse Cheshire cheese.
2. Small cubes of Edam.
3. A mixture of grated Parmesan and Gruyère.
4. Sage Derby cheese.
5. Any of the blue-veined cheeses, crumbled.

Use only sufficient sauce to moisten and hold the cheese together. When the puffs are cooked, place on a wire tray and slit them open. If there is any soft choux paste inside scrape it out. Fill the shells with the cheese mixture and place in a hot oven for 5–10 minutes just to warm the puffs through, and to bring out the flavour of the cheese. Serve with sauce and vegetables or with a salad. These can also be served cold.

Savouries

DECIE'S POTATO PIE

1–2 lb. creamed potatoes
1–2 chopped onions, fried in butter
4–8 oz. grated cheese
Seasoning, including a little cayenne pepper, or French
  mustard if liked

Method. Cream the potatoes using the butter from the fried onions and adding more butter if necessary. Beat in the onions, seasoning and most of the cheese. Place in a greased shallow fireproof dish and sprinkle with the remainder of the cheese. Bake in a hot oven, 400° F., M6 until nicely browned. Serve with green vegetables and tomatoes.

Variations

1. Add some chopped fresh herbs to the potatoes or sprinkle liberally with chopped parsley just before serving.

2. Skin and dice some tomatoes ($\frac{1}{2}$ lb.) and place in the bottom of the dish, season well. Cover with the potato mixture. Sliced mushrooms, aubergines, sweet peppers can be added to the tomatoes.

3. Omit the onions from the potato mixture and spread the potato over cooked leeks and onions moistened with white sauce.

4. The cheese potato mixture can also be used to top cauliflower, carrots, beetroot or celery; the vegetables should be partly cooked first as they will finish cooking in the oven. They are better moistened with a little sauce.

5. Rub the entire inside of a fire-proof dish with a cut clove of garlic before putting in the potato mixture. If more garlic is preferred crush 1 or 2 cloves and fry with the onion.

6. Dry mash the potato with the cheese and onion so that the mixture is firm and dry. Spread on a floured plate and leave to cool. Shape on a floured board into rissoles or croquettes, dip into beaten egg and then dried breadcrumbs. Either bake in the oven or deep (or shallow) fat fry.

7. Mix the potato with another root vegetable, e.g. parsnip, turnip, carrot, kohl rabi or swede.

Savouries

PIZZA

Make a fairly rich dough, omitting the sugar (see Yeast section) using 8 oz. flour. While the dough is rising prepare the topping. In Italy this varies according to the part of the Mediterranean coast in which it is being made. The local produce governs the variations.

Here is a general topping:

> Olive oil
> 1 lb. tomatoes
> ½ lb. onions, including some spring onion and garlic if desired
> Chopped fresh herbs, including basil and marjoram
> Seasonings
> 3–4 oz. dried Edam, Bel paese, Port Salut or grated Gruyère
> Stuffed black stoned olives

Pour enough oil into the bottom of a frying-pan to cover it, then heat. Chop the onions finely and cook slowly in the pan. When they are half cooked add the chopped skinned tomatoes, seasonings and herbs. Cook quickly until the mixture is fairly thick. When the dough has risen to twice its size, knead lightly on a floured board and roll or press into a circle about ¼-inch thick. Place on a greased baking sheet and spread with the tomato mixture, sprinkle with the diced or grated cheese and the olives. Leave to rise again in a warm place for 10–15 minutes. Heat the oven to 375–400° F., M5–6. Brush the top of the pizza lightly with oil and bake 20–30 minutes. Serve with green vegetables or with a green salad.

CHEESE FRITTERS

1. Cut small slices of cheese of even size (Cheddar, Gruyère, Edam). Heat the deep fat until it is smoking. While the fat is heating make a coating batter. When the fat is ready dip the cheese into the batter and fry quickly. Drain and serve immediately.

115

Savouries

2. Make a savoury drop scone mixture and add to this either grated or small cubes of cheese. A little chopped sweet pepper, tomato or fresh herbs are useful flavourings. Heat enough oil to cover the bottom of a frying-pan and drop the fritter mixture in spoonfuls into the pan. When set and brown on one side, turn with a palette-knife and cook the other side. Serve at once with a sauce and vegetables.

CHEESE PUDDINGS

Line a pudding-basin with some cheese suenut pastry and fill with any suitable vegetable mixture.

> Cauliflower, onion and carrot
> Leeks and carrots
> Onions and tomatoes, etc.

Season the vegetable filling and add a little stock. Put on the pastry lid and cover with greased greaseproof paper and a pudding cloth. Place in a saucepan of boiling water on a stand and simmer gently for 1½–2 hours. Serve with a sauce and a green vegetable.

CHEESE PIES

Make a good rich cheese pastry and use as follows:

1. Line a fire-proof plate with the pastry and cover with a layer or two of seasoned uncooked vegetables. Damp the edges of the pastry. Cover this with more pastry and press the edges together. Flute the edges and glaze the lid with beaten eggs. Make a hole in the centre to allow the steam to escape and decorate with pastry leaves. Bake in a quick oven 400° F., M6 for 15 minutes; then lower the heat in order to cook the filling without over-cooking the pastry. These plate pies or tarts are very good for picnics or served cold with a salad.

2. Prepare and cook some vegetables as for a stew or casserole. When they are half cooked turn into a deep pie dish and cover with cheese pastry. Cook as above.

Savouries

EGG AND CHEESE SAVOURIES

Soufflés

1 oz. butter
1 oz. 81 per cent extraction flour
¼ pint milk or milk and stock
3 egg-yolks and 4 egg-whites or 3–4 eggs
Seasonings
Flavourings as preferred

Grease a fire-proof dish and heat the oven to 375–400° F., M5–6. Soufflés need bottom heat so place a baking sheet on a shelf just below the middle of the oven to receive the soufflé dish.

Method. Separate the yolks from the whites of the eggs and beat the whites until very stiff. Melt the fat in a large saucepan and make a roux with the flour. Add the liquid, a very thick paste will result; this is called a panada. With gentle cooking this paste will leave the sides of the pan. Cook the panada gently for 2–3 minutes, then remove from the heat. Allow to cool a little, then beat in the egg-yolks and seasonings. With a metal spoon, cut and fold in the whites, spoon the mixture into the prepared dish. Bake for 30–40 minutes until well risen and browned. Serve immediately with potatoes, vegetables and sauce.

Plain soufflés are not often made. The cheese soufflé is regarded as the favourite. Variations may be made with the addition of vegetables.

Cheese soufflé Add 3 ozs grated cheese (Cheddar, Parmesan, Gruyère, Edam, Sage, Derby) to the egg-yolks. A little cayenne pepper or paprika pepper or French mustard brings out the flavour of the cheese. Be careful with the salt as many cheeses contain enough salt and no more is necessary.

Mushroom soufflé Add 4–8 oz. cooked, but dry, mushrooms to the cheese soufflé with the egg-yolks and cheese.

Cauliflower soufflé Parboil some sprigs of cauliflower and drain

Savouries

carefully. Place in the bottom of the dish and pour the cheese soufflé over. Bake.

Tomato soufflé Skin some tomatoes, cut in half and place in the bottom of the dish. Season well and pour over them a cheese soufflé mixture with a little chopped mint added. Bake.
Sweet corn soufflé Add some cooked well-drained sweet corn with the cheese.

Spanish soufflé Cook some onions, garlic, sweet peppers, and tomato in a little butter and when thick add to the panada with the milk. A little cooked brown rice stirred into this soufflé is a very pleasant addition.

Aubergine soufflé Cook some diced aubergine in a little butter with some finely chopped onion. When cooked add the mixture to the panada with the yolks and cheese.

Spinach soufflé Add 4–6 tablespoons of spinach purée to the panada using less milk to maintain the consistency. A little sorrel with the spinach gives an unusual but pleasant, sharp flavour.

Herb soufflé and Cress soufflé Add chopped fine herbs with cheese.
When adding vegetables or vegetable purées to the soufflé mixture, take care that they do not cause the panada to be too soft. See that they are well drained or use less milk in the panada. If the panada is too soft the soufflé will probably rise well, but will fall very quickly when cooked and removed from the oven.

If an equal quantity of yolks and whites is used a firmer soufflé will result. With 3 yolks and 4 whites it will be lighter.

Soufflés may also be layered; vegetables may be placed in a layer in the centre of the soufflé as a surprise, but the layer or layers of vegetables must not be too thick as this will impede the rising process.

CHEESE PUDDING

This is really savoury egg custard with cheese and breadcrumbs or cooked rice added.

Savouries

1 pint milk or ¾ pint milk and ¼ pint thin cream
4–6 oz. breadcrumbs or cooked rice
2–3 eggs or 2 eggs and 2 yolks
4–6 oz. grated cheese
Seasonings

Grease a fire-proof dish. Heat the oven to 325–350° F., M3–4. Heat the milk and pour on to the breadcrumbs or rice, add the beaten eggs, cheese and seasonings. Pour into the dish and bake until it is set. If rice is used, it is a good idea to stand the dish in a shallow tin of hot water while cooking. This dish can be varied in much the same way as can savoury egg custard. It is particularly good with onion and mushrooms or plenty of chopped fresh herbs.

CHEESE AND EGG FLANS

1. *Quiche lorraine* Method. Line a flan-ring or shallow fire-proof pie dish with rich shortcrust or flaky pastry. Cut some Gruyère cheese into fairly thin slices and cover the bottom and sides of the pastry with them. Pour into the flan case a well-seasoned custard mixture made from eggs and double cream. 2 eggs to ¼ pint of double cream is the correct proportion, but the cream can be single; or even top of the milk makes a good flan. The custard may be flavoured with cooked spinach or leeks. Bake in a moderate oven 375° F., M5 until it is set and nicely browned. Serve with vegetables or cold with salad.

2. Bake a flan case blind and when it is set, but not brown, pour in a mixture of beaten eggs, grated cheese, cooked vegetables and a little cream. For an 8-inch flan case use 3 eggs, about 4 oz. of grated cheese and a little top of the milk with enough cooked vegetables to fill the flan. Some savoury fillings are:

Cauliflower, mushroom and peas.
Tomato and mushroom.
Onion or leeks.
Carrot and onion.
Beetroot and onion.

Bake as a *quiche lorraine* and serve with parsley or nut sauce.

Savouries

3. Line some bun-tins or a flan case with a rich shortcrust pastry flavoured with curry paste. Heat the oven to 400° F., M6. Make a really thick béchamel sauce and flavour this well with cheese. Beat in 1 egg per ¼ pint of sauce and half fill the pastry cases. Bake until the pastry is cooked and risen, and the filling is brown. Serve immediately.

A thin layer of cooked vegetables can be placed under the cheese filling to give variety.

CHEESE D'ARTOIS

Heat the oven to 450° F., M8. Roll out some flaky or puff pastry thinly to an oblong. Spread half of it with a fairly stiff, well-seasoned mixture of beaten egg and finely grated cheese. Fold the other half of the pastry over it and mark the top into slices. Brush well with beaten egg and bake until well risen and brown, about 15–20 minutes. Divide into fingers and serve either hot or cold.

CHEESE SCOTCH EGGS

Cover hard-boiled eggs with a stiff, duchesse potato mixture which is well flavoured with grated cheese. Shape and coat with egg and dried breadcrumbs. Leave to set and then fry in deep fat. Serve with a green vegetable and tomato sauce.

CHEESE AIGRETTES

Make some choux paste; add 1 oz. of finely grated cheese to each egg used. The cheese is beaten in after the eggs. Heat some deep fat until it is just hazing about 320–330° F. and then drop the mixture in in small spoonfuls. Fry slowly for 7–10 minutes until golden brown and well puffed out. Serve immediately.

PASTA

Wholemeal macaroni can be bought in health food stores but even so it is better to make one's own noodles and ravioli from the nouille paste given in the Pastry section.

Savouries

To cook pasta have a large saucepan half–two-thirds full of boiling water which is sea salted. Throw in the pasta a little at a time so that the water does not come off the boil, then cook gently until the pasta is tender. Drain well. Heat some butter in the saucepan, return the pasta and toss it in the butter. Add seasoning if necessary and serve with:

(1) finely grated cheese;
(2) a thick onion and tomato sauce and garlic if liked;
(3) a green vegetable.

MACARONI CHEESE

Cook some macaroni; mix with enough mornay sauce to moisten it well, the mixture must not be too dry. Place in a greased fire-proof dish and sprinkle with cheese. Brown under the grill, or in the oven, and serve.

SAVOURY MACARONI

Fry some onions, mushrooms and sweet peppers in butter. Stir in some cooked macaroni and a chopped hard-boiled egg for each person. Moisten well with cheese, tomato or herb sauce and finish as for macaroni cheese. Alternatively the macaroni may be served without the sauce, sprinkled with cheese only.

NOODLES

These are cooked and used in the same way as macaroni. To make them: roll out the nouille paste as finely as possible. Flour it well and roll it up loosely. Cut into pieces about $\frac{1}{8}$–$\frac{1}{4}$-inch thick and shake the pieces in a floured cloth to separate them and unroll them a little. Put in a warm place to dry out and when quite dry, store and use as required.

RAVIOLI

Roll out some nouille paste very thinly into an oblong. Cut into two equal pieces. Make a thick paste from cooked spinach purée and grated cheese. Put teaspoonfuls of this mixture evenly over one half of the pastry. Damp the paste between the stuffings. Place the other piece of pastry over the top and press down on to the damped sections. Cut into squares with a sharp knife or a pastry cutter. Leave to dry on a floured board for an hour or two; then cook in boiling salted water. Serve with tomato sauce.

RICE

Whenever possible buy the brown (unpolished) rice from a health or other food store. The food value of the unpolished rice is much better.

First wash the rice well, then cook, either in the same way as macaroni (but keep the water boiling fast all the time) or by the following method.

Bring 4–5 oz. of rice to the boil in sea-salted water or vegetable stock. When boiling, transfer to the oven or to a double boiler and cook with the lid on in a moderate heat until the rice is tender and all the liquid is absorbed. Add more liquid if necessary.

RISOTTO

> 1–2 oz. butter
> 1 chopped onion and 1 crushed clove garlic
> 5 oz. brown rice
> 1 pint stock
> Bouquet garni
> Seasoning
> 2–3 oz. finely grated dry cheese

Fry the onion and garlic in the butter; when it is turning brown add the washed and well-drained rice. Fry for 5–10 minutes. Add the stock, seasoning and bouquet garni and bring to the boil, stirring gently to prevent sticking. Put it in a double saucepan, and cook with the lid on until all the stock is absorbed (if the rice is not tender add a little more stock). With a fork stir in the butter and cheese. Serve hot.

Savouries

Risotto can be varied by using a little saffron, tomatoes, mushrooms or pimentoes and serve with fried bananas.

RISOTTO SAVOURY

Allow some thick risotto to cool and shape into balls around some cubes of Gouda or Edam cheese. Coat with beaten egg and dried breadcrumbs. Leave to set and then fry in deep fat. Serve immediately.

SAVOURY RICE CAKES

Cook some rice as for risotto but beat in 1–2 eggs when cooked, instead of the butter and cheese. Spread on a plate to cool. When cold shape into flat cakes and coat with dried breadcrumbs. Fry in shallow fat and serve with vegetables.

RICE AND VEGETABLE PIE

Cook some rice as for risotto. Put a layer of the rice in the bottom of a greased fire-proof dish and cover with a layer of parboiled vegetables. Cover these with sliced and skinned tomatoes and grated cheese. Repeat the layers once more, finishing with a layer of rice. Dot the top with pats of butter and pour over it a little cream. Bake in a moderate-hot oven for 30–40 minutes or until the vegetables are tender. Sprinkle with chopped parsley and serve.

Pulses

The method for cooking pulses is given in the Vegetable section. They are generally used in soups, stews and casseroles or braised in much the same way as baked beans. They can be mashed and shaped into rissoles or croquettes, or they may be mashed with vegetables, plenty of onions, and baked in the oven. Cheese may also be added if desired. Most pulses seem to combine well with tomatoes, onions and mushrooms. When cooked they are often improved with a white, cheese or herb sauce.

6

Stuffings

Fillings for salads are given in the Salad chapter (page 77) and in the section on beginnings, which deal with small salads. One can really experiment with stuffings, using imagination and skill in a way which give that wonderful feeling when a complementary flavouring hitherto unknown to you, results. One of the main reasons for having a stuffing is that it shall enhance and complement the flavour of the finished dish. They are also used to prevent food becoming too dry and to add food value to the dish.

Two mistakes which are generally made in stuffings are:

1. Too much use of breadcrumbs as a main ingredient.

2. The stuffing is mixed too dry and does not contain sufficient fat.

Whole rice, potatoes, onions, chestnuts, pulses and apples make a welcome change and oatmeal and sweetcorn can be added to any of these to overcome the former error.

The fat content should be one-third to half to one part of the main ingredient, much the same proportion as pastry. Fat may be added in several ways: cream, melted butter, suenut, nut butters. Very often one or more of the ingredients will have been fried or sautéd in butter or oil, which will add to the fat content. The flavourings that can be added to the stuffings are legion, but here are just a few.

Herbs, fresh or dried, curry powder or paste, paprika or cayenne pepper, French mustard, sweet peppers or aubergine, olives, green and black, nuts and cheeses, fruits—fresh, dried or juice, mushrooms, garlic, grated zest of lemon or orange, chutney or chopped pickles.

As a general guide a bland vegetable such as marrow can take a strong flavouring but a sweet pepper or similar vegetable which has a distinctive flavour of its own is better with a mild or complementary stuffing.

We will give only a few recipes for general guidance then we hope you will experiment on your own.

The quantities can be increased or decreased as you wish.

STUFFINGS FOR NUT SAVOURIES

As nuts are rich in fats they need a sharp stuffing to complement them and to help their digestion.

APPLE AND POTATO STUFFING

1 tablespoon oil
½ lb. onions
½ lb. cooking apples
1 oz. butter
Flavouring herbs tied in a bundle—lemon thyme, parsley, savoury, mint, chervil and sage
Grated rind of orange or orange juice
Enough freshly mashed or sieved potato to make a fairly firm stuffing—about 2 large or 3 medium potatoes
Seasoning and brown sugar to taste

Heat the oil and sauté the chopped apple and onion slowly for 10–15 minutes. Add the herbs, orange juice and a little stock if necessary. Simmer until the onions are cooked, remove the bundle of herbs and sieve. Add the potato and butter, mix to a firm purée. Taste and adjust the flavouring if necessary with sea salt and brown sugar.

Stuffings

APRICOT STUFFING

1 cup dried apricots
1 cup water or apple juice
3–4 cups wholemeal breadcrumbs
½ cup chopped celery
2 oz. melted butter or nut butter
Seasoning

Cook the washed apricots in the liquid for 5–10 minutes. Strain but save the liquid. Chop the apricots fairly finely and mix with all the ingredients using the juice to moisten the mixture.

MIXED FRUIT STUFFING

½ cup chopped cooking apples
½ cup chopped soaked prunes
¼ cup seeded raisins
¼ cup chopped oranges
Salt, brown sugar, a little nutmeg to taste
2 cups toasted breadcrumbs
2 tablespoons melted butter or nut butter
½–¾ cup apple juice or grape juice

Mix all well together and leave for an hour or so before using. This is also a good stuffing for tomatoes as it is slightly sweet.

STUFFINGS FOR VEGETABLES

SAVOURY RICE
(especially good for sweet peppers)

4 oz. cooked and dried whole rice
Garlic if liked
Chopped fresh herbs to flavour
1 medium onion chopped finely and cooked in 1 oz. butter
1 tablespoon concentrated tomato purée
2 oz. grated or cubed cheese
Enough fresh tomato purée to moisten
Seasoning

126

Mix all the ingredients together to a soft consistency. Taste and adjust the seasonings. Use as required.

Mushrooms and peas are a good addition to this stuffing.

The cheese may be replaced with chopped hard-boiled egg.

NUT STUFFINGS

Any of the recipes given in the section on Nut Savouries (page 95) make good stuffings, but here are one or two more.

BRAZIL AND RAISIN STUFFING

4 oz. wholemeal breadcrumps
2 oz. chopped or grated Brazil nuts
2 oz. stoned or chopped raisins
1 tablespoon chopped parsley with 1 chopped sage leaf added
1½–2 oz. melted butter or Brazil nut butter
1 egg
Seasoning

Mix everything together. This is a good stuffing for onions.

ALMOND AND APRICOT STUFFING

1 oz. butter or suenut
2 large chopped onions
4 oz. coarsely grated or chopped almonds
6 fresh or about 12 soaked apricots, diced finely.
1 tablespoon chopped fresh herbs
Grated zest and juice of ½ lemon
Sea salt and brown sugar to taste.

Melt the fat and fry the onions until slightly brown, add the almonds and continue cooking for 3–5 minutes. Remove from the heat and add the remainder of the ingredients.

This makes a very good stuffing for cucumbers. If you want a more substantial stuffing add a little mashed potato and use for stuffing marrows.

Stuffings

CHESTNUT STUFFING

1 lb. peeled chestnuts
1 large chopped onion
1 oz. suenut
Milk or milk and stock
Sea salt to taste

Make a cut or cross in the chestnuts and place them in cold water. Bring to the boil and boil for 3–5 minutes. Turn down the heat so that the water keeps warm but does not boil at all. Remove a few chestnuts at a time and peel off both skins. Fry the onion in the fat, add the peeled chestnuts and just cover with the liquid. Add salt and simmer gently until the chestnuts are cooked. Mash with a potato masher and add more milk, or milk and stock, if necessary.

This stuffing may be enhanced by the addition of a little apple.

SWEET CORN STUFFING

1 oz. butter
1 medium-size chopped onion
2–3 boiled cobs sweet corn
2 eggs
Sea salt and brown sugar to taste
Grated rind and juice of $\frac{1}{2}$ lemon
1 tablespoon chopped parsley

Melt the butter and cook the onion in it without browning. Strip the cobs and add the sweet corn to the onion. Cook for a further 2–3 minutes. Remove from the heat and add the remainder of the ingredients. This makes a good stuffing for tomatoes.

HERB STUFFING

(If only lemon rind and parsley are used this is known as Maître d'hôtel stuffing.)

Stuffings

1 large onion and 1 leek
2 oz. butter or suenut
Grated rind and juice of 1 lemon
2 tablespoons other fresh chopped herbs
1 egg or 2 tablespoons cream
½ teaspoon curry paste if liked
3 oz. wholemeal breadcrumbs
1 oz. medium oatmeal
1 tablespoon chopped parsley
Sea salt and brown sugar to taste

Fry the onion and leek in the fat until they are cooked, add to all the other ingredients and mix until they are of a soft consistency. Use a little stock or apple juice if the stuffing is too firm. This makes a good stuffing for a whole cabbage.

MUSHROOM STUFFING

1 onion and 1 leek
2 oz. butter or suenut
8 oz. mushrooms or 4 oz. mushrooms and 4 oz. mushroom stalks
Enough potato, rice or breadcrumbs to make a soft stuffing
1 egg or 2 tablespoons cream
Season with herbs to taste

Fry the chopped onion and leek in the fat until they are brown. Add the mushrooms (washed and chopped) and cook rapidly until all the liquid from the mushrooms has evaporated. Stir in the rice, potato or breadcrumbs and add the herbs and seasoning. Moisten with egg or cream. Use as required.

Hard-boiled eggs, cheese, peas or chopped pimento can be added to this stuffing.

This stuffing may also be made with carrots, celery, tomatoes or asparagus tips in place of the mushrooms. The tomatoes are skinned first and then treated like the mushrooms. The carrots and celery are chopped and cooked with the onion and leek—a little more fat may be needed.

7

Vegetables

Vegetables are a most important part of our diet, they provide many minerals and vitamins and plenty of roughage. Some vegetables also give us carbohydrates and second-class proteins in varying amounts. It is important to try to eat some raw vegetables each day—we deal with this in the Salad section—the recipes following are for cooked vegetables to serve as an accompaniment to a Savoury dish. They are arranged alphabetically for convenience. Some so-called vegetables, e.g. tomato, marrow, aubergine, etc. are really fruits, but we have included them here as they are used as vegetables. For protein combined with vegetables, see Savoury section.

BUYING

1. Freshness—if possible grow in one's own garden without artificial fertilizers—further information on this point may be obtained from the Soil Association. Take from the garden no more than the daily need, as for each day produce is left unused after gathering there is a corresponding loss in flavour and nutritive value never to be regained. If you are not blessed with your own garden produce then try to purchase from the local grower, although this is easier in the country, unfortunately for town dwellers.

2. Buy in season—young tender vegetables are by far the best, but beware of the forced and so-called imported young vegetables Unfortunately labour problems beset the market gardener and

130

Vegetables

pickers are used only for the main crop, so we miss the first pickings. This is another good reason for growing your own if at all possible.

TABLE OF VEGETABLES IN SEASON

This, of course, is approximate as the weather can so easily affect the length of the season making vegetables earlier or later as conditions dictate. Home growers have the obvious advantage of being able to pick in small amounts early and late at the right time. Greengrocers so often have over-mature vegetables or a mixture of the season's produce.

	English	Continental
Artichokes (globe)	Aug.–Oct.	All year round
Artichokes (Jerusalem)	Oct.–Mar.	
Asparagus	April–June	Mar.–May
Beans, broad	June–Aug.	Mar.–May
Beans, runner	June–Oct.	
Beans, French	May–Aug.	All year round
Beetroot	May–Mar.	
Broccoli	Mar.–May	Dec.–Mar.
Brussels Sprouts	Aug.–Feb.	
Cabbage, all varieties, green	All year round	
Cabbage, red	June–Sept.	Sept.–April
Capsicums (green or red peppers)	Sept.–Oct.	All year round
Carrots, young	May–Aug.	Feb.–June
Carrots, old	Sept.–Mar.	
Cauliflower	Mar.–Nov.	Nov.–April
Celeriac	Oct.–Mar.	
Celery	July–Mar.	May–June
Cucumber	May–Sept.	Sept.–Jan.
Kale	Nov.–Mar.	
Leeks	Oct.–April	
Marrow	June–Oct.	
Mushrooms, field	July–Sept.	

131

Vegetables

	English	Continental
Mushrooms, cultivated	All year round	
Onions	Sept.–Nov.	All year round
Parsnips	Sept.–April	
Peas, fresh	June–Sept.	
Potatoes	All year round	
Samphire	Aug.–Sept.	
Seakale	Jan.–Mar.	
Spinach	Mar.–Dec.	Feb.-Mar.
Swedes	Sept.–April	
Tomatoes	May–Oct.	Oct.–May
Turnips	Sept.–Mar.	
	English	Continental

PREPARATION
General Rules

The golden rule is to prepare the vegetables immediately before cooking, and the sooner from garden to pot the greater the food value! Wash all vegetables well and quickly in COLD water, using a soft scrubbing-brush for root vegetables.

Do not peel root vegetables unless they are very old, either scrape or peel as thinly as possible. Very often most of the goodness lies just beneath the skin, but the exceptions are root vegetables such as turnips, swedes, celeriac, etc. which have a protective fibrous layer around the root.

If you need to cut the vegetables use a very sharp stainless steel knife to lessen bruising and do this immediately before cooking—straight from the chopping-board to the saucepan. It is advisable when possible to choose root vegetables of roughly the same size, this eliminates cutting them so that they all cook in the same time.

Try not to leave vegetables which have been cut, soaking in water, as the soluble vitamins and minerals dissolve out and the food value is thereby lessened. If you must prepare vegetables before they can be cooked immediately, either place in a covered container without water in a refrigerator or cool place, or place

132

Vegetables

in a bowl barely covered with water and use the water for cooking the vegetables. Onions should never be allowed to soak in water; they should be wrapped tightly in greaseproof paper when peeled.

GENERAL METHODS OF COOKING

These are only the general methods—special points for each vegetable will be given in its own section.

1. *Boiling* Place even-sized pieces of vegetable in boiling sea-salted water—just enough water to cover vegetable. Cook until just tender. Greens should be treated in a slightly different way. The water should be boiled and a handful of greens added. The water then goes off the boil and should be allowed to boil again before another handful of greens is added. Repeat until all is in and boil until tender. This method conserves the colour of the greens.

2. *Conservative method* This is considered to be one of the best methods for most vegetables. Melt a little butter or nut fat in a saucepan, about 1½ oz. per lb. of vegetables. Toss very finely cut vegetables in this and cook very slowly for 5–10 minutes. Add a ¼ pint of vegetable water or water to each lb. of vegetables and cook slowly until tender, stirring and turning vegetables if necessary. You may have to add more water, but this should be done in small quantities and only if necessary. Most of the water should have evaporated by the time the vegetables are cooked and the small amount remaining can either be served with the vegetables as it is or thickened with 81 per cent extraction flour to make a sauce. There is no need to add sea salt during the cooking because this method conserves the natural salts and flavour; usually no salt is required.

This method requires far more close attention than others, as the risk of the vegetables burning is so great, but the results are so much better that we think the effort is well worth while.

The fat can be omitted if desired.

3. *Steaming* This was a favourite method between the wars,

133

Vegetables

but since it has been discovered that the quicker cooking methods conserve the food value better, it has lessened in popularity.

Prepare vegetables in the usual way and cut into even-sized pieces if necessary. Place in a steamer with water boiling well and allow about half as long again as the time described in the boiling method. This is not a suitable method for green vegetables.

4. *Oven cooking* (a) Baking. This method usually means cooking in the oven without the use of fat. It is used mainly for potatoes in their jackets but parsnips can also be cooked this way and beetroot if they are wrapped in greaseproof paper.

(b) Roasting. Means cooking in the oven with the use of fat in an open dish so that browning can take place. The following are among the vegetables which roast well—potatoes, onions, Jerusalem artichokes, marrow, carrots and parsnips. The fat can be of nut or vegetable origin. Oil may also be used. Flavouring can be added by putting a small piece of onion or garlic or herbs in the fat, before being heated. When the fat or oil is well heated add the raw or partly cooked vegetables. Baste and turn the vegetables whilst they are cooking so that they brown well—length of cooking depends upon size and age of vegetables.

(c) Casserole. This is the oven equivalent of the conservative method; the cooking takes place in a fire-proof dish with a tight-fitting lid. The cooking may be started in a saucepan and then the saucepan transferred to the oven. Sometimes single vegetables are casseroled but more often a variety is used. The vegetables are sliced or diced. Start cooking as for the conservative method, adding stock or water three-quarters of way up vegetables; bring to the boil and then place in a slow oven until cooked, or place vegetables in a casserole, nearly cover with boiling stock or water, and cook as before.

5. *Braising* This is similar to the conservative method—the difference being that the vegetables are thoroughly browned before the liquid is added. The vegetables are generally kept whole and should be of even size. When the vegetables are cooked they must be kept warm while the cooking liquor is reduced to a coating glaze which is poured over the vegetables before serving

Vegetables

6. *Frying* This is cooking vegetables (either raw or partly cooked) in fat, either deep fat or shallow fat frying. If deep fat frying is preferred some form of coating is used to protect the vegetables. Small and regular-sized vegetables are usually cooked prior to frying. Shallow fat frying is often used for raw vegetables and many Chinese dishes are prepared this way.

7. *Pressure cooking* This should be an excellent way of cooking vegetables as it lessens the cooking time appreciably, but it has, however, a questionable disadvantage—to wit the high cooking temperature—which we feel may destroy some food values. We recommend it to people who have little time to prepare their meals.

SERVING VEGETABLES

1. Drain carefully and *keep* any vegetable water that is not being served with the vegetables. Much too often this valuable liquid is thrown away—it should be used for drinks, soups, sauces, moistening savoury dishes, gravies or for cooking more vegetables. If you know prior to the meal that you will have no use for the liquids it is better to use the conservative method of cooking.

2. If further mashing or chopping is desired do it just before serving.

3. Add further seasoning and accompaniments such as glazes, butter, chopped herbs or sauces as required.

ARTICHOKES (GLOBE)

These are becoming more popular and are seen mostly in high-class grocery shops. They should be firm and green and the leaves should be close-fitting and tight. They are really buds picked before they flower and consist of three parts. First the leaves, secondly the choke enclosed by the leaves which is the hairy fibrous part (it would normally become the flower) and thirdly under the choke the most delicious part, i.e. the bottom, or as it is more generally known by its French name, the *fond*.

To prepare them cut the stalks off close to the leaves at the base. Remove discoloured outside leaves and any dry tips with scissors. If you know they were grown in clean conditions then just wash them, otherwise soak in salt water for 5–10 minutes, this will remove any insects. The choke can be removed before cooking; if you do this then rearrange the leaves and tie firmly but not too tightly with thin string or tape so that they do not lose shape when cooking. Another method is to fill the space left by the choke with a purée of spinach or stuffing, rearrange the leaves and tie as before. Cook immediately in salted boiling water, the stalk end uppermost, until the leaves pull out easily—this depends on the size or maturity—small or young ones take about 20 minutes, but larger ones may take up to one hour, although they are generally cooked in 40 minutes. Remove from the saucepan very carefully—a 'holey' spoon is very useful for this purpose—drain well the right way up. It is useful to use a rack with a tin beneath to catch the drips, but if you are only cooking two or three a large colander will do.

Serve the artichokes on a warm napkin in a hot dish and hand melted butter, browned butter sauce or hollandaise sauce with them. To eat the artichokes, pull out the leaves one by one and dip in the melted butter or sauce. Suck the base of the leaves (rather like eating asparagus). If the choke has been left in, remove it, and with a knife and fork eat the *fond*.

The *fonds* are considered a great delicacy on the Continent and there are many recipes for their use. You will find tinned artichokes or *fonds* at any good delicatessen and although they are easier to use, having been prepared, like most preserved foods, the flavour is not as good as the freshly prepared.

Stuffed Fried 'Fonds'

To prepare the *fonds*: trim stalk and cut leaves off just above the *fond*—cut the leaves at the side close to the *fond* so that it is left a tidy shape. Cook as for the artichokes in boiling salted water until soft. You may also cook in wine, but this is a matter of personal choice. Sandwich two together with some stuffing of your own choosing (may we suggest a plain stuffing such as Maître d'hôtel, page 128 to begin with). Then egg and breadcrumb, fry in deep oil until a golden brown and well heated through. Serve with béchamel or tomato sauce.

ARTICHOKES IN WHITE WINE

Prepare some artichokes in the usual way and parboil them. Cut them in quarters and cut out the choke. Place in a casserole with some butter, seasoning and moisten with a glass of white wine (Sauterne or Sauterne type of wine or apple juice). Cook slowly in the oven with the lid on at M3 or 325° F. for 25 minutes or until the leaves come away easily. Cover with a good brown sauce and serve.

ARTICHOKES (JERUSALEM)

This vegetable is in no way related to the Globe artichoke; it is the tuber root of a plant belonging to the sunflower family. It has a very distinctive flavour, rather earthy or smoky. When buying be sure the tubers are firm and free from telltale wrinkles of age.

To prepare, wash and scrub well. If they are freshly dug they may need scrubbing in two or three changes of water. Place in boiling salted water to which a little lemon juice has been added and boil in their skins until tender; approximately 15 minutes for young ones and 30 minutes or more for older ones. They can be pierced easily with a skewer or sharp knife when ready for serving. Peel while still hot (rubber gloves or a fork are handy at this stage!), toss in melted butter and chopped parsley or cover with a white béchamel, mushroom or caper sauce immediately. These artichokes discolour very easily and so we feel this is the easiest and most nutritious method. If you feel you would rather peel the skin before cooking—peel or scrape, using a sharp stainless steel knife and place immediately in clean cold water to which some lemon juice has been added. Use the water for cooking the artichokes.

Vegetables

ROAST ARTICHOKES

Place some oil or vegetable/nut fat in a roasting-tin and heat
to about 400° F. Place peeled artichokes in tins and roast until
cooked. They will become discoloured but the flavour is very
good. You may prefer to roast them around a nut or similar
savoury. If they are roasted in their skins the skins are uneatable
as they become bitter but the flesh is good.

ARTICHOKE CHIPS

Peel artichokes, cut into thin slices and place immediately in
acidulated water—leave there for 20–30 minutes and then pat dry
with a clean absorbent cloth (a clean drying-up cloth is good but
should be cleaned after use). Fry immediately in deep fat or oil.
Serve at once.

CASSEROLED ARTICHOKES

Wash and peel artichokes, place in a boiling white stock with a
squeeze of lemon juice and some fried onions. Add herbs or a
bouquet garni if desired and place in a hot oven 372° F.–425° F.
until simmering well, then reduce heat to 300° F.–350° F. until
the artichokes are cooked. Remove bouquet garni. Either drain
the artichokes (use the stock for soup) and toss the artichokes in
butter, chopped parsley and seasoning if so desired, or drain the
artichokes and keep warm. Use the stock to make a sauce and
cover the artichokes with it. Serve in the casserole.

ASPARAGUS

It is a pity that so little is grown in England nowadays. In the
early nineteenth century there were hundreds of acres under culti-
vation around London. Fresh asparagus has a wonderful, delicate
flavour. It needs careful handling and cooking.

Wash the asparagus carefully and well, cut off the woody ends
so that all the stalks are an even length. Scrape the lower part of
the stalks with a sharp knife if necessary and tie in even bundles

with tape or string. If you are lucky enough to own an asparagus kettle this is perfect for cooking, otherwise try to improvise with a stand that can be lifted out of the saucepan without the asparagus being broken. A pudding-basin stand can be used or a stone jar with water at tip-level. The tips then cook in the steam rather than the water. The most delicate and choicest part is the tip. Great care must be taken in the preparation, cooking and serving that it is not knocked off or damaged. It is very important not to overcook the asparagus—one should be able to bite not suck the stalks. Place the prepared bundles in boiling salted water to which a pinch of sugar has been added and cook for 20 minutes from the time the water reboils. This depends on the size of the stalks of course—the very fine stalks (sprue) take much less time. Drain quickly and serve, eat immediately with melted butter, browned butter, hollandaise sauce or mousseline sauce.

The hollandaise sauce can be flavoured with the rind and juice of a sweet orange for variety.

Asparagus has a delicate flavour, it must not be masked by a strong sauce.

It is eaten with the fingers and each piece dipped into the sauce. The tough part of the stalk is not eaten.

ASPARAGUS ROLLS

Prepare some small rolls (from your favourite bread recipe) well cooked and crusty, remove from the oven and slice off the tops. Scoop out the inside and fill with asparagus tips and mousseline sauce. Replace the lids of the rolls and warm in the oven for 10–15 minutes. This is a good savoury, either for the beginning or end of a meal, or as a supper dish.

AUBERGINES

These are also known as 'Egg Plants', and there are two kinds, the purple and the white, the latter are usually smaller and rounder. This is another vegetable (or fruit!) which deserves to be used a great deal more in this country. It can be grown in the south of England under glass (we have managed to do this) or in sheltered warm corners of the garden. When buying them make sure they are firm and shiny—they should not be wrinkled or blemished. The ones we have grown had rather nasty prickles on the calyx and stems which necessitated wearing a pair of tough gloves for gathering and cutting off the calyx during preparation. Aubergines can be fried, sautéd, baked and stuffed and the method of preparation varies with the way they are cooked. First wash them and cut off the stem and calyx.

RATATOUILLE NIÇOISE

4 medium-sized aubergines
Olive oil and seasoning
2–3 medium tomatoes
1 small marrow
2 onions
1 clove of garlic (if desired)

Method. Pour in sufficient olive oil to cover thinly the bottom of a medium-sized saucepan. Skin the tomatoes (plunge in boiling water for a few minutes), after this the skins will come off easily. Chop coarsely, taking out the hard centre piece. Peel the marrow and remove the seeds, cut into 1-inch cubes. Cut the aubergine into 1-inch cubes and roughly chop the onions. If you do not wish to use a clove of garlic in the ratatouille but would like a mere hint instead, rub the saucepan with a cut clove. Heat the olive oil until it just begins to smoke and put in the garlic, salt, onion, aubergine, marrow and tomato; stir well. Turn down the heat and simmer for 20–30 minutes or until the vegetables are tender. Taste and season if necessary. This dish is usually served on its own but may be used as an accompaniment to a savoury. Sprinkle with chopped parsley before serving.

Aubergines can be served in the same way with just a little onion added for flavouring, then serve as an additional vegetable.

Vegetables

FRIED AUBERGINES

Peel the aubergines and cut into thick slices. Remove any large seeds. Dip the slices into seasoned flour, shake off the surplus flour and fry in butter, oil or nut fat in a frying-pan. Use enough fat to come half-way up the slices. When one side is brown and tender, turn and cook the other side. Serve immediately.

Slices of aubergine can also be fried in deep fat. Coat with seasoned flour and then coat again either in egg and breadcrumbs or in batter.

STUFFED AUBERGINES

Allow a ½ aubergine per person. Wash and cut the aubergine in half (do not remove the skin), remove any large seeds. Make cuts through the flesh but do not pierce the skin. Fry the aubergines for 5–10 minutes with the cut surface downwards until tender. Scoop out some of the pulp, leaving about ½-inch thickness of aubergine. Mix the pulp with either:

1. Tomatoes, onion or garlic.
2. Breadcrumbs and chopped hard-boiled egg and mushrooms.
3. Breadcrumbs, mushroom, tomato and onion.
4. Breadcrumbs, cheese, tomato and onion.
5. Breadcrumbs, grated Brazil nuts, tomato and onion.

Season well and add herbs to taste. Either parsley, mint, sage or thyme are good. If you use tomato in the stuffing try a little basil. Fill the aubergine with the stuffing. Bake in a moderate oven 375° F.–400° F., M5–6 for 15–20 minutes. Serve with a sauce or gravy and vegetables.

BEANS

Broad Beans

This bean is rich in protein, carbohydrates and vitamins B and C. It is more digestible served on its own with accompanying vegetables than when it is served with another protein dish. When the beans are young they are cooked with the outside pod as well, but as they become older only the bean is used. They are usually served with parsley and butter in England but winter or summer savory herb is the best flavouring. If you have no savory then try thyme instead.

Like the rest of the leguminous family, peas and beans are the better for being gathered just before use. They should not be shelled until just before being prepared as there is a considerable flavour loss if they are left standing.

BROAD BEANS MANGE TOUT
(eaten whole)

Wash some young broad beans and 'top and tail' them. Cut into pieces about 1-inch long across the pod and place into just sufficient boiling salt water to cover them; this must be done immediately or they will turn black. Some people prefer to salt the beans after cooking but we have not noticed any difference either way. Add a piece or two of savory and simmer until tender (20–30 minutes). Remove the savory and drain the beans, keeping a little of the water. Either toss the beans in butter and chopped parsley (or chopped savory) or make a thick white sauce with a little milk and bean water. Add the beans when the sauce is made. Reheat and add chopped parsley or leave plain.

N.B. The bean water is sometimes bitter and it is advisable to taste before adding to vegetable stock or using for any other purpose.

When the beans are older they should be shelled and served after cooking as above. If the beans are very old some people like to take off the outside pale skin—this is better done after cooking (to preserve food value)—then serve as above or puréed. Personally, we think they lose their flavour when the skin is removed, but this is a matter of individual taste.

PURÉE OF BROAD BEANS

This is another way of serving older beans. Shell the beans and

Vegetables

cook gently in white stock with a small piece of butter. Sieve and reheat with more butter, pinch of sugar and some cream. Do NOT boil (to avoid curdling) but serve hot.

French Beans

These should be cooked when young, so young in fact that they need only be 'topped and tailed' and do not need stringing. Unfortunately it is very difficult to buy them like this, they are usually old. When buying be sure they are springy and a good fresh green colour—when they are limp it usually means they are stale. French beans are always boiled or cooked conservatively first, although they may be served in a variety of ways.

First wash the beans and then break off the top and tails—if they are old the coarse fibres at the sides will also come away, and they should be strung by pulling the fibres along the centre vein on each side. With very young beans you will not find any string at all and these beans are best cooked whole. The older beans may be cut into three or four pieces. Place small handfuls into boiling salted water and maintain at boiling point with water just to cover the beans. Allow to cook until tender—about 15-20 minutes, depending on age and size—this method keeps the colour well. Do not overcook; they should be firm but tender.

Drain and serve them tossed in melted butter. Taste and add more seasoning if required. Warm through and serve immediately.

The beans have a fresh delicate flavour served this way which is easily lost when other flavours are introduced. However, they may be served with the following sauces: white (with a pinch of grated nutmeg and a little cream); cheese; onion; and tomato.

They may be casseroled either by cooking first and then warming through in the oven with a mixture of cooked chopped onion and tomato, some butter and seasoning; or by placing the raw strung beans in the casserole with chopped onion and parsley, a little butter and seasoning with chopped skinned tomatoes. Cook this slowly until tender, adding tomato juice if necessary. With the latter method the colour is lost but the flavour is good.

N.B. French bean stock is very good for summer soups.

Vegetables

Runner Beans

These are cooked in exactly the same way as French beans but the preparation is slightly different. When young they can be strung like French beans but when they are older they should be pared very finely all the way round with a knife. Then cut them into diamonds—rather long thin pieces so that the flavour is preserved. They can be served and casseroled in the same way as French beans although we think with melted butter is best.

The following recipes may also be used for French beans:

BEANS WITH CARROTS AND CELERY

Scrape and slice the carrots thinly, wash and cut the celery into 1-inch lengths. Boil for 10 minutes in boiling white stock then add the prepared beans with some oil or butter and simmer until tender. Taste and season, serve hot.

BEANS, SPANISH STYLE

Peel a large onion, skin 2–3 tomatoes, prepare a pepper by removing the stalk and seeds and slice them all finely. Heat some butter or olive oil (about 1 oz.), add 1 chilli and some pepper (these two items are optional) and cook, stirring until tender and brown. Stir in approximately 1 oz. of wholemeal flour and brown for another five minutes. Add enough stock (brown if you have some) to make a pouring sauce, cook until thickened. Taste and season. Add a pound of prepared beans. Cook the beans very slowly in the sauce until tender, either on top of the stove or in the oven. This takes about 1 hour. Serve hot.

Dried Beans

These are usually described in England as haricot or butter beans. Under the name of haricot you can get quite a variety; there is the small white bean and a larger red one and also a little green bean (called flageolet in France); unless you go to a delicatessen or high-class grocers you will probably get the small white haricot (used for baked beans) or the butter beans. The method for cooking and serving is the same for each type.

Wash the beans well and leave to soak in clean cold or tepid water for 24 hours—some of the water will be absorbed so have a look after a while to see the beans are not uncovered. The more thorough the soaking the less time the beans will take to cook. Drain the beans and rinse again, place in enough cold water just to cover and add salt, a peeled onion with four cloves stuck into it, a scraped carrot, 2 sticks of washed celery which can be used to enclose parsley, thyme and a bay leaf tied to prevent the herbs escaping. Bring very gently to simmering point (30–45 minutes), skim any scum from the surface and cook very gently until the beans are tender. This does depend on the type of bean and how long they have been dried, generally 2–2½ hours is sufficient time.

Do not use bicarbonate of soda: this does help to soften the beans and reduce the cooking time but it also reduces the food value. Drain the beans and toss them in melted butter or serve with parsley, béchamel, curry or tomato sauce. The water in which the beans have been cooked is a wonderful foundation for sauces or gravies, and should always be used. Quantities of it may be used to make the sauce in which the beans are served.

BEANS IN TOMATO SAUCE
BOSTON STYLE

¾ lb. dried haricot beans
1–2 oz. butter
1 finely chopped Spanish onion
1 teaspoon dry mustard (optional)
2 teaspoons black treacle
¼ pint fresh tomato purée
2–3 tablespoons concentrated tomato purée
2 teaspoons dark moist sugar
½ pint bean liquid (approx.)
3 teaspoons rum (optional)
Seasoning

Soak the beans overnight in cold or tepid water. Drain and place in a medium saucepan, cover with fresh cold water and bring very slowly to just under boiling point. Simmer until the skins burst

145

Vegetables

when you blow on the beans—about 1 hour. Drain the beans, saving the liquid, and place the beans in a casserole. Melt the butter in a saucepan and cook the onion gently until soft; add the mustard, treacle, tomato and tomato purée, sugar, and bean liquid; bring to the boil. Add the rum and seasoning and pour over the beans, mixing well. Put on the lid and cook in a slow oven 300–325° F., M2–3 for 5 hours. Stir the casserole about every hour and add more bean liquor if the beans are drying out. Serve from the casserole.

BEETROOT

This root vegetable is so often used for salads that we seem to forget that it can be served as an accompanying vegetable. It has a pleasant sweet flavour, so it can readily be served with a sharp sauce. It is also valuable in meal planning as it adds colour and eye appeal to the meal.

If the beetroot are to be served whole the young round beetroot should be used, but if they are to be sliced or diced they can be round or long, and older.

When buying, the root should be hard to the touch and the skin undamaged. The leaves should be left on young beetroot. When preparing, the leaves should be twisted off a little above the root to prevent bleeding. The roots should be well washed with a *soft* scrubbing-brush, making sure the skin remains undamaged. Do NOT cut the beetroot or remove the root or tail. Beetroot are normally boiled, but medium to large can be baked in greaseproof paper on the rungs of the shelves of the oven. The temperature should be 350° F.–400° F. and the time varies, but a rough guide would be two hours. The beetroot should feel tender when gently squeezed between thumb and forefinger.

To boil the beetroot put them in boiling sea-salted water and cook until tender. One way of judging this is to pull the root; the skin and root should slide off easily. As you may imagine this is hard on the fingers! It is better to judge by the size and age of the beetroot. Young beetroot cook in ½–1 hour, older ones take 2 hours or longer if large.

Vegetables

N.B. If you grow your own beetroot and find you have many leaves, try cooking them like spinach.

CONSERVATIVE BEETROOT

1 lb. beetroot
½ lb. onions
½ lb. celery
Butter or other fat
Stock
Seasoning

Peel the beetroot and cut into ½-inch cubes. Peel the onions and cube. Discard the outer stalks of the celery (use for making stock or soup if suitable) and cut the head into quarters—wash very well. Cut into ½-inch pieces. Melt the butter in a saucepan and make it hot but not brown. Put in the prepared vegetables and cook gently with the lid on for 10 minutes, shaking gently now and again. Add enough boiling stock to come just to the top of the vegetables and cook quickly until tender, 20–30 minutes. If there is much liquid left, you may prefer to cook with the lid off for the last five minutes to allow the liquid to evaporate or thicken it with 81 per cent extraction flour to make a sauce for the vegetables, whichever is preferable. Taste, and season if necessary—a squeeze of lemon and chopped parsley are a good finishing touch. Beetroot may also be covered with a sauce; such as white sauce, béchamel sauce, a cream sauce or a white sauce to which a little horseradish has been added. We particularly like them with herb sauce or caper sauce.

BROCCOLI

There are many types of broccoli; the large white heads that look like cauliflower have only been developed in the last 70–80 years and they are used in exactly the same manner as cauliflower.

The purple and white sprouting broccoli are unfortunately often cooked like cabbage and they lose much of their delicate flavour in this process. They should be cooked like asparagus, tied in

Vegetables

bundles and placed on a drainer so that they can be lifted out with ease. They are better served with melted butter or in a sauce from the water in which they were cooked.

During the winter months one can buy broccoli at Covent Garden which are equal in size to a small cauliflower. One broccoli makes a good serving for one person. These broccoli have a wonderful flavour—reminding us that spring is not too far away! Cook and serve them as for asparagus.

BRUSSELS SPROUTS

Brussels Sprouts are a variety of the cabbage family—but they have a distinct flavour of their own. To date unfortunately, they appear to be cultivated so that they get larger and larger—good from the harvester's point of view and possibly the preparer, but not from the point of view of flavour; they taste more like cabbage. If possible buy them small, tight, green and firm to touch; if they have a number of yellow leaves on the outside do not buy them. When freshly gathered there should be no need to discard many outside leaves. At the base of the sprout make a small cut into the stalk as if you were beginning to halve it. This is to help the stalk cook in the same time as the leaves. If there appear to be small insects or caterpillars inside, soak for 5 minutes in cold salted water (1 tablespoon to 1 pint) and then rinse, otherwise wash quickly in cold water and cook immediately. Sprouts are better cooked by the conservative method—this gives them a nutty flavour which we enjoy, but you may prefer to boil them. Place in enough sea-salted boiling water just to cover them—add them to the boiling water a few at a time so the water never leaves boiling point and cook quickly until tender.

Serve the sprouts with melted butter, hollandaise sauce, white sauce, cheese sauce, apple sauce or with butter, lemon juice and parsley. A little (only a very small amount) grated nutmeg may be sprinkled on just before serving and this makes a pleasant change. The best flavouring for sprouts we feel is chestnuts. The sprouts may be served with a savoury chestnut purée or they can be cooked together as follows:

148

Vegetables

Boil 1 lb. of sprouts until not quite tender. Skin $\frac{1}{2}$ lb. of chestnuts (see Chestnut section, p. 128) and place the sprouts and chestnuts in a saucepan. This sauce should contain 2 oz. of hot melted butter. Cook sprouts and chestnuts for about 10 minutes, shaking occasionally until the contents are a golden brown. If this is served with potatoes and tomato sauce it makes a good savoury course for a cooked meal. Sprouts (when cooked conservatively) can also have a little chopped onion cooked with them.

CABBAGE

(including kale, spring greens, turnip and sprout tops)

This is a most nutritionally valuable family of vegetables—their mineral and vitamin values are high. Cabbage is good whether eaten raw or cooked; some people find it more digestible when eaten raw.

Like all other vegetables they should be as fresh as possible —bright green and firm, not limp or tired-looking.

All the preparation and cooking should be accomplished as quickly as possible, the leaves are washed thoroughly, discarding any discoloured leaves, or if the cabbage is very solid, cut the head into quarters or eighths and wash the sections. Cover the bottom of a saucepan with melted butter or oil and heat. Shred the cabbage finely with a sharp stainless steel knife, taking out the thick parts of the stalks as these take longer to cook than the leaves. Toss the shredded leaves in the fat and cook gently for 5 minutes, stirring two or three times. A small amount of water should be left on the leaves after washing as this will prevent the leaves from sticking. Pour on a little boiling water, just enough to cover the pan bottom for $\frac{1}{4}$ inch and cook quickly until the greens are tender. If the cabbage or greens are young and tender this will only take 5–10 minutes, but when older or coarser (spring greens) they may take as long as 20 minutes in which case you may have to add a little more water if necessary. If there is any cooking liquor left, drain it off and use for sauce or stock—serve the greens immediately. We do not think this recipe needs the addition of salt— however, it is wise to taste them as you may not agree!

Vegetables

The cabbage or greens may be plain boiled as above without the preliminary cooking in fat, but adding some butter or margarine just before serving when the cabbage has been drained. Cabbage is not usually served with, or in a sauce, but you may like to try, for a change—sweet and sour sauce, tomato sauce, curry sauce or cheese sauce.

SAVOURY CABBAGE OR GREENS

Flavouring vegetables
1 medium finely chopped onion
1 medium finely diced carrot
2 stalks finely shredded celery
½ medium-sized finely shredded pimento
Garlic as required
1 oz. butter or oil
1–1½ lb. cabbage or greens
Seasoning
Water or stock

Prepare the cabbage or greens in the usual way. Heat the fat in a saucepan and put in all or some of the flavouring vegetables (you may not want to use as many as described and the recipe can be varied to personal taste). Cook the vegetables in the fat until half cooked (about 5–10 minutes). Do not allow them to brown. Add the shredded cabbage or greens. Cook for another 5 minutes, stirring well and then add a pinch of brown sugar and enough boiling water or stock to cook the cabbage or greens until tender. Taste and adjust seasoning.

STUFFED CABBAGE LEAVES

This can be used as a variation of the above recipe. Before cooking the cabbage take out about 6–8 of the outside leaves and keep whole. While the rest of the cabbage is cooking as above, put the cabbage leaves into the boiling water for a few minutes and then plunge them into cold water. This makes them pliable. When the savoury cabbage is cooked, drain if necessary and place

Vegetables

1–2 tablespoons in the centre of each leaf. Fold the cabbage leaf to form a round package and secure with skewers or string. Heat some fat in an oven-proof entrée dish and put in the stuffed cabbage leaves, basting them well-placed in a moderate oven and cook until brown—about 20–40 minutes. When they are nearly brown add some tomato halves and whole mushrooms, baste them in the fat and lightly sprinkle them with a little seasoning. Serve in the entrée dish.

Instead of the cabbage stuffing, nut, egg or cheese stuffing can be used. This will make it a savoury rather than an accompaniment.

SAUERKRAUT

This is a form of pickled cabbage associated with Germany. It has a sharp taste and is very pleasant served with fatty foods, such as nut bakes, savouries, sausages and fried foods. It is a very lengthy job preparing it at home; for the occasions one is likely to use it, it can be bought from a delicatessen. Choose the whitest as this will be the best of the freshly made sauerkraut or it can be purchased in a tin.

The freshly made sauerkraut needs washing and then cooking in boiling water for two hours—the tinned product is pre-cooked and only needs warming, either in water or butter.

RED CABBAGE

It is a great pity that most people know this only as a pickle, because it is very good both raw in salads and cooked. As it is not usually cooked in Britain the methods of cooking come from various parts of Europe and vary in small details. We have chosen the recipe we like best and have called it Continental Red Cabbage.

> 1 red cabbage about 1 lb.
> 1 oz. butter or nut fat
> 1 small chopped onion
> 1 tablespoon brown sugar
> 1 cooking apple

Vegetables

2 tablespoons apple vinegar
1 grated raw potato
¼–½ pint stock
Salt, cayenne pepper
Powdered cloves, cinnamon

Cut into eighths and wash cabbage, then shred finely. Heat the fat in a saucepan and fry the onion and brown sugar together until brown. Put in the cabbage, apple, vinegar, potato, stock and seasonings. Add the spices if you like them. Simmer gently until tender—about 2 hours, adding more stock if necessary. Taste, it should be a sweet-sour flavour; adjust if required. Serve hot.

Shredded red cabbage can also be simply cooked in a good stock with butter, salt and pepper until tender.

CARROTS

Again, a vegetable of very high nutritional value. Carrots contain vitamins A and C and plenty of mineral salts if they have been grown on good soil. They have a sweet pleasant flavour which makes them a good vegetable for young children, who sometimes dislike a distinct flavour in a vegetable. They are in season for most of the year but we would like to sound a note of warning about some of the so-called 'early' carrots. These are very often forced so that they have little flavour or they are second-year carrots which would be seeding during the coming summer, with the result that they have a hard woody core and again little flavour; the outrageous thing is that we are usually asked an exorbitant price for an inferior product; personally, we prefer to wait for the *really* new carrots.

When buying carrots try to get them as fresh as possible. Very often dirty carrots have a better flavour than those which have been washed, but be careful the dirt has not been left on deliberately. When buying new crop carrots in bunches have a good look at the leaves; a great deal can be told by the appearance of these leaves—freshness in particular. To prepare new carrots, top and tail them with a sharp stainless steel knife and scrub carefully with a soft brush. Do not scrape or peel—if the skins are discoloured after cooking they can easily be rubbed off.

Old carrots can be prepared in the same way but they may need gentle scraping or peeling very finely. If you have to peel them it must be done with a fine peeler.

To cook young carrots, place them whole in very little boiling sea-salted water to which has been added a good pinch of brown sugar and 1 oz. butter for each lb. of carrots. We like to add 3 or 4 sprigs of mint, tying the stalks together so they can be removed with ease after cooking is finished. Cook quickly until tender, 10–20 minutes, place in a warm serving-dish and keep warm. Evaporate the cooking liquor by boiling quickly until the mixture becomes syrupy and toss the carrots in this. Sprinkle with chopped parsley or mint. Serve immediately. Young carrots can also be cooked by the conservative method, or they can be boiled and tossed in melted butter and chopped parsley when cooked.

The period during which really young carrots are obtainable is so short that it seems a pity to cook them by methods other than those which bring out their own flavour.

Old carrots can be cooked conservatively, boiled or braised. They need not be cooked whole which would take a long time if they are large, but they can be diced, sliced or cut into quarters lengthwise to form long fingers. The cooking time varies from 20 minutes to 1 hour, depending on the size of the carrots. They may also be served in parsley, cheese, caper, curry or béchamel sauce.

CARROT FLAN

Bake a flan case blind and when cooked fill with a purée of cooked seasoned carrots; arrange some carrot slices decoratively to cover the top and glaze with the reduced carrot liquor, as in the first recipe for young carrots. Garnish with parsley and serve hot.

Vegetables

Carrots and Seedless Raisins

This is an unusual but very good recipe. Prepare 1 lb. of carrots leaving them whole if young or small, otherwise slice them. Heat 1 oz. butter in a saucepan and cook the carrots for 5–10 minutes, stirring well. Add 1 level dessertspoonful of flour, stir again and add 1 tablespoon of water or stock and 1 tablespoon red wine or red grape juice. Simmer very slowly, adding more stock if necessary and when the carrots are nearly done add 1–2 oz. of washed seedless raisins. Cover the saucepan and place in a slow oven (or transfer to a casserole) until the carrots are cooked. Taste and add seasoning if necessary. Serve.

Mashed Carrots

Prepare and boil some old carrots, drain well (save the stock). Melt some butter; ½–1 oz. to 1 lb. carrots, in the saucepan, return the carrots and mash with a potato masher. Add sugar, salt, chopped mint or parsley to taste. This is an unusually good way of serving old carrots—don't expect them to mash like potatoes, they remain far more nubbly.

CAULIFLOWER AND BROCCOLI

It is unfortunate that the leaves of this well-known vegetable are often cut off when offered for sale, they are so good cooked and served with the white flower head. It would be a great help when buying if the leaves had been left on, as they are a good guide to freshness; however, see that the green is as fresh-looking as possible and the white flower unblemished. When preparing, great care should be taken as the heads often harbour caterpillars. If you have the leaves, then cut them away and wash them well, the tender leaves can be cooked whole—the larger leaves need to be stripped from the main stem (which can be put in the stock-pot). If you want to cook the head whole then cut off the stalk just under the head and cut a cross in it. We feel that unless you want to serve the cauliflower as a centrepiece to the savoury course, the best way to cook it is to break it into little pieces, and serve these tiny 'heads' in one way or another. If you are *sure* there is no 'wild or tame life' in your cauliflower then just wash the cauliflower quickly in cold water; if there are doubts, soak in cold salted water for about 10 minutes and rinse. Cook, in just enough sea-salted water or white stock to cover, for 10–15 minutes until just tender. Use the water for stock, soup or sauce. Cauliflower is so easily over-cooked and if it is the florets become mushy. If the head is cooked whole it will, of course, need longer (20–30 minutes) and it should be placed stalk downwards in the water. The greens from the cauliflower can be cooked in the same way as cabbage and served separately. If there are only a few leaves these can be laid on top of the cauliflower head or sprigs, so that they are not quite in the boiling water, and they will cook at the same time. They are then served with the cauliflower. The cauliflower needs careful draining before being served as it tends to hold some of the cooking water.

The following sauces are usually served with cauliflower, either handed with it or poured over: white sauce, cream sauce, cheese sauce, tomato sauce, hollandaise, mousseline, mushroom or curry. We especially like mint sauce with cauliflower but it may be a little unusual for some palates!

POLISH CAULIFLOWER

Cook the cauliflower, drain well and place in a warm heat-proof serving-dish and keep warm. Brown 2–3 tablespoons of fine wholewheat breadcrumbs in a little butter ($\frac{1}{2}$–1 oz.) and add 1 tablespoon of chopped parsley and 2 sieved hard-boiled yolks of egg to the breadcrumbs. If the cauliflower has drained a little more then carefully pour off the water and sprinkle the cauliflower with the prepared crumbs. Serve immediately. This method may be used with a whole or broken cauliflower.

FRIED SPRIGS OF CAULIFLOWER

Divide a 'head' into sprigs, wash and parboil. Drain very well and allow to cool. Season if preferred. Prepare a good coating batter (see section on Batters) and dip the sprigs into this. Fry in a deep oil or fat until golden brown and crisp, serve immediately.

This recipe can be varied as follows:

1. When the sprigs are cool allow them to soak in a mixture of oil, lemon juice, chopped mint and seasoning for 20–30 minutes. Turn the sprigs in the mixture 2 or 3 times, or spoon the mixture over them so that the flavour soaks into the cauliflower.

2. Flavour the batter with grated cheese, herbs, onions or tomato purée.

CAULIFLOWER SURPRISE

Prepare a whole head and cook for only 10 minutes. Drain carefully. Make a stuffing (see section on Stuffings) which you like, and which will go well with cauliflower. Place a round of it about 1-inch thick on the bottom of a fire-proof serving-dish. Fill all the spaces between the stalks with the rest of the stuffing and place the cauliflower stalk downwards on the stuffing, if there is any stuffing left use it to fill in around the base.

Cover the cauliflower with a greased paper and bake in a moderate oven 325° F.–350° F., M3–4 for 30–40 minutes. That is, until the cauliflower is cooked and the stuffing is hot. Remove the greaseproof paper and cover with a coating sauce to complement the stuffing, such as:

(1) Cheese stuffing with tomato sauce.
(2) Carrot stuffing with cheese sauce.
(3) Mushroom stuffing with parsley sauce.
(4) Chestnut stuffing with brown sauce.
    ad infinitum with many variations.

Vegetables

CELERIAC

This is sometimes known as a 'turnip rooted' celery which is a very descriptive name for it. So many soils are unsuited for celery-growing that it is surprising celeriac is grown so little; it has a delicate celery, nutty flavour and some people prefer it because it is not so stringy and coarse as stick celery. Outside it has a very gnarled, pitted uneven surface and it is usually bought trimmed of leaves and roots. If you grow them they are best used immediately they are dug up. They vary considerably in size.

To prepare them, first scrub if necessary, and then peel as finely as possible; this cannot be very thin as the skin is so uneven on the surface. If they are small to medium sized, they can be cooked whole in boiling sea-salted water or white stock, in much the same way as beetroot and for the same length of time (1–2 hours). They can be tested for tenderness with a sharp knife. If they are large, or if you prefer, they can be cooked cut in dice or fairly thick slices in the same manner as above except that the time will be shorter, 30–40 minutes. The water in which they are cooked is very good for the stock-pot, etc.

Sauces to be served with celeriac are melted butter, white sauce, cheese sauce, béchamel sauce or hollandaise sauce.

Braised Celeriac

Heat some oil, butter or nutter in a saucepan and in it brown some chopped onion and diced carrots for 5–10 minutes. There should be enough onion and carrot to cover the bottom of the saucepan. Cut some prepared celeriac in slices and place over the browned vegetables, add white or brown stock just to cover. Add seasoning and a little bundle of parsley, thyme and one bay leaf tied with string (easier to remove). Bring slowly to the boil and simmer gently with the lid on until the celeriac is tender. The herbs can be removed at the end of or at any time during the cooking if you do not care for a strong herb flavour. Take out the celeriac and place in a warm serving-dish and strain a little or all of the liquor over; the remainder can go into the stock-pot. Sprinkle with chopped parsley and serve.

CELERIAC FRITTERS

Prepare and parboil some slices of celeriac. Allow to cool, dip in batter or coat with egg and breadcrumbs and fry in deep fat until golden brown and crisp. Serve immediately.

An interesting savoury can also be made by slicing celeriac thinly and cooking as above. When cold, sandwich two slices together with a stuffing, coat and fry as above. Serve hot or cold.

CELERY

We use celery so much for soups, salads and as a flavouring vegetable that we are apt to forget that it can be used as a vegetable in its own right. As new varieties come on the market the season for English celery extends but we still think the celery that has felt the nip of autumnal frost tastes crisper and better than any other.

When buying take particular note of the condition of the outside leaves and stems, these should be crisp, fresh-looking and firm. If the celery is trimmed a lot it means, in the majority of cases, that it is stale.

To prepare celery cut away the very coarse outside stems and leaves and roots, which can go on the compost heap. The green stems can be used for the stock-pot or soup. The heart and white stems are generally used for cooking and salads. Celery must be washed very carefully as the growing conditions require it to be earthed up for blanching; do not leave the stems soaking long in cold water.

Celery can be cooked conservatively, braised, boiled in stock, fried or stewed. Sauces served with celery are: white, cream, béchamel, cheese, tomato, and egg sauce. It combines very well with chestnuts, and equal amounts of each can be cooked together.

Vegetables

BRAISED CELERY

This is very similar to braised celeriac—the celery is cut into 3-inch lengths or into quarters and cooked and served in the same way. A pleasant variation is to add some skinned tomatoes and tomato purée or juice at the same time as you cook the celery. When the celery is cooked, drain well and place in a warmed serving-dish, keep warm while preparing the following sauce. Make a roux and add the braising liquor plus the sieved vegetable to make a thick sauce; pour over or around the celery and serve.

FRIED CELERY STICKS

Prepare and parboil some celery sticks and/or small hearts in a well-flavoured white stock. Drain very well and allow to cool. Roll in seasoned flour, dip in batter and fry in oil or deep fat until golden brown, serve immediately. These are very good served with a chestnut or celery purée. These sticks can also be fried raw if they are tender and cut into 3-inch lengths. They may need to be cooked a little longer so heat the fat until just before smoking point (if you have a thermometer this is about 330° F.–340° F.).

CHICORY

Generally used as a salad plant, but it can be used as a vegetable to give variety in winter. Chicory is the blanched shoot of a vegetable root and it is forced in the dark (to prevent bitterness) in winter to give these shoots. The shoots should only have a slight yellow colouring at the tip, the remainder should be white. Other names for it are succory, and Belgian endive. In France it is called 'endive' and what we call endive (green, crinkly salad plant) they call chicory which makes it very confusing—especially if you are following a French recipe book! Chicory has a rather bitter flavour when cooked and is found unpalatable by some people.

Prepare it by washing in cold water, trim the stalk and remove any loose or blemished outside leaves. If it seems very gritty (it is forced in sand on occasions) then halve lengthwise and wash quickly under the tap.

Vegetables

BOILED CHICORY

If the heads are loose tie them with string or tape, drop them into enough boiling water to cover them well and cook quickly for about 20–30 minutes or until tender. Do not overcook or they become flabby and have no 'bite'. Slice and allow to drain well—you need not slice them but if you do not the draining will take longer—heat the chicory through in plenty of melted butter with seasoning (generally takes 5–10 minutes). Be careful not to brown it. This recipe may be altered as follows: cook the chicory for 5 minutes in boiling sea-salted water, drain and then cook slowly in plenty of butter until tender—about 30 minutes–1 hour, dependent on the size.

The chicory can be coated or served with white sauce (just a little lemon juice added to the sauce is pleasant), béchamel sauce, cheese or brown sauce.

BRAISED CHICORY

Prepare some even-sized heads and cook for 5 minutes in boiling salted water, drain well. Melt 1 oz. of butter; chop a peeled onion, dice a carrot and slice two sticks of celery (add a small piece of diced turnip if you like the flavour) and cook these gently in butter for 5–10 minutes. Place the drained chicory on top of the vegetables, add enough brown or white stock to cover and season to taste. Add a good pinch of brown sugar and a small bundle of herbs (parsley, bay leaf, thyme, tied together with string) if you like. Cook very gently on top of the stove or in the oven until the chicory is tender, generally about 1 hour. Either reduce the cooking liquid and serve with the chicory, or thicken the liquid to make a sauce to accompany the chicory.

N.B. Chicory stock tastes bitter and it is not generally used unless of course you like this type of flavouring!

CORN-ON-THE-COB
(See Maize)

Vegetables

CUCUMBER

Yet another vegetable that always appears to be associated with salads, but it can be very good cooked. It has a delicate flavour and requires careful cooking and seasoning. When buying cucumber choose those which are both green and firm, the skins should be free from damage. The cucumber should be the same circumference for the whole of its length. If it is bulbous at one end it means the seeds inside will be big and tough.

Most recipes for cucumber say that the skins should be removed, whilst we, being contrary, say they should be left on because we feel the flavour and food value is thereby unimpaired. They should be carefully washed, the stalk end and tip removed with a stainless steel knife and having done so, taste to make sure the cucumber is not bitter.

Cucumber is better cooked in its own juices in a similar manner to mushrooms, marrows and tomatoes. Either slice or dice the cucumber, remove the seeds only if they are tough, melt enough butter or oil just to cover the bottom of the saucepan and heat. Put in the cucumber and add a little seasoning, place the lid on and cook very gently for 5–10 minutes or until tender. Holding the lid tightly, shake the saucepan while cooking. Taste and adjust the seasoning (a pinch of brown sugar is sometimes an improvement) and serve the cucumber immediately with any liquid that is left.

BAKED CUCUMBER

Wash and dice some cucumber. Grease a fire-proof dish. Make a mixture of brown breadcrumbs, melted butter, a very small amount of finely chopped onion and either (1) a little grated lemon rind or (2) paprika pepper or (3) celery salt. Add seasoning and, starting with the cucumber, make layers of the cucumber and breadcrumbs until the dish is full. Finish with breadcrumbs. Bake for about an hour in a moderate oven 350° F.–375° F., M4–5 covered with a greaseproof paper. The paper can be removed at the end to allow the top to brown. A pleasant variation is

161

Vegetables

achieved if you pour in some tomato juice or fresh tomato purée and cook as before.

Wash, dice or slice some cucumber and cook in a little boiling water or stock until tender; it is most important that the stock should be of a very delicate flavour otherwise the cucumber flavour is completely lost, cook for about 5–10 minutes. Drain the cucumber and place in a warm dish. Make a sauce, using the cooking liquid and a little milk. When the sauce is cooked add some cream or an egg-yolk, stir well (do not reboil otherwise it will curdle), season if necessary. Pour over the cucumber, serve immediately. Try a little parsley, chives, chervil or tarragon in the sauce.

ENDIVE
See Lettuce

KOHL RABI

This is grown rather more on the Continent than in Britain, but used preferably young and tender, either raw or cooked it has good dietetic value. It makes a good 'catch' crop in the garden but it should be grown quickly otherwise it becomes very tough. It looks like a smooth green turnip with the leaves growing like side-shoots out of the top of the root instead of at the centre. The preparation also follows the same pattern as for turnip; cooking and serving are the same with the added advantage of the leaves being used as a green vegetable to serve with the root (see section on Cabbage for cooking). Any of the turnip recipes can be used for Kohl Rabi although the flavour is quite different—'nutty' by comparison.

To prepare, take off the leaves (use as greens) and wash. If desired they can be cooked in their skins, but the tough skins must then be taken off after cooking. Otherwise, peel fairly thickly to remove all the tough outside. If they are small in size you can leave them whole, but larger ones should be cut into slices or quartered.

Cook in just enough boiling salted water, or stock to cover until tender.

Vegetables

They are usually served with a covering of white sauce (made with part of the cooking liquid) or tossed in melted butter and chopped parsley.

LEEKS

Are very much appreciated by those who find onions a little strong! They have a delicate flavour and possess all the advantages of the onion without any of the disadvantages.

When buying look for freshness (this is not necessarily cleanliness, since vegetables that have not been washed retain their freshness and taste better) and try to buy leeks that have not been trimmed too much. The tough green leaves are good for stock, or they can be cooked with the leeks to give them flavour, but do not serve them unless you are prepared to purée these leaves.

Leeks have one fault. Because they are blanched the stem seems to accumulate a fair amount of grit and this requires very careful cleaning. First cut off the fibrous roots and trim the green leaves. With a sharp stainless steel knife slit the leeks from the green part right down to the white base. allowing the tip of the knife to pierce the centre, but do not split them in half. It is then possible gently to open the leek out so that cold water can run through each leaf from the root to the green stem. The centre is usually clean. The leek can then be reshaped and cooked whole or cut into sections or slices as desired.

Leeks can be used as onions for flavouring in any recipe that specifies onions and they also answer this very useful purpose in salads and soups. They can be boiled, cooked conservatively, braised, steamed and covered or served with the following sauces —white, cream sauce, cheese, béchamel and caper. They can also be partly cooked and finished in melted butter, oil or vegetable fat until they are brown.

CREAMED LEEKS

Prepare some leeks, the coarse green leaves should be saved for soup. Cut the leeks into thick slices. Cook in boiling stock or boiling salted water, until tender. Drain well (leeks take a lot of

Vegetables

draining) and melt some butter or other fat in a saucepan, add the leeks, seasoning, a little grated nutmeg and about 1 tablespoon of 81 per cent extraction flour. Cook for about 5 minutes, stirring all the time, do not let the flour burn. Add a $\frac{1}{4}$ pint of double cream and $\frac{1}{4}$ pint of milk (or $\frac{1}{2}$ pint of single cream) and one egg-yolk. Heat well to thicken the sauce but be careful not to allow to boil or it will curdle—it is a good idea to do this in a double saucepan, but if you do it takes appreciably longer time to thicken.

Leek Pudding

Line a pudding basin with some wholemeal crust and place inside some washed and prepared leeks cut into thick slices. Add seasoning and small pieces of butter, cover with more crust and stand in a saucepan of boiling water; cook for about three hours.

If this is served with a good cheese sauce and another vegetable (not potatoes), it makes a very good savoury course.

LENTILS
See Peas

LETTUCE
(including endive and Batavian lettuce)

Personally we would not cook these at all as we much prefer them raw—they all have a tendency to become bitter when cooked, especially endive. However, when there is a glut in the garden or when one wants variety in the winter amongst the cooked greens (endive and Batavia are usually imported from France during the winter months) then it is useful to have some recipes for cooking them.

They should be as fresh as possible; if you do not cut them from the garden use lettuce the same day as they are bought. Cut off the dried stumps and with the tough and discoloured leaves, put these on the compost heap. Wash the lettuce in cold water, cut into quarters if the recipe demands this. If there are green fly then leave in cold salted water for 5–10 minutes and then wash well.

164

Vegetables

Many recipe books give recipes for lettuce which require hours of cooking—we feel that lettuce, etc. need much the same cooking as spinach, and other green vegetables, i.e. as quickly as possible. In the following recipes the time will vary with the type of lettuce you may be using; beginning with the shortest time and ending with the longest the list would read like this:

Cabbage lettuce, Webb's Wonderful lettuce, Cos lettuce, endive, and Batavian lettuce. If you have never come across the Batavian lettuce it looks rather like a 'cross' between lettuce and endive, it has a fairly bitter flavour and the leaves are tougher than the ordinary lettuce or endive.

CONSERVATIVE LETTUCE

Cut the heads into quarters and place in a saucepan with no more water than that which the leaves hold after washing. Cook over a gentle heat for 5–10 minutes with the lid on, then take the lid off and turn lettuces, cook until tender, 5–30 minutes. Drain if necessary and season, adding melted butter and serve.

Lettuce may also be served with cheese, béchamel or cream sauces.

MAIZE

This is a vegetable which is becoming increasingly popular, so much so that market gardeners have started growing for the markets and it has become easier to obtain from the greengrocers. It can be grown outdoors in the south of England if we get a reasonable summer with plenty of sunshine!

It certainly tastes better for being freshly picked and when buying, choose the young cobs, the grain being a green/pale yellow to mid-yellow in colour, dependent on the variety. If the grain looks orange and full it means it has ripened and is too tough to be edible. The husks (the green outside covering) and the 'silk' (green-red silky threads at the top of the cob just beneath the husks) should be fresh in appearance—particularly the green part of the silk.

Vegetables

To prepare, cut off the stalk close to the bottom (which is tough) and take away the husk and the silk; if there is a tip with no grain or miniature grain this can be cut off also; sometimes this becomes necessary to fit the cobs into the saucepan! Generally the cobs do not require washing. Heat some water to boiling and put in the cobs, use just enough water to cover the cobs. Time the cooking period from when the water reboils, giving young cobs 8–10 minutes and older and larger ones 15–20 minutes. Do not overcook as they become tough and lose their sweetness. It is sometimes said that to cook them in salted water also makes them tough, but we have found cooking them with or without salt makes no difference. The flavour is improved a little with a small amount of sea salt added to the water.

The corn is then drained and served on a warm napkin in a warm serving-dish. Melted butter can be handed round or iced pats of butter. The corn is held in the hands or with two forks and the grain is stripped off with the teeth—much to the delight of the youngsters! You may prefer the use of two sticks which are inserted at each end and used as supports. If you want to use the grain or serve it without the cob it can be cut off with a sharp knife when the corn is cooked, but it is easier with one's teeth. Cut the corn off the lower half of the cob first and then using the 'cleaned' half as a handle cut off the grains from the other half. The grains can then be reheated in melted butter and/or cream and seasoning. Serve in individual dishes or as an accompanying vegetable. It can also be used in savouries such as flans, soufflés, etc.

When fresh corn is unobtainable it can be bought in tins either whole grains or cream style; needless to say the flavour is not so good. The cream style is very useful for soups and baked savouries and the whole grain should be used as you would fresh. If, however, you want to eat sweet corn out of season try the frozen cobs, they are better flavoured than the tinned.

Sweet corn is usually served by itself, either at the beginning of the meal or as a separate course. It can be served as an accompanying vegetable either in melted butter, browned butter, cream or white, parsley or cheese sauce, or from the following recipes:

Vegetables

BAKED CORN

(a)

Prepare the cobs and place in a fire-proof dish, cover with milk. Put in a moderate oven 375° F., M5, and bake until tender, this usually takes 40–45 minutes. Drain, season the corn and serve. Use the milk for sauce or soup.

(b)

Use young corn and do not remove the husks. Place in a hot oven 400–425° F., M6–7, and bake until tender—about 30 minutes. Serve in the usual way.

SWEET CORN FRITTERS

1 tin sweet corn or 12 oz. sweet corn stripped off the cob
4 tablespoons sifted flour
1 teaspoonful baking powder
2 eggs and seasoning

Chop the sweet corn and stir in the flour which has been sieved with the baking powder and seasoning. Separate the eggs and stir in the yolks. Place some nutter in a frying-pan (about 1 oz., depending on the size of the pan) and start to heat it. Whip the egg-whites until stiff and fold into the fritter mixture until you cannot see any lumps of egg-white. When the fat is smoking hot, drop spoonfuls of the mixture into it and cook until brown. Then with a slice or palette-knife, turn the fritter over and cook on the other side. Keep warm in oven while making other fritters and then serve immediately.

SWEET CORN WITH TOMATOES

1 oz. butter
1 lb. tomatoes
Thyme and parsley
Seasoning
Pinch brown sugar
12 oz. corn stripped from the cob or tin

167

Vegetables

Melt the fat in a saucepan and add the chopped and peeled tomatoes, simmer with the chopped herbs and seasonings for 5–10 minutes with the lid off. Add the corn and cook for another 5 minutes. Serve hot.

MARROWS

The younger and smaller the marrow, the better they are to eat; the enormous harvest-festival type are fine specimens to look at but they are inclined to be tough and tasteless, all the goodness having passed into the seeds. On the Continent this has been recognized for a long time and the French have a special name for small marrows *courgettes* and the Italians *zucchini*. These small marrows are about 4–8 inches long and they can be cooked and eaten whole. If the marrows are larger but still young and tender, they are also good to eat but need to be prepared and cooked in a different way.

Do try and buy marrows that have been freshly cut or try to grow your own. People frequently look upon the marrow as a tasteless vegetable; this is probably because they lose much of their flavour within hours of picking and a second reason might be because they are boiled, which tends to make them tasteless.

We will start by giving some recipes for the smaller marrows and follow these with recipes for the larger ones.

Baby Marrows, Courgettes or Zucchini

Although the following is a method which requires boiling, the skin of the small marrow left on keeps in the flavour.

Cut off the stalk as close to the marrow as possible without damaging the skin. Place as many marrows as you may require in a saucepan of boiling sea-salted water (only enough water to cover) and cook for 10–15 minutes until just tender. Drain carefully and serve with melted butter, hollandaise sauce, mint sauce or the following brown butter sauce:

Vegetables

2 oz. butter
Seasoning
1–2 tablespoons chopped fresh herbs (parsley, thyme or
   mint)
2 tablespoons apple vinegar or lemon juice

Melt the butter and heat until it browns and froths—add the
other ingredients and pour over the marrow immediately.

FRIED BABY MARROWS

1. Wash and cut into thin rings—dip in seasoned 81 per cent
extraction wholemeal flour and then in a good batter (see chapter
on Batters) and fry in deep fat until cooked crisp and brown.
Serve immediately.

2. Wash and cut into thin rings and pat dry with a cloth if
necessary. Fry in butter or vegetable fat in a frying-pan until
golden brown. Serve immediately. The rings can be egg-and-
breadcrumbed if you prefer.

BABY MARROWS FROM PROVENCE

6 baby marrows
2 oz. butter or 2 tablespoons olive oil
1 clove garlic (onion or shallot may be used instead)
1 lb. tomatoes
A little grated cheese
Seasoning

Wash and cut the baby marrows into thick slices, cook them
gently in the butter or oil with the crushed garlic (or chopped
onion) for about 5–10 minutes. Meanwhile skin the tomatoes and
quarter them if small, cube if large. Grease a fire-proof dish and
arrange the tomatoes and courgettes in layers, sprinkling with
seasoning, starting and finishing with tomatoes. Sprinkle the top
with grated cheese (grated cheese may also be put between layers
making the dish into a savoury) and cook in a moderate oven
375° F., M5 for 45 minutes–1 hour. Cover the top with a piece
of greaseproof paper if it should become too brown.

Vegetables

Large Marrows

Peel the marrow thinly, slice into ¾-inch rings and remove the seeds. Cut the rings into even-sized pieces—(they should look rather like pineapple chunks). Melt 1 oz. of butter or vegetable fat or 1 tablespoon of olive oil in a saucepan, add the marrow and seasoning with some freshly chopped herbs (parsley, chives, marjoram or mint) if you like. Put the lid on, which should fit tightly and cook over a gentle heat until tender, 10–15 minutes approximately; shake the pan vigorously at first to prevent the marrow from sticking. The marrow is then served in its own liquid thus retaining as much of the flavour as possible. This is the best way to cook the marrow if it is to be served on its own.

Baked Marrows

Prepare and cook the marrow as above but without the herbs. Lay the marrow in a fire-proof dish which has been rubbed with a cut clove of garlic (grease the edge of the dish to assist in the washing-up!) and cover with a thick white sauce, béchamel or caper sauce. If there is any liquid left from cooking the marrow use this in the sauce. Cover the surface with breadcrumbs and/or cheese and bake in a moderate oven 375° F., M6, for 30–45 minutes.

One of the best ways to serve the larger marrows is to stuff them and then either bake or steam them. They can be prepared for stuffing in a variety of ways.

1. If the marrow is fairly tender, leave the skin on and then slice it lengthwise; scoop out the seeds so that you are left with two canoe-shaped pieces. Fill each piece with stuffing and bake; or stuff and tie the marrow together as near its original shape and steam.

2. Peel the marrow and cut off both ends. Scrape out the seeds first with your fingers and then with the handle of a spoon. Fill the hollow with stuffing and cook. If the stuffing has been packed very firmly you can cut the marrow into slices and bake them in the oven.

3. Peel the marrow and cut across the middle. Cut a piece off

170

Vegetables

each end of the marrow so that the marrow will stand upright and scoop out the seeds. Fill the hollow and bake or steam. The stuffings can be taken from the chapter on Stuffings. Serve the finished dish with a good thick gravy, tomato or onion sauce.

A sage and onion or sage and leek stuffing is very complementary and a savoury rice stuffing is good.

MUSHROOMS

Nowadays it appears to be easy to buy cultivated mushrooms all the year round, but those of you who know where you can find field mushrooms in the autumn are really lucky (and should keep their whereabouts a secret!). Mushrooms must be freshly picked and not over 24 hours old to retain their full flavour and still be wholesome. We have found that the mushrooms provided for our open market are the best buy as they are despatched after picking the evening before and we use them as soon as we buy them. The mushrooms should be undamaged and the stalks should be of an even length, the ends of which have been cleanly cut. The gills should be a pinky or mid-brown colour and the cap should be white or white only very slightly tinged with brown-grey. Neither the cap nor the gills should look grey or black as this may mean the mushrooms are stale, they should also be quite dry as dampness again means old age. There are various stages in the growth of a mushroom.

1. When they are young they are small and round with little or no gill showing—if the gill does show it should be a pale grey, pink—and these are called button mushrooms. They are very useful for garnishing soups, and sauces which are to be kept as white as possible, but being very young the flavour is not so pronounced as it is in older mushrooms.

2. In the middle age the cap has opened out more with the gills showing a pink or brown colouring, dependent on variety. The flavour is better and these are used for savouries, fillings, and as a vegetable. They may also be used as the button type although they are called cups.

3. When still older the gills are fully exposed and the cap is flat

171

Vegetables

(hence their name 'flats'); the gills are a lovely soft deep brown in colour. These mushrooms usually have a good strong flavour and are wonderful when stuffed, and since they are so much larger they are ideal for stuffing. If you wish to introduce a dark colour into your vegetable course they are invaluable as they turn practically black when cooked. A mixture of mature mushrooms, tomatoes and green peas is most appetizing.

Apart from whole mushrooms one can buy the stalks separately and since the growers can only sell the mushrooms with a certain length of stalk, there are always plenty of 'stalks' about. They are not to be looked down upon at all, as they are well flavoured. Although slightly tougher than the mushroom to eat, they can be used to make stock, sauces, savouries, stuffings, etc. in fact anything that does not require the use of whole mushrooms. In most of the recipes which follow, stalks may be wholly or partly substituted for whole mushrooms which proves a great economy as they are much cheaper to buy. Authorities seem to be divided on the method of preparation. Some say peel and dust or rub with salt, etc. but never put anywhere near water, and others suggest that it is better not to peel and wash quickly in cold water. We think the second method is the better as we have strong views on the question of peeling anything without need; so much goodness can be lost both in the peel and the vegetable when it is cooked. Field mushrooms must be very carefully washed and they require very close examination since they attract grubs, maggots and other insects!

Mushrooms can be baked in the oven, fried and grilled whole; cut up they are used in the manner the dish demands. They are generally cooked and served with butter or cream or white sauce. Remember that mushrooms usually shrink in cooking and produce some liquid.

BAKED MUSHROOMS

Place the mushrooms, after preparation, in a greased baking-dish (one which has a fitting lid) stalk side upwards. Pour a little cream or place a flake of butter in each cap and season well. Put

172

on the lid and bake in a moderate oven until tender. This generally takes from 10–20 minutes, depending on the heat of the oven and the size of the mushrooms. Remove the lid just prior to serving. This method is very good for retaining the flavour, but if you have a nut savoury or a similar dish, baking in the oven, then the mushrooms can be placed around or on the top of the savoury to cook.

FRIED MUSHROOMS

1. Melt a little butter, vegetable fat or oil in a frying-pan, put in the mushrooms when the fat is really hot and cook as quickly as possible until tender without burning. If the mushrooms are large they will need to be turned with a slice, otherwise tossing and stirring will be sufficient. This should take only 5–10 minutes. Season, sprinkle with chopped parsley if you desire. Serve immediately. If there is much liquid left save it for soup, gravy or sauces, only a little should be served with the mushrooms.

2. Use either a saucepan or a frying-pan with a lid. Melt and heat some butter, oil or vegetable fat (a little chopped onion, leek, or shallot can be cooked in it first, or rub the saucepan with a cut clove of garlic), add the mushrooms with seasoning and cook gently with the lid on for 5–10 minutes, shaking occasionally to prevent sticking. On removing the lid, you will find the mushrooms have cooked and produced quite an amount of liquid. If you want the mushrooms glazed then boil them very rapidly for 3–5 minutes until most of the liquid is gone and then serve immediately. If you want to thicken the mushrooms, sprinkle with a little flour from a dredger when the mushrooms are off the heat, stirring all the time and then cook gently until the mixture thickens. This can be enriched by adding cream and/or egg-yolks as desired and then gently heating but not boiling.

3. Prepare mushrooms of an even size and not too large. Heat the deep fat and make a coating batter (see chapter on Batters).

Dip the mushrooms in the batter and fry. Serve immediately. They are very good when served with a sauce; try sauce tartare.

4. Choose even, and medium-sized mushrooms, remove the stalks and cook gently in butter, drain well and add the chopped

stalks to the liquid. Thicken the juice with sufficient flour to make a panada and beat in an egg. Allow the sauce to cool and sandwich the mushrooms together in pairs with a little of the sauce and then coat all over with the sauce. Roll in a little flour and knock off any surplus. Leave to get really cold and firm. Dip first in batter and then in breadcrumbs and fry in deep fat until golden brown.

GRILLED MUSHROOMS

Grease the grid in the grill pan and arrange the prepared mushrooms on the grid, dome side uppermost. Brush with melted butter or oil and season. Place under a hot grill for 4–5 minutes and then turn and brush again and cook for another 4–5 minutes. Use as required.

STUFFED MUSHROOMS

Choose large flat mushrooms. Wash thoroughly and remove the stalks. Grease a baking-dish and place the mushrooms in it. Prepare any stuffing mixture you may like and pile it on top of the mushrooms. Bake in a moderate oven for 20–30 minutes and serve with a sauce.

ONIONS
(Shallots and Garlic)

Where would we be without them! They are used so frequently to flavour dishes that we often forget to use them as a vegetable. Imported onions ensure a good supply all the year round. While on the subject of onions, we must mention shallots and garlic both of which belong to the onion family; they are used for flavouring, shallots are mild and garlic strong!

Shallots are chopped and generally used for flavouring of soups, sauces, gravies, stuffings and savouries. They can be used as a garnish when cooked and so can pickling onions if and when you are able to find them.

Vegetables

Garlic is such a health-giving vegetable (as are all the members of the onion family) that it seems a great pity so many people should dislike it. Used in very small quantities it can transform a salad, vegetables or savouries without being objectionable. There are several ways of preparing it: (1) peel a clove of garlic and cut it in half. Rub firmly around a saucepan, baking-dish or salad bowl so that a little of the juice is extracted. In good kitchen-utensil shops you can purchase a garlic crusher which enables the juice to be used as required. (2) Make a garlic paste by peeling a clove and crushing it with sea salt until a paste is formed. Use as required. (3) Peel as many cloves as required and chop very finely and use as desired.

Perhaps it should be explained that garlic is sold in bulbs—they have the same appearance as bulbs too, and are covered with a fine white papery tissue. These bulbs can be broken into cloves—when you buy a bulb feel it firmly with your fingers and you will feel the cloves underneath. Choose the clove nearest the surface and strip the white papery tissue, it will be joined to the bulb at the base but will come away quite easily when lifted upwards and outwards. The final layer before the clove itself is more like onion-skin.

Spanish onions deserve a special mention, they are large and of milder flavour than the usual onion. Onion enthusiasts eat them raw, but they are generally used and cooked as other onions, making excellent stuffings—and good onion rings. Sometimes in the spring, onions sprout green shoots, these should not be thrown away. Allow the onion to continue sprouting until the green shoot is 4–6 inches long, then cut off and use raw and finely chopped. The parent onion is by this time in a pretty poor state but it can be used in the stock-pot.

When buying onions see they are firm, free from mould or sprouting and that the papery layers are whole and unblemished.

To prepare onions cut off the bottom and the top with a sharp stainless steel knife and carefully pull off the papery layers until the onion proper appears. If there is a purple or greenish colouring this is edible and need cause no concern. Prepare onions just before you need them, but never, repeat never, soak in water. If you have many onions to prepare and they are particularly strong you will no doubt find your eyes watering. It does sometimes help to rinse the knife and your hands in cold water frequently, but a great help, funnily enough, is wearing glasses! Although even this does not always stop the tears completely.

Cutting an onion

Skin and cut off base   cut down to near base and   cut across sections
then in half right through

The cutting or chopping of onions can be quite an art. If you find it a very trying job then invest in an onion chopper which is easily obtainable from a kitchen-equipment store. Never use the board for anything else after chopping onions or garlic or shallots. If you want pieces of onion to show in the finished dish then cut in rings, cubes or slices from top to bottom, leaving a small part of the root section at the bottom to hold the slices together.

Onions can be boiled, steamed, fried, cooked conservatively, braised, baked or stuffed. They are good served in or coated with practically any sauce.

BOILED ONIONS

Prepare and either cook whole or cut as desired. Place in a saucepan of boiling sea-salted water, only enough to cover, and cook until tender. Up to two hours for large whole onions and as little as 20–30 minutes for small or sliced onions. The cooking water is then used to make an accompanying sauce, or it can be used for gravy, broth or the stock-pot, but never throw it away.

FRIED ONIONS

Cube or slice the onions as preferred. Melt some butter, vegetable fat or oil in a frying-pan and heat. Put in the onions and stir well. Cook gently, turning frequently until tender and browned. They need close attention! Season to taste and serve.

Or, you can add half a teacup of water or stock and let the onions boil or cook in the steam. When the liquid has evaporated then stir as before until the onions are browned.

2. Slice some onions into rings and separate the rings. Dip into milk and drain, then dip into seasoned flour and shake well. Fry in smoking deep fat until golden brown, this will only take a second or two and drain well. Serve immediately. You may like to try another coating of seasoned flour, then beaten egg-white and then flour again, or they can be dipped in batter.

PARSNIPS

This vegetable is not very popular; it has a distinctive sweetish flavour, and like brussels sprouts and celery, it is the better for having been frosted.

When buying see that the roots are undamaged and not too large as the large roots tend to be coarse.

The parsnips should be well scrubbed and topped and tailed. They should always be cooked in their skins and the skins rubbed off afterwards or left on as desired. They can be boiled, baked, roasted, fried, cooked conservatively and steamed. They can be served with white, parsley or cheese sauce or melted butter.

Old parsnips develop a hard core which is easily removed when the parsnip has been cooked.

BOILED PARSNIPS

Prepare the parsnips, cut into even pieces if they are large, and place in just enough boiling water, sea salted, to cover. Cook until tender, from 30 minutes–1½ hours. Drain, and either serve with butter and chopped parsley or a sauce. The parsnips can also be mashed when cooked, but if they are old the core should be removed first.

ROASTED PARSNIPS

Scrub and trim the parsnips—parboil, place in a hot oil or vegetable fat, baste and roast until tender. Turn and baste while cooking.

BAKED PARSNIPS

Scrub and trim the parsnips and bake in their skins on the oven shelf or on a baking-sheet. Serve in the same way as baked potatoes with butter and seasoning.

FRIED PARSNIPS

1. Boil and drain some parsnips, fry in butter with a sprinkle of brown sugar until brown and crisp.

2. Cut into thin slices. Heat the deep fat to smoking point and fry until golden brown.

3. Cut some cooked parsnips into slices or even-sized cubes, dip in a coating batter and fry in deep fat until golden brown.

MASHED PARSNIPS

Remove the hard core from some boiled parsnips and either mash on their own or with an equal amount of potatoes. Add butter and seasoning to taste.

PARSNIPS IN BATTER

Cube some boiled parsnips and sprinkle them over a tin which contains a Yorkshire pudding mixture. Bake quickly in a hot oven until batter has risen and is brown on top. Cut into squares and serve.

PEAS
(including dried peas and lentils)

These are at their best when young and freshly picked and in these circumstances there are not many vegetables to equal them for flavour and tenderness. We tend to disregard fresh peas nowadays as frozen peas are so plentiful but the fresh peas are far superior. Frozen peas contain only half the usual amount of vitamin C by the time they are cooked. When buying peas look for a firm, fresh green and unblemished pod—neither too flat nor so full that the skin is wrinkled and paling in colour.

Shell the peas just before cooking them as they lose some of their flavour soon after shelling. If you do have to leave them prior to cooking, cook them with the clean empty pea-pods in the water for extra flavour. As the peas become older, watch for the little grubs that eat the peas. If the peas vary a great deal in size shake them through a large-hole colander or a riddle.

Young peas should be cooked very little, for 5–10 minutes in very little boiling sea-salted water. When tender, drain (use the water, if possible, it is very good indeed) and toss in a little melted butter or margarine. Serve immediately.

Young peas are so tender and have such a delicate flavour that they need no other flavouring.

When peas are older a good pinch of brown sugar and 3–4 sprigs of mint can be added to improve the flavour (tie the stalks together with a piece of string to make them easier to remove). Older peas may take longer to cook, but they are served in the same way.

There are other methods of serving peas, some of which follow. Personally we feel they are best cooked and served as above, but if you are lucky enough to grow your own and there is a glut then it is useful to vary the method.

PEAS IN FRENCH STYLE

1–2 oz. butter
1 medium-small lettuce, shredded
4–6 chopped spring onions
1 teacup cold water
1 pint shelled peas
Seasoning and brown sugar (mint optional)

Heat the butter and add the lettuce and onions. Cook for a minute or two and then add all the other ingredients and stir well together. Bring slowly to the boil and simmer gently until the peas are tender (10–20 minutes, dependent on age). Serve immediately all together; if there is too much liquid then remove the lid for the last 3–5 minutes and cook quickly to reduce it.

CREAMED NEW PEAS AND CARROTS

1 bunch new carrots
1 pint shelled peas
½ oz. butter
¼ pint cold water
Seasoning and brown sugar
4–5 sprigs mint
3 tablespoons whipped cream

Prepare the carrots and shell the peas. Melt the butter and gently cook the carrots in it for 5 minutes. Add water, seasoning, sugar and a bunch of mint, put on the saucepan lid, bring to the boil and simmer for 10 minutes. Add the peas and cook until tender. If the cooking liquid is not reduced by this time, finish cooking with the lid off to reduce it. Keep an eye on the cooking as the liquid may evaporate *too* much—vegetables should not be browned at all. When the vegetables are cooked and the liquid evaporated remove the mint and add the cream. Stir together and serve immediately.

The following is a good recipe if you have large amounts of old peas to cope with.

GREEN PEA PUDDING

2–3 new potatoes
4–5 sprigs mint
1 pint peas
½ oz. butter
1 onion or 3–4 spring onions
1 lettuce
1 egg
Seasoning

Vegetables

Prepare the potatoes and place in sufficient boiling sea-salted water to cover; put in the mint bundle, cook for 10 minutes. Add the shelled peas and cook until tender. Melt the butter and cook the onions and shredded cleaned lettuce for 5 minutes. Put the potatoes, peas, onions and lettuce through a sieve; add the beaten egg and taste. Season to taste. Place in a greased pudding basin and cover with a pudding cloth or greaseproof paper. Stand on a rack in boiling water and steam for about 1 hour.

Dried peas

Used mainly in soups and stews, dried peas can also be used, especially in winter, as a vegetable or they may be a good substitute for lentils in recipes. They are soaked in the same way as dried beans—for 24 hours in cold or tepid water. Wash very carefully and inspect closely before soaking. The cooking is also similar but the flavouring vegetables are generally omitted. When they are cooked they may be served with melted butter or in a white parsley sauce, but the traditional and oldest way of serving them is as a

PEASE PUDDING

Wash, soak and then cook ½ lb. of dried peas. Sieve and add ½ oz. of butter, 1 egg and seasoning to taste. Beat all the items together for 3–5 minutes until it is very well mixed. In days gone by it was then placed in a floured pudding cloth and boiled for another hour. We put it in a greased pudding basin and deep fireproof dish and cover with greaseproof paper or a cloth, stand on a rack in a saucepan of boiling water and steam for ¾–1 hour.

PEAS AND RICE

Wash, soak and then cook ½ lb. of dried peas. Wash and cook ½ lb. of natural rice. Melt 2 oz. of butter in a saucepan and heat, add the peas and rice and stir together with a large fork. Add some concentrated tomato purée, just enough to give a pinkish colour; or fresh tomato purée may be used. Stir all together with a fork until well heated through; it will take about 10 minutes. Taste and

Vegetables

season as necessary. This recipe can be varied by adding a little chopped mint or basil.

SPANISH PEAS

Wash, soak and then cook some dried peas. Add salt and paprika pepper to taste and serve with pats of cold butter. Chopped fried Spanish onions added to this also make a fine flavour.

Lentils

This is also a pulse, but it is useful because it does not require soaking. The lentils should be washed and inspected carefully as there are sometimes small stones in their midst. They are generally used in 'made up' dishes and are very nutritious, but they can be cooked plainly as follows: place the lentils in enough sea-salted water to cover and bring to the boil (stir occasionally to make certain they do not stick); add a bouquet garni of parsley, thyme and bay leaf, place the lid on the saucepan and simmer gently until tender. Remove the bouquet garni, strain and taste. Season if necessary and serve with butter.

Lentils can also be puréed; sieve the lentils when they are cooked and add some of the cooking water if necessary. They can be flavoured by the addition of some chopped onion, carrot and celery which has been cooked in butter, vegetable fat or oil and when nicely browned the mixture can be added to either the purée or the boiled lentils. Purée of lentils flavoured like this makes a good stuffing.

FRIED LENTIL CAKES

Make some thick lentil purée as above and add one or two eggs. Beat well together and cool. Shape into cakes or rolls or balls. Coat with egg and breadcrumbs and fry in deep fat until brown and heated through. Serve immediately.

CURRIED LENTILS—DAHL

Melt some butter, oil or vegetable fat in a saucepan and fry

Vegetables

chopped onions and a little garlic until golden brown. Add the lentils and stir in the fat for a minute or two (they stick if you leave them!). Add curry powder and/or paste to taste and leave on a VERY LOW heat for 5–10 minutes, stirring as necessary. Add sea salt, a pinch of brown sugar and enough stock just to cover the lentils (tomato juice or purée is good if added to the stock) and simmer until the lentils are cooked. Add a little lemon juice, taste and serve.

This is very good if served with a green vegetable; we sometimes cooked dice carrots with the onion at the beginning.

PEPPERS
(also known as Capsicums and Sweet Peppers)

These vegetables are becoming increasingly popular. They are good in salads when raw and excellent cooked and stuffed. They can be bought green mostly but also yellow and red and are usually imported; though we have grown them under glass in this country. They have a pleasant fresh flavour (particularly raw), quite unlike anything else, and are well worth trying. Prepare them by slicing off the stalk end (save this stalk if you are stuffing the pepper). Inside you will find it almost hollow save for a centre piece, which is covered with tiny flat discs. Remove this centre core and the discs, which are the seeds, and any other seeds you may find, as they are very hot and should not be eaten under any circumstances. The centre piece is supported by three or four ribs which come up the sides of the pepper and these can be removed if they are tough or large. Some recipes tell you to skin the peppers but we have found this unnecessary. Wash the peppers quickly in cold water.

STUFFED PEPPERS

Prepare the peppers and parboil them and their 'lids' in boiling salted water for 10–15 minutes. Drain, and use the liquor for a sauce or gravy to accompany the peppers. Prepare some stuffing while the peppers are cooking and fill them when they are cool enough. Replace the 'lids' and bake in a greased dish, covered

Vegetables

with a greased paper for 20–30 minutes. Remove the paper towards the end of the cooking period. The peppers can be brushed with oil or vegetable fat to keep them from browning too much.

Serve with gravy or sauce.

Ideas for stuffings and sauces

1. Whole natural rice, flavoured with tomato, onion or garlic and herbs—serve with cheese sauce.

2. Whole natural rice, flavoured with mushrooms, peas and egg—serve with tomato sauce.

3. Whole natural rice flavoured with cheese, onion and garlic —serve with parsley sauce.

4. Tomato, aubergine and cucumber with onion—serve with béchamel sauce.

5. Brown breadcrumbs, ground Brazil nuts, mushrooms and herbs—serve with gravy or tomato sauce.

6. Brown breadcrumbs, ground cashew nuts, onions and herbs —serve with gravy or tomato sauce.

7. Mashed potato, peas, diced carrots, onions—serve with cheese sauce or mild curry sauce.

We hope you think of many more—good experimenting!

POTATO

Books have been written (but perhaps not read very much) about this vegetable! In spite of this it is still surprising how badly treated the potato can be. There are two golden rules: (1) try to grow your own or buy compost-grown; (2) never peel them before cooking, otherwise flavour and food value are lost. We will try to give you some basic methods and different ways of serving them.

We will first deal with new potatoes which are treated quite differently from old.

When buying make sure you *are* buying new potatoes as so often the potatoes which appear so early in the year (and for which we pay a lot of money!) do not behave at all like really new potatoes. We think the first Jersey potatoes are worth waiting for

Vegetables

and you can always judge whether or not the potato is new by the skin; it should come off when rubbed with the thumb and forefinger. The skin should look fresh and papery, not dry and tough.

To prepare, scrub the potatoes with a soft brush, remove any blemishes with a sharp knife. Place in just enough sea-salted boiling water to cover. Cook gently for 15–25 minutes, depending on the size. Add a few sprigs of mint if you desire. Save the water for future use and either serve the potatoes in their jackets with butter to be used separately or quickly remove the skins with a knife and toss the potatoes in melted butter and chopped parsley.

New potatoes have such a short season and so delicate a flavour that it is best to serve them plainly. They are waxy rather than floury and cannot be treated in many of the ways which we use for old potatoes. However, here are some recipes to use for new potatoes.

CREAMY NEW POTATOES

Wash and cook some new potatoes. Peel and cut into slices. Put the following into a saucepan:

> $\frac{1}{8}$–$\frac{1}{4}$ pint single cream
> Juice of half a lemon
> 1–2 oz. butter
> Seasoning

Add the potatoes, mixing well together and heating through. Serve hot. This is very good with chopped parsley and mint added.

NEW POTATOES WITH LEMON
(Pommes Maître d'hôtel)

Prepare and cook the potatoes in sea-salted water to which has been added lemon juice. Drain and serve with melted butter, a few shreds of lemon rind, a squeeze of lemon juice and chopped parsley.

This is very good with orange rind as a pleasant change.

Vegetables

CURRIED NEW POTATOES

1 lb. small new potatoes
1 oz. butter, nut fat or oil
2 tablespoons chopped onion
2 teaspoons curry paste
1 oz. (approximately) 81 per cent extraction flour
1 pint milk
Salt and brown sugar to taste
1 tablespoon mango chutney
Squeeze of lemon juice

Wash and boil the potatoes for 10 minutes. Heat the fat and fry the onions until soft but not brown, add the curry paste and cook gently, stirring for a few minutes. Add enough flour to make a roux and then add the milk. Bring to the boil and simmer until it thickens, add the seasoning and flavouring to taste. Then add the potatoes and simmer over a gentle heat until they are cooked. The sauce should thicken during the cooking until it becomes a creamy consistency.

FRIED NEW POTATOES

Scrub some even-sized small new potatoes and rub off the skins gently. If they are really new the skins will come off when scrubbing. Heat plenty of butter in a frying-pan and add the potatoes, keep turning them until evenly cooked and golden brown—this takes about 30 minutes. Season, add chopped parsley and serve hot.

Old potatoes

These can be boiled, steamed, baked, roasted, creamed, mashed or fried—they can also be used to make cakes, scones, pancakes, etc.

To prepare, scrub them well in cold water with a soft vegetable brush and inspect for blemishes. Remove any of these with a sharp stainless steel knife. If you have any potatoes with a whole skin, make a small cut somewhere on the potato so that the skin does not burst in cooking.

Vegetables

BOILED POTATOES

Wash and prepare the potatoes, which should be of a nearly even size if possible. Place in enough sea-salted water just to cover the potatoes and cook until soft, 25–40 minutes. They can be tested with a skewer or a sharp knife. If you like potatoes very floury and dry, then try boiling them for two-thirds of the normal cooking time, drain well and cover with a clean cloth. Replace the lid and stand in a warm place for 10–15 minutes, by which time they will have finished cooking in their own steam. If you wish to remove the skins before serving, peel them immediately they have been drained, using a stainless steel knife. This is an easy task save that the potatoes are very hot! We find that wearing a thick rubber glove on the hand that holds the potato is a great help. Serve with melted butter and chopped parsley, or mint sauce or dry with chopped parsley.

To dry mash potatoes

Potatoes sometimes require to be dry mashed before being made into special dishes. First prepare and boil the potatoes, while they are still hot remove the skins and put through a potato-ricer or sieve. Use the mashed potato as required.

To cream potatoes

Boil or steam the potatoes and remove the skins. Either press through a ricer or a coarse sieve or mash very well with a potato masher while hot; if they are left to cool they will become gluey. In another saucepan heat some butter and milk together, 1 oz. of butter and $\frac{1}{8}$–$\frac{1}{4}$ pint of milk to 1 lb. of potatoes (you can be more or less lavish as you wish!). With a wooden spoon beat the prepared potato over a gentle heat and add the milk mixture, stirring all the time. Add seasoning to taste and serve hot, garnished with a sprig of parsley.

Flavourings for variety: (1) lemon or orange rind grated finely; (2) chopped parsley, chives or mint; (3) chopped watercress; (4) chopped spring onions; (5) grated nutmeg; (6) paprika pepper; (7) chopped cooked peppers; (8) chopped mushrooms.

Potatoes will blend with any vegetable and equal quantities of

Vegetables

creamed potatoes and mashed vegetable make a pleasant change, e.g. potatoes and swedes; potatoes and carrots; potatoes and peas; potatoes and onions are a few examples.

Potatoes can also be steamed. Prepare as before and place in a steamer with the water under the steamer boiling well. Steaming takes half as long again as boiling.

BAKED POTATOES

Wash, scrub, and remove any bad parts. Cut a cross in one side of each potato. If the potatoes are uneven or very large cut them into sizes as required. Place on a baking-sheet or on the rungs of the oven shelf and bake for 45–75 minutes, according to the size and the heat of the oven 375–425° F. or M5–7. They are cooked when the skins brown and the potato feels soft when pressed between thumb and forefinger. When cooked press the potatoes gently in a cloth so that the cross opens and put them in a serving-dish. Place a pat of butter and sprig of parsley in each cross and serve immediately.

Variations

1. After preparing the potatoes dry them in a clean cloth and rub with butter or nut fat. Bake as before on a baking-sheet.

2. After rubbing with fat as above roll in coarse sea salt or caraway seeds and bake on a baking-sheet.

3. Bake the potatoes without the cross but with a cut right around the widest part, so that when they are baked they can be cut in half, scoop out the potato and cream it, adding any of the flavourings for creamed potatoes. The addition of grated cheese or nuts makes a good savoury dish. Pile the potato back into the skins and place on a baking-sheet. Sprinkle with grated cheese or breadcrumbs and a few small pieces of butter, brown under the grill or return to the oven to brown and warm through.

ROAST POTATOES

Prepare and parboil some even-sized potatoes, drain and save the water for stock, skin them if you prefer to do so or leave with

188

skins on. Have ready for use some oil, vegetable or nut fat heated in a baking-tin in a moderate oven 375–400° F. or M5–6 and place the potatoes carefully on the tin. Either baste or turn the potatoes in the fat so that all the surfaces are coated in fat and return to the oven. Cook until tender and golden brown, 20–40 minutes approximately; the potatoes will probably need turning two or three times. They are very good if roasted around and together with a nut savoury, particularly if the fat is flavoured with onions, garlic or herbs.

FRIED POTATOES

Potatoes are more frequently fried as 'chips' than in any other form. The method is as follows:

Scrub some old potatoes thoroughly, removing any blemishes. We leave the skins on but you can peel them off very thinly if you wish (use them to make stock). Heat deep fat until 330–340° F. or until a small cube of bread just sizzles. While the fat is heating, cut the potatoes into the shape you require, ½-inch cubes, or large chips made by cutting the potatoes in half, then into quarters and then eighths; or the usual size for chips made by cutting into sixteenths. The secret is to cut the pieces as nearly the same size as possible, so start with even-sized potatoes. Potatoes to be prepared for deep fat frying are usually soaked in cold water and then dried very thoroughly in a clean cloth—this is to wash away the starch grains from the cut surfaces so that the pieces of potato will not stick together during cooking. This can be omitted (from the nutritional point of view it is better if it is) but when cooking the potato pieces, fry fewer than usual and shake gently and constantly during the first frying. Put the prepared potato into the wire basket and lower gently into the fat, cook until the potatoes are tender but not brown. A good guide is when the edges start to turn brown. It is very difficult to give a time for this as so much depends on the quantity involved, but 5–10 minutes is the average. Drain the potatoes very well. When this point is reached, heat the fat until it is really hot, 390° F. or until a good blue haze rises from the surface. Fry the potatoes a second time in the hot fat and you will find they brown almost immediately—drain when they

Vegetables

have reached the right colour and serve as quickly as possible. Place them in a warmed serving-dish but never cover with a lid as this will cause all their crispness to be lost. If you are cooking a large quantity, keep them warm in a slow oven, again without a lid. This may seem a lot of bother but it is well worth it. Potatoes may also be cut into fine matchsticks (*pommes paille*), finely sliced (potato crisps) or cut into fine ribbons (*pommes copeaux*) with a potato peeler, in this case the pieces of potato are fried in very hot fat only as they are small enough not to need the slower cooking first.

Some other ways of frying potatoes are as follows:

1. Nearly cook some even-sized small or medium old potatoes. remove their jackets and place in hot fat 370–380° F.; fry until golden brown and crisp, and serve immediately.

2. Sieve some hot cooked potatoes and add to each 1 lb. of potatoes 1 oz. of butter and 1 egg. Season and flavour well. Flavourings can be: cheese, nuts, onions or garlic, herbs, mushrooms, tomatoes and nutmeg. Allow to cool. Shape into balls, croquettes or cakes and roll in seasoned flour. The potato mixture should be firm and easy to handle. Coat with egg and breadcrumbs twice and fry in hot fat 390° F. until brown, crisp and heated through. Handle with care as they break rather easily. Serve immediately.

SAUTÉ POTATOES

Melt 1 oz. of butter in a frying-pan and when foaming add 1 lb. of cooked potatoes sliced when cold. Add seasoning, allow the potatoes to brown a little and turn them over carefully with a slice. Continue until the slices are nicely browned, sprinkle with chopped parsley and serve.

POMMES LYONNAISE

This is a variation of sauté potatoes. First cook two onions cut into rings, in 3–4 tablespoons olive oil, and when cooked and brown remove the onions from the pan. Sauté 1 lb. of cooked sliced potatoes in the oil and when browned add the onions, mix and sprinkle with parsley to serve.

Vegetables

POMMES À LA PROVENÇALE

Yet another variety of sauté potatoes. Heat some oil and add two crushed cloves of garlic and one or two rosemary leaves. Add sliced parboiled potatoes and seasoning. Cook until brown and sprinkle with chopped parsley. Serve.

There are many other ways of serving potatoes, but space permits only a few more.

DUCHESS POTATOES

1 lb. potatoes
1 oz. butter or margarine
1 egg
2–3 tablespoons of cream
Seasoning

Prepare potatoes and boil. Put them through a ricer or sieve while hot. Melt the fat in a saucepan and add the potato with the egg, seasoning and 1 tablespoon of cream. Beat well over a gentle heat; the potato should be firm but not too stiff. If it is, add more cream. There are two ways of finishing Duchess potatoes: (1) grease a round or square flat tin or fire-proof dish and spread the potato evenly in it. Mark into squares or eighths and brush with beaten egg. Bake in a moderate oven 375° F. until brown and crisp. Pile the pieces on a serving-plate and garnish with parsley and watercress. (2) Place the mixture prepared as above in a piping bag and pipe large rosettes on to a baking-sheet. Glaze with egg and bake. Garnish and serve.

COLCANNON

This is a mixture of dry mashed potatoes with well-drained partly cooked cabbage. Two parts potato to one part cabbage. Mix the cabbage and potato together and season well, adding just a little beaten egg or milk if it will not bind. There is, however, usually sufficient moisture in the vegetables. Melt 2 oz. of butter or vegetable fat per lb. of vegetables in a frying-pan and when foaming, add the vegetables and spread evenly over the pan. Cook gently until the bottom is nicely browned, then turn with a slice. Continue cooking until the mixture is heated through and full of crisp browned pieces. This dish is also known as 'bubble and squeak' because so much butter was used in preparation that it used to bubble when cooking and squeak when turned!

Colcannon can be varied in many ways:

(1) by adding onions, leeks or herbs.

(2) by adding other vegetables than cabbage or a mixture of vegetables, but there should always be twice as much potato as added vegetables. Other vegetables: cabbage and carrot, leeks, cabbage and onions, turnip and swedes, swedes and carrots, brussels sprouts and kale.

HUNGARIAN POTATOES

1 oz. butter
1 large chopped onion
¾ pint stock
1 tablespoon concentrated tomato purée
1 lb. potatoes
Salt and brown sugar to taste
1 teaspoon–dessertspoon paprika

Melt the butter in a saucepan and add the onion; cook gently until soft. Add the stock and the purée. Bring to the boil and add the potato cut into ½–¾-inch dice. Add seasoning and paprika, cover and cook gently until tender, about 20–30 minutes. Taste and adjust the seasoning if necessary. Serve with garnish.

POMMES BOULANGÈRES

1 lb. potatoes
½ lb. onions
Salt and pepper
½ pint milk
½ pint stock or Marmite and water
Butter

Vegetables

Prepare the potatoes and onions and slice thinly. Place alternate layers of potato and onion in a greased fire-proof dish, starting with a potato layer and finishing with same. Sprinkle a little seasoning on each layer. Fill the dish with the mixture of stock and milk to the level of the top layer of potato. There will be a little left which should be used to top up half-way through the cooking. Flake a few pieces of butter on top and bake in a moderate oven 375° F. for an hour or longer if necessary. Serve in the dish.

PUMPKIN

This vegetable is used more in America than here, but it can be seen in greengrocers' shops in the late summer or autumn months.

Preparation and cooking are as for marrows.

SAMPHIRE

This is a sea plant, not unlike seaweed, which grows on certain parts of the coastline of Great Britain. We serve it in our restaurants in late August and September having it sent direct from Norfolk. It has branching stems covered with a green succulent flesh.

The preparation is simple in that it should be washed in cold water—you may have to take off some parts of the plant which have become discoloured. Cook in boiling water for about 15 minutes and serve with melted butter. It may also be served with a vinaigrette sauce or lemon juice.

You eat it rather as you would asparagus with forefinger and thumb, holding the base of the stems and pulling the fleshy part away with the teeth.

The taste is very pleasant and salty and it has a high iron content.

Vegetables

SEAKALE

This plant is like chicory, it is a blanched young shoot which is forced during the winter months so that it arrives at the time of the year when fresh vegetables are short. Like all blanched stems it quickly loses its freshness and should be gathered just before use. When buying seakale try bending one of the stalks a little; if it snaps this is a sign of freshness, but if it bends then it has been cut a day or two and has probably lost some of its flavour.

To prepare, cut the root off as close to the leaves as possible and remove any discoloured or limp leaves. Wash under a running cold tap and shake gently to remove surplus water. It is cooked rather like asparagus, tied in bundles and placed on a rack in boiling sea-salted water to which the juice of a lemon has been added. The lemon juice helps to keep the stems a good colour. Use as little water as you can without burning; if the seakale is steamed it will take a little longer than boiling which takes 20–30 minutes. The seakale can be drained well and served with melted butter, browned butter or hollandaise sauce. Another good way is to make a sauce from the cooking liquid—adding, if necessary, some creamy milk—taste and season if necessary, add some chopped parsley, green peas and sliced cooked mushrooms. Coat the seakale with this and serve immediately.

Polish Seakale

Prepare, boil, drain and place the seakale in a warm serving-dish. Sprinkle with a mixture of chopped parsley, chopped hard-boiled egg and fine wholemeal breadcrumbs fried until crisp in plenty of butter or vegetable fat.

Fried Seakale

Prepare and boil the seakale until it is nearly cooked. Drain well and separate into stems; if the stems are large cut them in half. Dip in seasoned flour and then either in batter or in egg and breadcrumbs, fry in hot deep fat 380–390° F. until crisp and golden brown. This will only take a few minutes. Serve immediately without a cover.

Vegetables

SORREL

Has a sharp acid flavour and is usually mixed with spinach, lettuce or young nettles. It is used in salads. Prepare and cook it as you would spinach.

SPINACH

This vegetable is available all the year round and it is valuable because it is rich in minerals and vitamins. It has a decided flavour which some people dislike, particularly the habit it has of 'furring' the teeth; if this is so we would suggest trying young spinach raw in salads, the flavour is much less pronounced; the spinach is easier to digest and there is no 'furring'.

Spinach cooks down tremendously so that you will need what may appear to be a 'mountain' for just a few people. Young spinach and summer spinach are tender and generally need less cooking time than the coarse variety (known as 'beet' spinach on the market) which is grown during the winter months. When buying see that the leaves are fresh and green, not wilted or yellowing. Since spinach grows near the ground-level it collects a lot of soil, especially after rainy weather.

To prepare it, first pick it over, taking out the coarse stems and any large pieces of grass or weed and then throw it into a sink full of cold water. Quickly but gently wash it and put in handfuls into another sink or bowl of cold water. Meanwhile refill the sink and rinse again until there is no more sand or grit at the bottom of the sink. This may take seven or eight washings.

There are two methods of cooking.

1. The following is the older method and is not good from a nutritional point of view, but it does take away some of the strong taste and some of the 'furring'. Have ready a large saucepan $\frac{1}{2}-\frac{3}{4}$ full of boiling sea-salted water and throw in the spinach a handful at a time so that the water never stops boiling. Cook for 10–20 minutes or until just tender. Drain well—chop coarsely with a sharp stainless steel knife and drain again, or sieve the spinach. If possible the spinach water should be used, either for spinach

Vegetables

soup, a sauce to accompany the spinach or the savoury with which the spinach is being served. Any remaining can be used in the stock-pot. Melt some butter in the saucepan and gently warm the spinach. Taste and season. Serve. Here are some points which may be of interest:

(a) Seasoning—spinach benefits from a little grated nutmeg and brown sugar.

(b) Spinach is very difficult to drain as it tends to hold the water between the leaves; the chopping reduces the coarseness in old spinach and helps with the draining. If you are using young spinach, you need not chop it, but you will have to drain in small quantities carefully.

(c) Many people prefer spinach sieved so that it becomes a purée—this changes the flavour and texture, so experiment to see which you prefer.

2. The second method may be termed the 'modern' method as it is advocated by all concerned with food values. The spinach is prepared in the same way as the first method. Melt some butter, 1 oz. per 1 lb. of spinach, in a large saucepan and add the spinach in handfuls, turning it in the butter. Put on the lid of the saucepan and cook very gently until some water (from the washing) and juice have collected at the bottom of the saucepan; this takes about 5–10 minutes but allow longer for large quantities.

Then cook on a medium heat until tender, looking at the spinach from time to time. If it is producing a lot of liquid cook with the lid off to reduce it for a little while. Drain, saving any liquid and chop or purée. Taste and serve.

CREAMED SPINACH

Prepare the spinach as above. When cooked add, for each 1 lb. of raw spinach, the following:

$\frac{1}{8}$ pint white or béchamel sauce
$\frac{1}{2}$ teaspoon brown sugar
Nutmeg or salt to taste
2 tablespoons cream
$\frac{1}{2}$ teaspoon lemon juice

Vegetables

Mix these items together with the spinach and reheat, not too much as the cream tends to curdle.

SPINACH WITH MUSHROOMS OR TOMATOES

Prepare some cooked, drained dry spinach, about 2 lb. when fresh; this depends on the size of your mould; add one of the following:

(1) 2 oz. butter, seasoning to taste
(2) ½ pint white or béchamel sauce
    2–3 tablespoons cream
    1 beaten egg, seasoning
(3) 6 tablespoons cream
    1 oz. butter, seasoning to taste

Then arrange on a warm dish in a ring, or in a ring mould, packed firmly with the mixture. If you have used the ingredients in 1 or 3 it can be turned out straight away, but if you have used number 2 it should be gently baked, stood in warm water until set, and then turned out.

Fill the centre with mushrooms in a white sauce or skinned tomatoes, cooked in butter with onions and seasoning until a purée is formed (this usually takes about 30 minutes).

SPINACH PANCAKES

1. Mix a little dry cooked spinach purée with a pancake batter. Season to taste and cook as you would for ordinary pancakes. These pancakes can be served with a filling or a sauce. A soft creamy cheese filling served with tomato sauce makes a good savoury dish.

2. Make some pancakes and sandwich them in layers with a tasty spinach purée until you have a good-sized cake shape. Cut into wedges and serve tomato or cheese sauce with the slices.

3. Cook some pancakes and spread the centre with a good spinach purée. Roll up the pancake and keep in a warm oven whilst others are being made. Serve with a sauce of your own choice.

197

Vegetables

SWEDES

This root vegetable, together with parsnips and turnips, appears to have lost favour recently, which is a pity because it can give variety of flavour and colour in winter. The swede is more nutritious than the turnip but is cooked in exactly the same way as for old turnips, so see the Turnip section for cooking. Sometimes in the spring, swedes sprout some orangy red shoots—when these are fairly large they can be cooked like asparagus.

SWEET CORN
See Maize

TOMATO

This is of course a fruit, but it has been served for so long in a savoury fashion that it is included in the vegetable section.

Tomatoes really are delicious and it sometimes seems a pity to cook them, but since they are so useful for flavour and colour the savoury course would lose a lot through their absence. They have another attribute, they will blend with practically any vegetable; they are also very juicy, particularly when cooked, and can be served in place of a sauce.

When gathered warm from the greenhouse or garden they have a wonderful flavour and aroma. If you are lucky enough to grow your own, do try to experiment with one or two of the more unusual varieties—the yellow tomato and the small red ones which grow in bunches.

Tomatoes can be cooked in their own juice, fried, puréed, grilled, baked and stuffed. They also make very good soup and sauces.

To skin tomatoes

Remove the stalks and wash—they need only be wiped if you know they have been grown without spraying treatment. Use a very sharp-pointed knife to cut out the green part where the stalk was attached. Put in a bowl and pour over enough boiling water

Vegetables

to cover. Leave for a minute or two, pour away the water and the skins will slip off easily.

Tomato seasoning

Tomatoes require some brown sugar to bring out their flavour. We make up a mixture of equal parts sea salt and brown sugar especially for tomatoes and this is very good flavoured with basil or mint.

BAKED TOMATOES

1. Place whole tomatoes in a greased, shallow oven-proof dish and make a small cut somewhere on the skin. Sprinkle with tomato seasoning and add some extra butter or vegetable fat or oil. Bake in almost any heat from a slow to hot oven, the time taken will depend on the heat and the size of the tomatoes, varying from between 10–30 minutes. Whilst they are cooking spoon the fat over the tomatoes once or twice. Serve in the baking-dish.

2. Use the same method as above but cut the tomatoes in half and place a small piece of butter on each half, or brush each half on the top with oil. Serve in the dish.

3. Slice the tomatoes and lay them in a greased baking-dish. Sprinkle the layers and the top with tomato seasoning and pieces of butter, fat or oil. Sprinkle some chopped parsley, mint and basil on the top and bake as before. Serve in the dish.

FRIED TOMATOES

1. Heat some butter or other fat in a frying-pan, place either halves or slices of tomato in the pan and sprinkle with tomato seasoning. Cook quickly until just brown and turn with a slice so as to brown the other side. Serve immediately.

2. Choose small even-sized tomatoes, remove the stalks and wash thoroughly. Melt and heat some fat in a frying-pan. Add the tomatoes and cook very gently for about 10 minutes. They must be cooked thus because the skins so easily burst and they must be turned whilst cooking. These make a very good garnish.

3. Take even-sized tomatoes, firm preferably, skin them and

199

then let them get quite cold. Coat with seasoned flour, dip in a coating batter, and fry in deep fat.

GRILLED TOMATOES

Grease the grill pan and allow it to heat up under the grill. Choose even-sized tomatoes, remove the stalks and cut in half— brush with melted butter, vegetable fat or oil and sprinkle with tomato seasoning. Grill under a moderate grill for 5–10 minutes, until golden brown and tender. This is a good alternative to baked tomatoes if the oven is not in use!

STUFFED TOMATOES

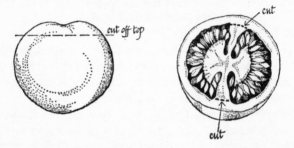

Choose large ripe tomatoes, wash and remove the stalks. Cut off the top and place this top piece to one side. Inside the tomato in the centre is the core with 2–3 dividing walls. With a pair of scissors make a cut in these walls near the outside. Then with a spoon gently twist out the centre with the walls. Place in a bowl and spoon out the seeds and the liquid too. Turn the tomato shells upside down and allow to drain. When they have drained and are ready for stuffing sprinkle the insides with a little tomato seasoning. The hard part of the core can be disposed of but the rest of the inside can be used for the stuffing, sauces or in vegetable juice.

Any suitable stuffings from the section devoted to this may be used or stuff with mushrooms, peppers, onions and corn or a mixture of these, all of which are very good with tomatoes.

Vegetables

Tomato Purée

This can be bought in tins or in tubes and usually contains Italian tomatoes puréed and with much of the water driven off. Tomatoes do not, as is the case with other vegetables, lose a lot of food value when preserved, so this purée is very good to use with fresh tomatoes (particularly winter crop tomatoes) adding natural colour and flavour.

In the summer fresh tomato purée can be made by cutting up tomatoes and cooking them in their own juices with appropriate flavourings and brown sugar. When enough water has evaporated pass them through a sieve and use as required.

TURNIPS

 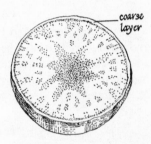

coarse layer

When these vegetables are young and fresh, in middle or late summer, they have a wonderful flavour. They can be bought in shops with their green tops (which are a very good vegetable cooked in the same manner as for spinach), and are sometimes called *navets*, though this is the French word for turnips. These very young turnips should be peeled and cooked in the same way as young carrots or cooked conservatively. They are also very good cooked *with* young carrots, glazed with the reduced cooking liquid and sprinkled with parsley.

Old turnips including swedes

Cut off the tops and bottoms, discard any turnips which are woolly. If a turnip is cut in half (*see diagram*) it is seen that there is a thick coarse outside layer. Usually turnips are peeled to

201

Vegetables

remove this; however, they can be boiled or steamed and the skin removed afterwards. Cut the turnips, if necessary, into even sizes and boil in sea-salted water until tender. This will take from 25–45 minutes, depending on the size and age. They can then be mashed with butter and seasonings, or they can be coated with a good white or béchamel sauce. Turnips hold a lot of water when they are cooked and they need to be drained very carefully or they will be sloppy when mashed.

(Swedes are very good mashed and served with fried onions or onion rings.)

Turnips are more often used as a flavouring vegetable, with onions, swedes, carrots and celery than by themselves. Here are one or two ideas for serving them.

FRIED TURNIPS

Mash some dry cooked turnip with an equal amount of potato and season well. Add 1 beaten egg or 2 egg-yolks and allow to cool. Shape into croquettes and flour them. Coat with egg and breadcrumb and fry in deep fat. Serve immediately with parsley or watercress and wedges of lemon.

STUFFED TURNIPS

Choose even-sized, young turnips and cook until nearly tender. Cut off the top and scoop out the inside. Sauté the turnip case in butter until just brown; a little chopped onion and a leaf of rosemary added to the butter makes a good flavour. Remove the turnips and place on a fire-proof dish. Add the brown butter, having strained out the onion and rosemary, to the scooped-out turnip; add some mashed potato or carrot. Season well, adding just a pinch of nutmeg or cayenne. Egg, cheese, or nuts can also be added if desired. Fill the turnip cases with the mixture, replace the tops. Bake in the oven 350–400° F., M4–6 until warmed through 15–30 minutes. If any stuffing is left over, make a bed of this in which to stand the turnips. Tomatoes and mushrooms can be added when the dish is placed in the oven and they make a good garnish.

Vegetables

MIXED VEGETABLE DISHES

These dishes are particularly useful if you wish to use protein in the sweet (e.g. fruit meringues), and not in the first course. They are usually attractive because of the mixture of colours, textures and flavours, so they lend themselves to attractive presentation and garnishing. Some of them, such as the casseroles and stews, can be left to cook on their own; served with a green vegetable they make a complete course. The details of cooking each kind of vegetable will be found in the various sections and are not repeated here.

Casseroles, Hot pots and Stews

These are similar as far as the ingredients are concerned but differ in the method of cooking.

Casseroles are cooked slowly in a deep heat-proof dish with a tight-fitting lid, in the oven.

Hot pots are casseroles finished with a layer of sliced potato on the top. The lid is removed for the last $\frac{1}{2}$–1 hour so that the potatoes can brown and crisp.

Stews are cooked slowly and entirely on the top of the stove in a saucepan or stew-pan. As it is a slow-cooking method, green leafy vegetables should not be cooked by it but peas and beans can be used.

VEGETABLE CASSEROLE

Prepare and cut into slices or medium-sized pieces any of the following fresh vegetables (needless to say one does not use all the vegetables at once, in fact a great variety of casseroles can be made by simply varying the ingredients). Do not allow too much of any one vegetable to predominate and use vegetables having a strong flavour very sparingly.

Vegetables

Jerusalem artichokes	Marrow (preferably young ones)
Broad beans	Mushrooms
French beans	Onions
Runner beans	Parsnips
Carrots	Peas
Cauliflower	Peppers
Celeriac	Potatoes
Celery	Shallots
Sweet corn	Swedes
Kohl rabi	Tomatoes
Leeks	Turnips

In place of or with potato, pearl barley, haricot beans, macaroni, butter beans or lentils can be used; with the exception of lentils and potato they should be cooked beforehand and the cooking water used in the casserole.

For flavouring, use fresh or dried herbs and garlic (if liked) and include one of the onion family. If liquid is required use vegetable stock or water with vegetable extract added, e.g. Marmite, Vesop, Vecon, etc. Remember to season with care as this method conserves and tends to concentrate the natural salts and flavours.

To continue with the method—melt a little butter or heat some oil in a large frying-pan or saucepan and gently sauté the vegetables for 5–10 minutes together. This improves the flavour greatly and reduces the cooking time as the casserole is already hot when it is put in the oven. If you have an ingredient such as lentils or a lot of potato, butter beans, etc. which will absorb the fat and slightly thicken the liquid, then just add the flavourings, seasonings and stock. Bring to the boil, place in the casserole, add more stock if necessary, to come half-way up the casserole, cover and bake in a slow–moderate oven 300–375° F.,M2–5, until tender. The time varies enormously, depending very much on the oven temperature and the size and kind of vegetables which are used. The average time is about 2 hours. If a lot of liquid collects then let the casserole cook with the lid off towards the end; add more liquid if the casserole gets too dry.

Vegetables

If you want to cook the vegetables in a thickened liquid sprinkle the vegetables after they have cooked in the fat with wholemeal or 81 per cent extraction flour, stir it in adding more if there is still some unabsorbed fat and continue cooking for 3–5 minutes. Then add the liquid, etc. and continue as before.

HOT POT VEGETABLES

The ingredients as before and the method as follows. Grease a deep fire-proof dish and its lid. Place the vegetables in layers, sprinkling a little seasoning on each layer, ending with a good layer of sliced potato. Add boiling stock $\frac{1}{2}$–$\frac{3}{4}$ to the top. Place some shreds of butter on top or brush with oil and cover with the lid. Bake as above but remove the lid at the end so that the potato is brown and crisp.

STEWS

These are generally prepared as for casseroles but cooked in a saucepan, with a tight-fitting lid, very slowly. They can also be brown stews or ragouts. These are made by allowing the vegetables and then the flour to brown gently in the fat. Take care to brown but not burn the vegetables as this can easily be done. If the liquid has been thickened then the stew must be stirred fairly frequently. Stews should not boil, but just simmer; asbestos mats can be used if you have difficulty in getting a low heat. Stews are very good when finished with dumplings.

POTATO DUMPLINGS

2 oz. 81 per cent extraction self-raising flour
Seasoning
1 oz. fat
6 oz. dried mashed potato

Sieve the flour and seasoning. Rub in the fat and add the potato. Mix together until soft dough is formed—if you want a little more liquid add a little beaten egg. Form into small balls about the size of a walnut or slightly larger. Place in the stew, cover and cook for 20–25 minutes.

Vegetables

Herb—add 2 tablespoons of chopped mixed herbs.
Onion—add 2 teaspoons of finely chopped onion or chives.
Cheese—add 2 oz. of grated cheese.

WHOLEMEAL DUMPLINGS

6 oz. 100 per cent wholemeal flour
Seasoning
1½ oz. butter
1 beaten egg
Cold water to mix

Sieve the flour and seasoning through a coarse sieve and rub in the fat. Mix with the egg to a soft but easy-to-handle dough, using some of the water if necessary. Roll into balls and cook them in boiling water. Use as required.

VEGETABLE CHOP SUEY

For this dish it is important to cut all the vegetables into small pieces of the same size as they should be cooked very quickly, first in oil and then in a little water.

1–2 lb. assorted vegetables
½ lb. shredded cabbage
¼ lb. mushrooms
Bean or bamboo shoots
Oil for frying
¼ pt. stock or water
Sea salt
Soy sauce or Vesop

Heat the oil until it is smoking hot and add all the chopped mixed vegetables except the mushrooms and bean or bamboo shoots. We find a large frying-pan with a lid is very good for this but it can be cooked just as well in a large saucepan. Cook at medium to hot temperature, turning the vegetables all the time so that they start cooking without browning; this will take about 5–10 minutes.

Vegetables

Add the water, or the stock, and the seasoning to taste. Bring to the boil and cover. Stir occasionally and add more liquid if necessary, cook until almost tender. Add the mushrooms and the bean sprouts or bamboo shoots and finish cooking the whole lot. There should be very little liquid left at the end and the vegetables should be only just tender, they should have a definite 'bite'. Serve immediately in a warm dish.

VEGETABLES IN BATTER

Make some Yorkshire pudding mixture (see chapter on Batters). Parboil some carrots, potato, onion, turnip, parsnips and swedes or a mixture of any of these. Place in a baking-tin with some oil or vegetable fat and place in a hot oven 400–425° F., M6–7 until the fat smokes and the vegetables are hot; this will take 10–15 minutes. Pour in the batter, return to the oven immediately and cook until the batter is well risen and brown. Serve with a green vegetable and sauce or gravy; the pudding should be cut into squares and placed on a warm plate.

COLCANNONS AND CHAMPS

These are a mixture of equal parts of potato and some other vegetables or a mixture of vegetables. The whole thing can be puréed or it can be mashed together.

The other vegetables can be: cabbage, brussels sprouts, kale, turnip and swedes, swede and onion, carrot, onion and peas.

In colcannon the vegetables are mixed with seasoning and perhaps a little milk so that the mixture is quite stiff. Heat some butter, vegetable fat or oil, in a frying-pan until quite hot. There should be enough fat to cover the bottom. Add the potato and vegetables and smooth down so that the pan is evenly covered with the mixture. Turn down the heat when the bottom of the mixture is brown, then turn with a slice and allow to brown again on the other side. Continue to do this until the mixture is hot and has a good proportion of browned pieces through it. In champs a much larger proportion of milk to potato is used and the mixture is not fried. The milk is heated until nearly boiling (chives and herbs can be added) and then beaten into the potato and other vegetables until a very creamy light mixture is obtained; the consistency should be such that it will drop from a spoon or masher easily. Add seasonings to taste and serve on hot plates with a good piece of butter or nut butter in the centre of each portion.

MIXED VEGETABLE FRITTERS

In the vegetable recipes we have given directions for making vegetable fritters. An assortment of these makes an interesting dish, particularly for a party. Here are some points that will add to the interest.

1. Do not fry all the vegetables in the same coating. Fry some without a coating, some coated with egg and breadcrumbs, some in batter.

2. Fry some small bunches of tender herbs in batter and serve with the vegetables.

3. Use some vegetables whole (e.g. cauliflower sprigs) and some puréed, flavoured, bound with egg and shaped into balls or croquettes, e.g. potato fritters.

4. Have *everything* ready before you start frying and then serve the dish as soon as it is assembled, taking care with arrangement and garnishing.

5. Have as large an assortment as possible. Here is a list of vegetables that can be used:

potato	cauliflower	carrots
parsnips	onions	beetroot
brussels sprouts	broccoli sprouts	seakale
spinach	runner beans	mushrooms
tomatoes	peppers	chestnuts
celeriac	Jerusalem artichokes	

6. Some of the vegetables can be marinaded before coating to give added flavour. Care must be taken to drain and dry them well, otherwise the marinade may come through the coating and spoil the oil or fat used for frying.

Vegetables

Mixed Stuffed Vegetables

This is another very attractive assortment and it is easier to make than the fritters. When served with a green vegetable and a sauce it makes a very good savoury course.

The following vegetables can be used:

tomatoes	small marrows	mushrooms
onions	globe artichokes	cabbage lettuce
vine leaves	chicory (cut in half and	cucumbers
aubergines	the filling piled on	peppers
potatoes	the cut side)	turnips

The stuffings can vary too, they need not always include a protein. It is a good idea to use the unstuffable vegetables, e.g. peas and asparagus, etc. to stuff the others.

Vegetable Rings

In a shallow fire-proof dish make a ring of creamed potato or duchesse potato mixture; glaze with a beaten egg and bake in a moderate to hot oven 375–400° F., M5–6 until browned and warm. Fill with a mixture of vegetables either in a sauce or glazed with melted butter. Garnish with parsley and serve.

The ring can be piped if a duchesse potato mixture is used and this adds a more decorative finish.

Vegetable Pies

Use any of the casserole or stew mixtures and cover with any of the following:

1. Shortcrust pastry.
2. Cheese pastry.
3. Savoury pastry.
4. Flaky, rough puff or puff pastry.
5. A cheese scone mixture.
6. Mashed potato which can be flavoured with cheese, onions or herbs.

Vegetables

VEGETABLE FLANS

The flan can be made from shortcrust, potato or one of the richer pastries and can be round, oblong or square.

It can be filled with:

1. A purée of the vegetable with pieces of the vegetable arranged as a garnish on the top, e.g. carrots for carrot flan.

2. A mixture of vegetables arranged colourfully, either in straight lines or in sections.

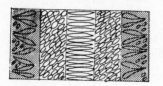

The vegetables are then covered with a thin sauce so that the colour shows through or can be glazed with melted butter or oil.

3. A mixture of vegetables in a thick white/brown or tomato sauce; the top can be sprinkled with cheese and browned under the grill.

VEGETABLE ROLY-POLY

Make some suenut or savoury pastry and roll out to an oblong. Either slice some vegetables very finely or grate them coarsely, season them and place on the oblong (see diagram).

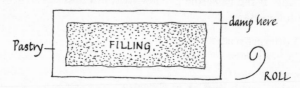

Damp the edges with water or beaten egg and roll up. Tie loosely in a floured cloth and steam for 2–2½ hours, or place on a greased baking-sheet and bake in a moderate–hot oven 375–

Vegetables

400° F., M5–6 for 1–1½ hours or until the vegetables are cooked and the pastry is brown.

STUFFED PANCAKES

Make some pancakes in the usual way (see chapter on Batters) and have ready a filling of mixed cooked vegetables which are finely chopped, well flavoured and moistened with a little sauce. Warm the filling and as the pancakes are made spread with the filling and quickly roll up. Place the filled pancakes in a warmed greased oven-proof serving-dish and replace in the oven to keep warm. When all the pancakes are made garnish the dish and serve with cheese and egg sauce.

STUFFED WHOLEMEAL ROLLS

Take some wholemeal rolls and cut off the tops. Scoop out as much of the inside crumb as you can (use this for stuffings, nut savouries or for making breadcrumbs) without making a hole in the walls or base. Butter the inside of each roll and its lid, and then butter the outside. Bake in a moderate oven until crisp and brown. Fill with a mixture of cooked vegetables in sauce and replace the lids. Serve immediately.

MIXED VEGETABLES

Cook as many vegetables as you have, very carefully and separately. Have ready a well-warmed shallow serving-dish and place the vegetables on it attractively. Either glaze with butter, nut butter, tartex, or pour over a well-flavoured white sauce. This sauce should be thin enough to show through the colour and type of vegetables.

This kind of vegetable dish is very good in summer when there are so many young vegetables obtainable (although it can be attractive at any time of the year).

8

Sauces

Sauces for salads are given in the Salad chapter. Sauces can be classified under four headings: sweet and savoury, hot and cold.

They are used for the following reasons:

1. They add moisture to dry foods and give a contrasting texture.
2. They provide flavour.
3. They improve the appearance of the dishes and can provide a colour contrast.
4. Food value is added.

HOT SAVOURY SAUCES

The basic savoury sauces are white and brown, but there are many, many sauces derived from these.

WHITE SAUCE

For a coating sauce:

> 2 oz. butter or margarine
> Approximately 2 oz. 81 per cent extraction flour
> 1 pint liquid
> Seasoning if needed

For a pouring sauce:

> 1 oz. butter or margarine
> Approximately 1 oz. 81 per cent extraction flour
> 1 pint liquid
> Seasoning if needed

Sauces

Melt the fat in a medium-sized saucepan, but do not brown. Draw aside from the heat and add enough flour to make a paste. This paste is called a 'roux' and it takes about equal quantities of flour and fat to make it. The amount of flour varies slightly with its moisture content. It is therefore better to measure the fat first and then add sufficient flour to give the correct constituency. The paste should be soft but fairly firm; it must not run, or the sauce will be greasy (if it is add more flour); nor should it be like breadcrumbs, this is too stiff and will give a lumpy sauce because each starch grain has not been coated with fat. If there should be a breadcrumb texture add enough butter to make the roux moist but remember a little more liquid will also be needed. When the roux is made cook it very gently, stirring all the time, until it starts to sizzle around the edges and looks a paler fawn when turned over. It should take 3–5 minutes to get it to this stage. Continue cooking for another 2–3 minutes, but on no account must it be allowed to brown as this would affect the colour of the sauce. Draw the saucepan away from the heat and add a little of the liquid (this may boil at once as the pan will be hot) and stir it well, when the mixture is smooth, add a little more liquid and stir again. Continue this process until all the liquid has been added. Bring to the boil, stirring all the time and when thick enough remove from the heat. Beat well to remove any lumps; this will also give a gloss to the sauce. If there are lumps which cannot be beaten out with the spoon (though it is surprising what the beating will do) change to a heavy wire whisk, which should break them down. If lumps have formed before the mixture has boiled, a wire whisk may be used, but it should be remembered that once the lumps are cooked they will not break down. Simmer the sauce for 3–5 minutes to cook the flour, add more liquid if this is necessary and then taste. Adjust the seasoning and serve in a warmed sauceboat or use to coat the prepared food. Pouring sauces are served with the meal and handed separately. Coating sauces are part of the dish, e.g. cauliflower au gratin, and are served at the table with the food they cover. Here are a few of the most useful white sauces made by this method. The quantities are for 1 pint of sauce, and can be halved or doubled as required.

Sauces

ALLEMANDE

First prepare 1 pint of velouté sauce and allow to simmer very gently for 10–15 minutes in order to reduce it slightly. Turn into a double saucepan and add 4 egg-yolks, 2 oz. of butter (in small pieces) or 4 tablespoons of double cream. Lemon juice to taste. Cook gently until thick and creamy.

BÉCHAMEL

This is a wonderful sauce which is to be preferred to a plain white sauce. Add ½ a chopped onion, 1 diced carrot, 1 chopped stick of celery, a crushed clove of garlic, 1 bay leaf, some parsley stalks and 8 peppercorns (if liked) to 1 pint of milk. Bring slowly to the boil and infuse for 5–10 minutes at the back of the stove. Strain the milk and use this to make a sauce with 2 oz. of roux. Season to taste; add 2–4 tablespoons of cream just before serving. Do not reboil after adding the cream.

BUTTER SAUCE

A roux sauce made with vegetable stock instead of milk. It can be used to coat or serve with a particular vegetable and is very useful as it uses the cooking liquid. It can also be made with a general vegetable stock and served with a savoury.

CAPER SAUCE

Add 2 tablespoons of chopped capers to a white or butter sauce. A good pinch of brown sugar brings out the flavour.

CELERY SAUCE

Chop a heart of celery very finely. Sauté for 5–10 minutes in 2½ oz. of butter, add enough flour to make a roux and make a sauce with a pint of milk and stock. Simmer until the celery is cooked, then adjust the consistency and flavouring.

Sauces

CHEESE SAUCE

Add 3–4 oz. of grated cheese to 1 pint of white sauce. Any dry, full-flavoured cheese will do. A little French mustard, or a small pinch of cayenne pepper will bring out the flavour.

CHESTNUT SAUCE

Skin 1 lb. of chestnuts and then cover with 1 pint of stock and cook. Mash or sieve them. Make a roux with 3 oz. of butter and 2 oz. of flour, stir in the chestnut purée to make a thick chestnut sauce. If it tends to be too thick add more stock or milk. Season and add 2–4 tablespoons of cream just before serving.

CREAM SAUCE

Add ½ pint boiled cream to 1 pint hot béchamel sauce.

CUCUMBER SAUCE

Add a cooked and sieved cucumber to 1 pint of béchamel sauce. A little spinach purée may be added with some cream.

CURRY SAUCE

(see section on Curries, p. 229)

EGG SAUCE

Add 2–4 chopped hard-boiled eggs to a white or béchamel sauce.

HERB SAUCE

Add 2–3 tablespoons of chopped fresh herbs to a white or béchamel sauce.

MORNAY SAUCE

Add 3–4 oz. of mixed Gruyère and Parmesan grated cheese to 1 pint of béchamel sauce.

Sauces

MUSHROOM SAUCE

Have ready 1 pint of hot béchamel sauce. Wash 6 oz. of button mushrooms, cut these into quarters and cook quickly in 1 oz. of foaming butter for 3–4 minutes. Add seasonings and stir into the béchamel sauce. Add a quarter of a pint of cream immediately before serving. Do not reheat.

ORANGE SAUCE

Make 1 pint of butter sauce, add the grated rind of 2 oranges and then the juice. Simmer for 10 minutes. Add 2 egg-yolks. Adjust the seasoning. Strain and serve.

ONION SAUCE

1. Chop 4–6 onions and fry in $2\frac{1}{2}$ oz. of fat until golden brown. Add 2 oz. of flour, cook and add 1 pint of stock. Season and flavour to taste. Simmer for $\frac{1}{2}$ an hour, remove the flavourings if desired, adjust the seasonings and serve.
2. Add 3–4 chopped boiled onions to 1 pint of white sauce or béchamel sauce.

PAPRIKA SAUCE

Add sufficient paprika to a white or béchamel sauce to produce a good colour and flavour.

PARSLEY SAUCE

Add 2–3 tablespoons of freshly chopped parsley to 1 pint of white or béchamel sauce, just before serving.

PIQUANTE SAUCE

Add finely chopped fresh, parsley, pimento, gherkins and capers to 1 pint of white sauce.

Sauces

Soubise Sauce

Sieve 4–6 cooked onions and add the purée to 1 pint of thick white sauce or béchamel.

Supreme

Add ¼–½ pint of cream to 1 pint of velouté sauce.

Velouté

Sauté some parsley stalks, 2–4 oz. of button mushrooms, and 6–12 peppercorns in 2 oz. of butter without browning. And 2 oz. of flour, cook and add 1 pint of white stock. Simmer for ½–1 hour. Strain and adjust the seasoning. Add a little cream just before serving.

Watercress Sauce

Wash a bundle of watercress well and chop very finely. Add to the white sauce just before serving.

White Wine Sauce

Make 1 pint of thick white sauce, add up to a ¼ pint of white wine, bring to the boil and draw away from the heat. Add 2 oz. of butter (in small pieces) and 2 yolks of eggs. Season, taste and add a little lemon juice. Serve immediately.

Wholemeal Sauce

Use 2½–3 oz. of fat and flour to 1 pint for a coating sauce and 1½ oz. of fat and flour to 1 pint of stock for a pouring sauce. (The bran does not thicken the sauce.)

Brown Sauce

This dish can be made for coating, but is generally used for serving with a dish. By decreasing or increasing the proportion of roux to the liquid it will be suitable for one use or another.

Sauces

1½ oz. butter or white vegetable fat

1 onion

1 carrot

1 stick celery

¾–1 pint well-flavoured vegetable stock, made brown with Vesop, Marmite, Yeastrel, etc.

1 oz. 81 per cent extraction flour. (If wholemeal is used, the amount of fat and flour must be increased.)

Herbs to flavour, tied in a bundle (bouquet garni)

Pinch of brown sugar

Melt the fat in a saucepan and add the chopped vegetables. Brown the vegetables slowly without burning—this may take up to 20 minutes or ½ an hour but the slower the better. They should be stirred fairly constantly. Add the flour and brown it gently for 5–10 minutes. Do not on any account burn it as this will not only leave a bitter flavour, but the flour will lose its power to thicken the sauce. Add the stock, herbs and sugar, simmer for 30–40 minutes. Strain and taste the sauce, adjust the consistency, reheat and serve. A little sherry can be added just before serving if liked.

A small amount of chopped mushroom stalks and a little tomato purée may also be added to enrich the sauce.

Here are a few variations, which contain a little wine; this may be replaced with apple juice or grape juice, if preferred.

DEVIL'S SAUCE

Soften some chopped leek or shallot in a little butter and allow it to brown. Add 1 wineglass full of brandy and let it slowly reduce. Add 1 pint of brown sauce, tomato purée to taste, and simmer. Before serving add enough French mustard and cayenne pepper to make the sauce hot and spicy. A little chopped parsley or chervil may be added.

BROWN MUSHROOM SAUCE

Sauté 2 chopped onions in butter and brown them slowly. Add 4–6 oz. of chopped mushrooms, and cook quickly for 1–2 minutes.

Sauces

Add 1½ gills of white wine or apple juice, reduce by half. Add 1 pint of brown sauce with a tablespoon of tomato purée. Simmer for 5–10 minutes. Adjust the seasoning and consistency.

BROWN HERB SAUCE

To ½ pint of white wine or apple juice add 2 tablespoons of chopped parsley, chives, chervil and tarragon and 2 tablespoons of chopped onion. Bring to the boil and simmer for 15 minutes. Add 1 pint of brown sauce and simmer for 10 minutes. Add a few drops of lemon juice to some extra chopped herbs and add to the sauce. Taste, adjust seasoning and consistency. Beat in a little butter before serving.

ITALIAN SAUCE

Sauté 4–6 oz. of chopped mushrooms and 2 chopped onions in a little olive oil for 5–10 minutes. Add ½ a pint of white wine or apple juice. Reduce by half. Add 1 pint of brown sauce and 1 tablespoon of tomato purée and 1 tablespoon of chopped parsley. Adjust for seasoning and consistency.

BROWN ONION SAUCE

Chop 2–3 onions very finely and brown in a little butter. Add 1 glass of sherry and reduce slightly. Add 1 pint of brown sauce and simmer for 10 minutes. Strain if preferred and adjust for seasoning and texture if desired, before serving.

BROWN PIQUANTE SAUCE

Make a brown onion sauce as above and just prior to serving add some chopped gherkins, chopped parsley and French mustard.

CASHEW OR ALMOND SAUCE

Chop 4 oz. of cashew or almonds very finely and brown them slowly in 2 oz. of butter. Add flour and brown the roux. Add 1 pint of brown stock and simmer for 5–10 minutes. Season with sea salt, a little paprika, powdered mace and lemon juice. Add 2–4 tablespoons of cream. Serve immediately.

Sauces

The following is a Chinese sauce which is a good accompaniment to vegetables:

SWEET AND SOUR SAUCE

2 oz. butter or oil
2 medium grated carrots
6 skinned diced tomatoes
Approximately 2 oz. 81 per cent extraction flour
½ pint water or stock
4–6 tablespoons apple, vinegar or lemon juice
3–4 tablespoons soy sauce (from delicatessen stores),
    equivalent to Vesop, but made from soya beans
3 tablespoons brown sugar
3 tablespoons sherry or grape juice

Melt the fat and sauté the vegetables for 10 minutes. Remove the saucepan from the heat, add the flour, and stir well. Add the water (or stock), vinegar, soy sauce and brown sugar. Bring to the boil, stirring all the time and simmer for 5 minutes. Add the sherry and adjust to taste. The taste should be as contradictory as the name!

Reheat and serve.

If you find the taste of the sauce too strong, the amount of soy sauce, vinegar and sugar should be reduced.

Tomato sauce is made in the same way as a brown sauce. In winter a larger proportion of concentrated tomato purée can be used, but even in summer a little helps the flavour and colour. We find the tomato purée in tubes is better.

QUICK TOMATO SAUCE

2 oz. butter or margarine
1 desserstpoonful tomato purée
Brown sugar and sea salt to taste
2 oz. (approximately) 81 per cent extraction flour
1 19-oz. can tomato juice
2 teaspoons cream
A little freshly chopped basil and parsley

Sauces

Make a roux and add the tomato juice and purée. Bring to the boil and simmer for 5 minutes. Season, add the herbs and the cream. Serve *without* reboiling, otherwise the cream will curdle.

TOMATO SAUCE

1 oz. butter or margarine or oil
1 carrot
1 onion
1 stick celery
1 oz. 81 per cent extraction flour
½ pint stock
1 dessertspoonful tomato purée
Bouquet garni and a little basil and ½ a bay leaf
Sea salt and brown sugar

Brown the chopped vegetables in the fat, add the flour and allow this to brown. Add the washed and chopped tomatoes, the stock and the herbs. Season slightly and simmer, stirring occasionally, for 30 minutes. Remove the herbs, sieve and adjust for seasoning and consistency. Serve hot. This tomato sauce can be varied considerably.

1. Add 1 crushed clove garlic (crushed in salt).
2. Add mushrooms.
3. Add parsley.
4. Add some cream or egg-yolks just before serving.
5. Add some sherry or grape juice, and so on.

MELTED BUTTER SAUCE

Melt 1 oz. of butter per person very gently so that it does not brown. Skim if necessary and pour into a hot sauceboat so that any sediment remains in the saucepan. Seasoning may be added.

BROWN BUTTER (1)
(*beurre noirs*)

Cook 2 oz. of butter until nut brown and then allow to cool. Reduce 1 tablespoon of apple vinegar to half quantity and add 1 tablespoon of chopped parsley. Draw aside from the heat and pour in the butter, reheat and season if necessary. Serve immediately.

BROWN BUTTER (2)
(*beurre noisette*)

Cook 4 oz. of butter until evenly nut brown, add the juice of ½ a lemon, pepper and salt if you like, and serve immediately.

Here are two very rich sauces which are usually served with asparagus, seakale, other delicate vegetables and vegetable savouries. They both require a double saucepan. They are served warm rather than hot and in small quantities.

SAUCE HOLLANDAISE

4 tablespoons water or stock from the vegetables with which the sauce is to be served
1 tablespoon wine, apple or herb vinegar
4 egg-yolks
4 oz. butter
Salt and brown sugar, a very little cayenne pepper for seasoning
1 tablespoon lemon juice

Place the first three ingredients in the top of a double saucepan and cook gently until thick, using a small whisk. The water in the bottom should never boil, just simmer. Remove the mixture from the heat and add the butter cut into small pieces, whisking well and always in the same direction. Season and add the lemon juice to taste. Serve.

This sauce should never be boiled or it will curdle—it is a fine emulsion, rather like a hot mayonnaise.

The Allemande sauce, given in the white sauces, makes a good mock hollandaise sauce.

Sauces

Sauce Mousseline
(*Savoury*)

This is a hollandaise with cream added, the quantity can be halved.

6 egg-yolks
Sea salt and brown sugar
Small knob butter
Juice of 1 lemon
5–6 oz. unsalted butter
¼ pint stiffly whipped cream

Place the yolks, seasoning, the small knob of butter and half the lemon juice in a double saucepan and whisk until quite thick. Remove from the heat and whisk in the butter. If the sauce gets cold, warm over the water for a few minutes. Add seasoning if necessary and lemon juice to taste, then fold in the whipped cream. Serve immediately.

COLD SAVOURY SAUCES

Mint Sauce

4 tablespoons finely chopped fresh mint
½–1 tablespoon brown sugar
2 tablespoons boiling water
½ tablespoon wine, herb or apple vinegar
1 tablespoon lemon juice

Dissolve the sugar in the boiling water and allow to cool. Add all the other ingredients and adjust for seasoning. Allow to stand a little while before serving.

In place of the lemon juice the grated rind and juice of an orange is a pleasant change, but a little more vinegar or lemon juice may be required if the orange is a sweet one.

Sauces

APPLE SAUCE

1 lb. cooking apples
A little apple juice
½ oz. butter
Brown sugar or honey if needed

Wash the apples and remove any bruises. Cut into pieces, and cook in a covered saucepan with sufficient apple juice to prevent the apples from sticking. Sieve and beat in the butter and brown sugar (or honey) if the sauce is very sour. This sauce should be pleasantly sharp. It makes a wonderful contrast to fried foods or rich nut savouries.

A little quince cooked with the apple gives a pleasant flavour, as does some mint, added in the last five minutes of cooking.

GOOSEBERRY SAUCE

This is made in the same way as apple sauce. If it is made with ripe dessert gooseberries, no sweetening will be needed.

SWEET SAUCES

WHITE SAUCE

Made in exactly the same way as a savoury white sauce except that 1–2 oz. of brown sugar and/or honey are used to sweeten it when cooked. Obviously no salt is added.

The sauce can be served plain or flavoured as follows:

Vanilla Infuse a vanilla pod for 10–20 minutes in the milk before using or use vanilla sugar to sweeten the sauce.

Spice Add cinnamon or nutmeg to taste.

Hazelnut Brown 2–4 oz. of hazelnuts in the oven and allow to cool. Grate these nuts into the sauce just before serving.

Creamy sauce Add up to a quarter of a pint of cream (whipped if preferred) just before serving.

Chocolate Melt 2–3 oz. of raw sugar chocolate gently in the milk and make the sauce in the usual manner. Taste the sauce before adding any sweetening as it usually requires less than the others.

Coffee Dissolve 1 tablespoon of powdered coffee in a little boiling water and add this to the sauce.

Lemon and orange Add finely grated rind and juice of either lemon or orange to taste. Or the zest may be removed with a peeler and infused in the milk.

EGG CUSTARD

1 pint milk
Vanilla pod or strip of lemon rind for flavouring
2 eggs and 2 yolks (this makes a creamier custard) or
  3 eggs
1–2 oz. brown sugar or honey

Heat the milk with the flavouring and sugar until they are hot but not boiling. Pour on to the beaten eggs, whisking well. Return to a double saucepan and whisk over hot water until the sauce thickens. Remove from the heat immediately, take out the flavouring and serve, either hot or cold.

SABAYON SAUCE

3 egg-yolks
3 oz. brown sugar
1 wineglass fruit juice, wine or sherry

Beat the yolks and the sugar together until they look like creamy coffee; do this in the top of a double boiler. Add the liquid and place the pan over almost boiling water, whisk vigorously until it nearly thickens, then remove from the heat and whisk for 1–2 minutes. Serve immediately or it will lose its frothiness.

SAUCE MOUSSELINE
(*Sweet*)

2 eggs and 2 yolks
3 oz. brown sugar
4 tablespoons strong coffee, fruit juice or rum

Sauces

All the ingredients are whisked over very hot water until thick and frothy. Use immediately.

HARD SAUCE

> 3 oz. unsalted butter
> A good 3 oz. dark brown sugar

Warm the bowl and cream the fat and sugar until light, fluffy and coffee coloured. Add any of the following and beat in gradually:

> Vanilla—use vanilla sugar
> Rind and 1 tablespoon orange or lemon juice
> Spice
> Coffee essence
> 2–3 tablespoons fresh fruit purée—apricot, strawberry, raspberry, etc.
> 3–4 tablespoons rum and a few drops lemon juice
> 2–3 tablespoons brandy

Pile this up in an attractive bowl and leave to harden. Serve with Christmas pudding, mince pies, baked apples and rich fruit puddings.

FRUIT SAUCES

These are made from purées of fresh or cooked fruit, the fruit provides its own thickness, or it may be thickened with a little agar-agar or whipped cream. Apple is one which requires no thickening, but strawberry and raspberry will require it. Whenever possible use the ripe fresh fruit and purée just before serving, a little lemon juice can be added to preserve the colour, e.g. banana and peaches. If the fruit is perfectly ripe there should be no need to sweeten; if, however, sweetening is necessary, use a thin honey which dissolves easily. These sauces may be served hot or cold.

CREAM

This is hardly a sauce but is so often used in place of that one it seems reasonable to describe here how to use it.

Sauces

It can be served in a sauceboat, each person taking what he requires. Do see that the cream flows easily and that it is fresh. Very often double cream needs to be liquified by adding some top of the milk to it.

Whipped cream

If the cream is very stiff, as is the case with Jersey and Guernsey cream in summer, it must be liquified with the top of the milk or plain milk. Turn this into a cream basin and beat with a wire whisk until thick and creamy. If it starts to thicken very quickly then add more top of the milk or plain milk otherwise it will become more like butter. Whipped cream should be light and fluffy but stiff enough for piping if desired.

The cream may also be whipped with a rotary whisk but great care must be taken to stop before it is over-whipped. The cream may be flavoured as follows:

Chantilly cream Add some vanilla sugar.

Ginger cream Add some finely chopped preserved ginger and a little syrup.

Orange and lemon Add a little grated rind of either.

Coffee Sprinkle with a little powdered coffee before whipping.

Chocolate Add some grated raw sugar chocolate.

Nut Add some grated nuts.

Fruit Add some mashed or puréed fresh fruit, but only enough to flavour and colour slightly.

Nut creams

These can be bought concentrated and in jars from health food stores. They need to be well stirred and diluted with water or fruit juice; add a little water for nut cream, more water for nut milk.

If you have a liquidizer attachment these can be quickly and easily prepared at home. Blanch some nuts and place these in the liquidizer with sufficient liquid just to cover. The liquidizer should not be more than one-third full, a quarter full is better. Switch on the machine slowly at first, then increase the speed to maximum. Run the machine until the mixture is smooth and free from lumps. (Please read the instructions delivered with the machine as some state a specified time for maximum running.)

9
Curries

We always feel that a lot can be learned from the dishes of the Far East, particularly as strict Hindus and Buddhists are vegetarians and have been for many thousands of years. Unfortunately most people think of curry as a yellowish brown sauce with an assortment of food floating about in it, and so hot that it burns the mouth. In point of fact it need not be hot at all and it need not be a sauce! Curry is prepared in India from fresh herbs and spices and the curry powder or paste is made freshly for each meal, much as we use fresh herbs in parsley or mint sauce.

The amounts and varieties of herbs and spices used with each dish are wide in range, whereas in England we often stick to one curry powder or paste and the inevitable result is that all our curries taste alike! Nowadays, there is no need for this. With the revival of interest in food, high-class grocers, delicatessen and supermarkets all stock the various spices needed; and in big towns and cities Indian stores may be found. If you live in a small town try the chemist, as he often stocks unusual spices and flavourings in the purest form.

For making curries you will need
1. A main ingredient such as eggs, vegetables or fruit.
2. Curry powder, paste or various spices.

CURRY POWDER
The best kinds to buy are the Indian varieties, some are milder than others so inquire when purchasing them as to their

potency! It is a common mistake to think that you only have to add more curry powder to make the curry hotter. It is the amount of chillies, ginger, cayenne and mustard which make the difference, and if you add too much of a mild curry you will produce a predominantly large proportion of the other flavourings which is not good. If you are fond of curry and use it frequently then it is much better to make your own powder and keep a small amount in an airtight tin or jar.

Indian 'Garam-masala'

1 oz. black peppercorn
1 oz. coriander seed
$\frac{1}{4}$ oz. cloves
10–15 cardomoms
$\frac{1}{2}$ oz. black caraway seed
$\frac{1}{4}$ oz. ground cinnamon

Remove the papery skin from the cardomoms. If you have a coffee grinder, grind all the ingredients together except the cinnamon which is mixed in afterwards. The spices should be ground finely but not to powder. If you have no grinder, with the exception of cinnamon, pound in a pestle and mortar. Sieve through a fine sieve (carefully, or you will be sneezing). Then recrush what is left in the sieve until fine enough—lastly add the cinnamon to the sieved spices. Store in an airtight jar. This recipe does not include the turmeric and chilli powder which is present in most curry powders.

Medium Curry Powder

2 oz. turmeric (yellow colour, aromatic but not a strong flavour)
4 oz. coriander seed (spicy, can easily be grown and used fresh)
2 oz. curnin seed (aromatic and slightly hot)
1 oz. ground ginger (hot!)⎫
1 oz. black pepper (hot!) ⎬ these quantities can be reduced

Curries

½ oz. fenugreek (mild flavour and resembles celery)
½ oz. chillies (capsisums—red, very hot and pungent)
½ oz. cardomoms (bitter-tasting seed, should be freshly
    ground)
½ oz. mace (outside of nutmeg, very pleasant but not hot)
¾ oz. mustard seed (hot!)
¼ oz. cloves
¼ oz. poppy seed

It is not essential to include the last five ingredients. The method
of making and storing is the same as above in the previous recipe.
By varying the amounts of ginger, pepper, chilli and mustard you
can make it milder or stronger as you please.

CURRY PASTE

This includes some aromatic oils and liquids which cannot be
preserved in powder form. We use a mixture of powder and paste
and sometimes paste alone. We feel that this is a 'must' when
making curry.

3. If you are making a 'wet' curry, you will need a curry sauce
in which the main ingredient is either cooked or reheated. The
basis of this sauce is: onions, shallots, leeks or garlic, fried in oil
or clarified butter and it is sometimes thickened with flour or
potato but it is best to allow it to thicken with long slow cooking.

4. Some kind of 'nut milk'. Coconut is the common type, but
it can also be made from other nuts. The nuts are grated and
boiling water, milk or stock is poured on and allowed to stand
for 30 minutes. The mixture is then strained through butter muslin
or similar clean cloth and the cloth is squeezed to extract all the
'milk' possible. This milk is always added just before the curry
is served otherwise the delicate flavour is lost.

The proportions are:

4 oz. grated nuts (this is about ½ a coconut) to ½ pint boiling
    liquid.
3–4 tablespoons of desiccated coconut or ground almond to
    ½ pint boiling liquid.

Curries

The dry grated nut which remains after being squeezed can be infused again with boiling liquid and the result used in the actual cooking of the curry; it is useful if you have no stock available.

5. A curry needs ingredients which will give it both a sweet and sour flavour. Although this may sound contradictory, it is a possibility which enhances the curry and gives a most interesting flavour—balancing the spices as it were. The simplest way to arrive at this is by the addition of lemon juice and brown sugar, but here are some more suggestions:

Sweet	Sour
Dried almonds	Lemon juice
Dried currants	Tamarind (these can be bought
Dried raisins	dried, they are then cooked
Apples (replacing mangoes)	and used)
Seedless jams (apricot, plum, etc.)	Orange sections
	Grapefruit sections (the skins should be removed and the fruit added just before serving)

Sweet chutneys ⎫
Mango chutneys ⎬ these are sweet and sour together

6. Fresh herbs. We are fortunate in being able to use our own fresh herbs in curries, and they give an excellent flavour. We grow coriander and fenugreek ourselves. Dried herbs can be used but they do not give such a good flavour and they must be used in smaller quantities.

Serving curry

In the Far Eastern countries the curry is served with many other side (accompanying) dishes. Rice is served on a separate dish and it is beautifully cooked so that each grain is separate. In Britain we often serve the curry surrounded by rice on the same dish. Curry should be eaten with a spoon and fork and it must be prepared so that this is possible.

Curries

Dishes to accompany curry

1. Rice. The cooking and serving of this commodity is dealt with under the section on Rice.

2. Chapatis. These are made from 100 per cent wholemeal flour kneaded to a soft dough with water and a pinch of salt. They should be well kneaded to make them light, and then left for an hour or so before rekneading. Break off a small portion of the dough, form it into a ball, and roll it out on a floured board until thin and round, 4–5 inches across—rather like a small pancake. They may be either fried in smoking fat or oil until brown and puffed up, then drained and served, *or* cooked on both sides on a lightly greased solid electric hot plate or girdle. The baking should be fairly quick (so they must be rolled thinly) otherwise they become hard. If the hot plate method is used and many chapatis are to be made, place them in a cloth and keep them warm in a slow oven.

3. Poppadoms or porpadoms. These are generally bought already prepared at a delicatessen or a good grocer. They look like fine wafers and they can be cooked in two ways:

(a) Place under a heated grill and when puffed and slightly brown, turn and grill the other side. The grill should be at a medium heat—if it is too hot the poppadoms will burn.

(b) Heat some oil and press the poppadoms into it with a slice; when the poppadom has risen and puffed and is brown, turn it and cook the other side. Drain very well; for this use a large cake-rack standing on a baking-sheet. They are served cold and generally broken over the curry.

4. Side dishes or 'sambols'. We use hors d'œuvre dishes for these but any small attractive dishes or bowls can be used. Just a few of these may be served, or as many as you like, or can manage.

Mango chutney.
Any home-made fruit chutney.
Sliced banana.
Sliced or chunked cucumber.
Sliced or quartered tomatoes.
Grated coconut.

Curries

Pieces of lemon or orange to squeeze.

Purée of curried lentils.

Gherkins.

Green olives.

Guava jelly.

Preserved ginger.

Water melon or ordinary melon.

If you want to attempt something more ambitious try some of the following ways with vegetables and fruits cut up finely and mixed with lemon juice, a little brown sugar and salt, fresh herbs, in particular mint, a little chopped fresh green chilli, green or preserved ginger. The last is optional and is added to give a hot flavour. A little crushed garlic may also be added.

Apple, green or red peppers and raisins..

Apple and onion.

Pineapple

Beetroot and horseradish (this is very hot, only add lemon juice and brown sugar).

Tomato and chive.

Cooked potato and onion.

Cucumber, onion and parsley.

Dessert apples and bananas.

Dessert apples, oranges and dates.

Soaked prunes stuffed with orange and apple.

It is customary to serve a cool drink with curry—lager, white wine, or if you prefer it, apple juice or lemonade flavoured with mint.

We hope you will enjoy trying the recipes and if you like them, do hunt for more, there are many to be found.

CURRY SAUCE

2 oz. butter or oil

2–3 onions, leeks or shallots

1 clove garlic (optional)

1 good teaspoonful curry powder*

1 good teaspoonful curry paste*

* Increase or reduce as desired.

1 oz. wholemeal flour (approx.)

½–¾ pint stock or water from the boiled rice

1 large or 2 small apples

3 skinned tomatoes or 2 teaspoons tomato purée

A squeeze of lemon

1 teaspoon brown sugar or to taste

½ teaspoon sea salt or to taste

2 teaspoons chopped fresh herbs

1–2 teaspoons mango or lime chutney (chop the mango
if in large pieces)

1 oz. seedless raisins

¼ pint nut milk

Method. Heat the fat and cook the onion slowly for 5–10 minutes
(if you are not using the sauce to curry the vegetables, add a
chopped carrot and a piece of celery which improves it), then add
the curry powder and paste and cook for another 10 minutes,
stirring when it seems to be needed. It is important to cook the
curry powder slowly in the fat as this takes away the rough
powdery taste and gives a mellow flavour. Add enough flour to
absorb any surplus fat and then add the stock and/or rice water.
Bring slowly to the boil and add the finely chopped apples,
tomatoes or tomato purée (a little of each can be used), lemon
juice, seasonings, herbs, chutney and raisins. Cook very slowly
for 30–45 minutes. It will need to be stirred frequently if it is
cooked in a saucepan on the stove, as it tends to catch or burn on
the bottom; if the oven is on it is very easy to cook it en casserole
at 275–350° F., M1–4. The time will depend largely on the oven
heat, from 40 minutes to 1 hour approximately. If the sauce
appears to be too thick add more liquid; curry sauce is used fairly
thinly. Just before serving add the nut milk. Taste and adjust for
sweet/sour with the seasonings.

How to use the sauce

1. If it is to be used for eggs then just allow the eggs (medium
hard-boiled) to warm in the sauce and use immediately. Serve
with rice and accompaniments.

Curries

2. This is a very good foundation for currying any vegetables or vegetable. Remember that the vegetables should be fresh and not left-overs. It is the juices from the vegetables, as they cook in the sauce, which give the curry the distinctive flavour. The vegetables can be parboiled in very little water (the vegetable water can be used for the curry sauce), then the vegetables finish cooking in the sauce; or the vegetables can be added raw to the sauce and thus entirely cooked in it.

3. If you are currying potatoes, lentils, rice or want a very liquid sauce, reduce the butter or oil to ½–1 oz. and leave out the flour. Allow the sauce to simmer to the consistency required.

Suggestions for vegetables to curry

1. Mushrooms (these can be added to any curry with advantage).
2. Potatoes.
3. Green Peas.
4. Carrots and Peas.
5. Leeks and dried bananas
6. Cauliflower, tomatoes and French or runner beans.
7. Broad beans and tomatoes.
8. Aubergines, cucumber and tomato.

These are only a few of the many combinations that can be used—it is most exciting to find others.

CURRIED NUTS

Nuts can be curried on their own or with a mixture. The best nuts to use are almonds, Brazils or hazelnuts. They should be allowed to brown in the oven (this improves the flavour) and then they are added to the sauce and simmered in it. It is also good to make a curry with one vegetable and one kind of nut, such as carrots and hazelnuts; potatoes and almonds; and so on.

CURRIED RICE

Cook some rice and add enough thin sauce to give a good flavour and colour. This can be served with vegetables. It is also a useful mixture with which to stuff vegetables.

Curries

CURRIED LENTILS
(*Dal or Dahl*)

6 oz. lentils
A good ½ pint water or stock
Sea salt to taste
1 teaspoon turmeric
½ teaspoon chilli powder (optional)
½ oz. butter or oil
1 chopped onion or leek
1 teaspoon curry powder
1 teaspoon curry paste
1 teaspoon 'garam-masala'
2 teaspoons chopped fresh herbs

Method. Wash lentils and cook slowly in the water with salt, turmeric and chilli powder (if used) until tender and all the liquid is absorbed. This will take approximately 30 minutes; the lentils will need stirring towards the end of the cooking period, as they may burn. Stir lightly with a fork so that they do not become too mushy, add more water or stock if necessary. Heat the butter or oil in a frying-pan and cook the onion or leek gently, add the curry powder or paste if used. Just before the onions are cooked, add the garam-masala and chopped herbs. Cook a few moments more and stir into the lentils. Serve hot with more fried onion as garnish if liked.

DRY CURRIES

CURRIED PEAS AND BROAD BEANS

½ lb. peas or beans
1 oz. butter or oil
1 chopped onion, leek or shallots
1 teaspoon chopped fresh herbs
1 teaspoon 'garam-masala'
½ oz. ginger (fresh or root)
1 teaspoon turmeric
Sea salt to taste

Curries

CURRIED PEAS AND BROAD BEANS *cont.*

½ teaspoon chilli powder
1 dessertspoon lemon juice

Heat the butter or oil in a saucepan or frying-pan with a lid, and cook the chopped onions, herbs and ginger gently until the onion is nearly cooked. Add the turmeric, salt and chilli powder and cook them a little. Mix in the peas and cover with a well-fitting lid—this can be done in a fire-proof covered dish in the oven—cook very gently until the peas are tender. A few minutes before the cooking is finished add the 'garam-masala' and lemon juice. If there is too much liquid take off the lid and allow it to evaporate. Serve with rice and accompaniments. If you wish to use curry powder and paste, cook them with the onions and omit the ginger, turmeric, 'garam-masala' and chilli powder. You are likely to need about 1 teaspoon of each for this recipe but it depends on how hot you like the curry.

Dry curries are very good and make a pleasant change from using curry sauce. One must be careful to see that they do not burn, but if this difficulty is experienced use the oven method.

Other vegetables which can be used for dry curries

1. A mixture of vegetables such as potatoes, peas, cauliflower, onions, garlic and tomatoes or any mixture that you may particularly prefer.
2. Mushrooms.
3. Cauliflowers.
4. Potatoes, and in particular new ones. As the new potatoes are inclined to stick they are definitely better cooked in the oven.
5. Potato, aubergine and tomato.
6. Peas and carrots.
7. Runner or French beans.
8. Young broad beans cooked in their pods (mange tout).
9. Marrow—evaporate the liquid to make it dry.
10. Cabbage (shredded) or brussels sprouts (whole).

Bananas can be dry curried and make a good accompaniment to a main curry.

10

Batters

There are two types of batter; thin batter for pancakes and Yorkshire puddings and thick batters for coating. They are usually a mixture of egg, flour and milk and can be quite plain or rich, depending on what may be added to them.

Here are the basic recipes and the general method.

<table>
<tr><td>THIN BATTER</td><td>COATING BATTER</td></tr>
<tr><td>4 oz. 81 per cent extraction flour</td><td>4 oz. 81 per cent extraction flour</td></tr>
<tr><td>Pinch sea salt</td><td>Pinch sea salt</td></tr>
<tr><td>1 egg</td><td>1 egg</td></tr>
<tr><td>About ½ pint milk and water or milk</td><td>About ¼ pint milk and water or milk</td></tr>
</table>

The only difference, as you can see, is the proportion of liquid to flour.

First sieve the flour and salt into a bowl, using a wooden spoon or a small wire whisk, make a hollow in the middle of the sieved mixture. Crack the egg into a cup, pour into the hollow, and add a little of the liquid. With the spoon or whisk break the yolk of the egg and gently mix into the milk; as you do this a little flour will be drawn in. Continue mixing, gradually drawing in more flour from the sides. The mixture will get stiff as the flour mixes in, so add a little more liquid; to allow the mixture to get too stiff will make the batter lumpy. To make a coating batter, add nearly all the liquid; adjust the consistency so that the batter will coat well the back of a wooden spoon, but not too thickly; the amount

Batters

of liquid depends on the water content of the flour and so a little more or less may be required. If you are making a thin batter, add about half the liquid. Now beat well with a wooden spoon until the surface is covered with bubbles; this may take 5–10 minutes. A whisk or rotary beater is quicker. For the thin batter, add enough liquid to make it the consistency of pouring cream.

There are two schools of thought as to whether the batter should be left to stand or not. It used to be thought that if the batter was left to stand for an hour or so, the starch grains softened and burst more quickly; but provided the cooking is quick enough, there seems to be little difference between a batter which has stood, and one which has not. If left to stand, keep it covered in a cool place or in a refrigerator.

Liquidizer method: if you have a liquidizer, making batter is very simple indeed. Place the liquid egg and seasoning in the liquidizer and switch on at a slow speed until the egg is mixed in. Take the lid off and spoon in the sieved flour. When it is mixed in, increase to maximum speed for 45–60 seconds, then use as required.

Yorkshire Pudding

Prepare half a pint of batter (batter made with a half-pint of liquid). Place a shelf near the top of the oven allowing room for the batter to rise, then heat the oven to 425° F., M6–7. Take a shallow tin (a gingerbread tin is best as it has sides 1 inch or more deep; a Swiss roll tin is too shallow), and put 1 oz. of oil or white fat into it. Heat the tin in the oven until the fat is just smoking and quickly pour in the cold batter; return to the oven as quickly as possible and cook until well risen, crisp and golden brown. You will find that the pudding rises and browns best around the edges and takes 35–45 minutes to cook. Cut into squares and serve on a hot dish.

We find it is quicker to cook the pudding in a tin, and then serve on a dish. If you prefer to use a glass or oven-proof dish then stand it on a baking-sheet and be certain it is very hot before adding the batter.

Batters

Variations

1. Make small Yorkshire puddings either in bun-tins or in individual fire-proof dishes—made in these, the puddings are very good, and tend to be lighter and crisper than the larger pudding. They take less cooking time, about 15–20 minutes, depending on the size, and need only a little fat in each container.

2. When heating the fat in the tin, add small pieces of nut savoury or small parboiled vegetables (carrots, onions, parsnips, etc.) then add the batter and cook as before.

3. Just before cooking the batter add some diced or grated cheese (about 2–3 oz.). More than this amount will make the batter heavy; add two tablespoons of chopped fresh herbs, mixed. Cook as before.

4. Chopped raw onion, chive or garlic added.

5. Add 2 oz. of currants, raisins or sultanas to the batter and cook as before. Serve with brown sugar or honey and cream.

6. The batter can be flavoured with orange or lemon rind and/or spices.

7. Heat some butter in the tin and add 1 lb. of washed, cored and thinly sliced ripe apple (leave the peel on), sprinkle with lemon rind or spice to flavour and a little sugar or honey to sweeten. Pour on the batter and cook until the batter is brown and the apple soft. If the apples are ripe eating-apples, you need not add any sugar when cooking, or you can add dried fruit to sweeten. Do not be tempted to add the sugar to the batter as it will make it heavy.

There are other fruits which can be cooked with batter; apricots, bananas, oranges and dates are but a few. For variety some of these flavourings can be used together, for example—the nut savoury and herbs; vegetables and cheese; apple, dried fruit and spice.

PANCAKES

If you are fond of pancakes and make them fairly often, keep a special pan for them; it is sensible to use the omelette pan for pancakes since they both need the same sort of pan. Details of

241

this pan and its use will be found in the section on Omelettes.

Method for making pancakes: you will need (1) the pan; (2) a small jug of hot oil or fat; (3) a palette-knife; (4) a larger jug holding batter; (5) a board on which to roll the pancakes; (6) the filling; (7) a serving-dish in a warm oven.

Heat the pan with some of the fat in it; when the fat just begins to smoke pour it back into the jug. Although it may not look as if there will be enough grease left to prevent the pancake from sticking, if you leave any more than a smear of grease, the pancakes will fry.

Before the pan loses heat, pour in a 'disc' of batter which covers a third to half of the pan, then with a twisting motion of the wrist, run the batter around the outer edges of the pan and tilt the pan to cover any holes which appear. When the bottom of the pan is covered with the set batter, there should not be any liquid batter left; if there is, the pancakes will be too heavy and thick. It is a good idea to use a graduated jug which will indicate an even amount of the mixture for each pancake (we use a tiny cream ladle which is perfect for an omelette pan). Let the pancake cook until the underside is brown and of good appearance, then turn with a palette-knife or toss it.

Tossing pancakes is not nearly as difficult as one may imagine, but be sure to have a good pan so that the pancakes will not stick. When first trying, toss over a table or sink. Do not toss the pancake too high or it may end up on the ceiling!

Cook the other side of the pancake until brown and then turn on to a board for filling and rolling up.

The side which is cooked first and is therefore usually the more attractive should be outermost when the pancake is rolled up. All this appears to take a long time but actually takes only about a minute. The first one or two may not be so good as the rest, but handling the pan becomes easier with practice. A little trial and error is needed to get the heat adjusted correctly. From half a pint of batter we get twelve pancakes, using a $7\frac{1}{2}$-inch omelette pan.

Pancakes should be eaten immediately they are cooked and filled, but if this is not possible, keep them warm in an oven until served.

Batters

SWEET	SAVOURY
Lemon and sugar or honey	Thick creamy sauce with egg, mushroom, asparagus, etc. in it
Apple purée with lemon flavouring	
Bananas mashed with honey and ground nuts	Mashed vegetables with grated cheese
Bananas mashed with orange Juice and grated chocolate	Spinach purée
	Cabbage in sweet or sour sauce
	Chestnut purée with onion

Fruit liqueurs may also be used for flavouring, if you like them. Most of these fillings should be kept warm in a small double saucepan or in a basin standing in hot water. When the pancake is cooked (and the pan reheated with more fat), spread the pancake with the filling and roll up and keep warm. Or sprinkle with lemon or orange juice and sugar, roll up and keep warm. If you use honey, warm it gently until it runs easily, fill the pancake with a slightly sour filling and then run the honey over the pancakes prior to serving. After filling one pancake you will find the pan is warm enough for another pancake to cook.

The savoury pancakes can be served with an appropriate sauce, e.g. tomato, cheese, mushroom, etc.

Fritter batter

This is made as for the pancake batter. Vegetable fritters are dealt with in the Vegetable chapter.

Fruit fritters

First prepare the batter and then the fruit. The fruits which can be used are as follows:

Apples Wash, core with an apple corer and cut into rings about ¼-inch thick, leave to soak for 30 minutes in lemon juice, cognac or grape juice with cinnamon. Add brown sugar or honey to the liquid for sweetness.

Apricots Wash, halve and stone. Marinade for 30 minutes in lemon juice, kirsch or apple juice, with a sweetener.

Fillings

Bananas Peel, and if small, cut in half lengthwise; if large cut into three chunks. Marinade 30 minutes in rum or lemon juice with cinnamon or orange juice, with a sweetener.

Oranges Peel and divide carefully into sections, removing as much pith as possible. These are easier to fry without marinading, but they may be soaked in curaçao or cointreau for 30 minutes.

Peaches Wash and cut into quarters. Soak in lemon juice or brandy or apple juice plus a sweetener for 30 minutes.

Pears Wash and cut into quarters or eighths. Marinade in kirsch or cherry brandy, apple juice and cinnamon or ginger, orange juice or ginger syrup for 30 minutes.

Pineapple Remove top and bottom and tough outside skin. Cut into quarters. Slice away hard core and cut each quarter into slices. Soak in rum or orange juice and cinnamon or grape juice with sweetener for 30 minutes.

Strawberries These are best when picked from your own garden and used unwashed. If you buy them they should be washed but dried very carefully. Do not marinade.

The fruit must then be drained very carefully (the marinading liquid is a wonderful base for a fruit cup, fruit salad or fruit soup), dipped and coated all over with batter. This may best be done with the fingers. Fry in oil which is just smoking (without the frying-basket). Lift out with a drainer-spoon or flat wire whisk. Drain well and serve immediately.

A mixture of fruit fritters is a gorgeous sweet and is not much more work than making one kind only.

We have given the most economical recipes for batters, but there are many ways to make them richer, lighter and crisper.

1. The addition of more eggs (take away the equivalent amount of mixing liquid). We make our pancakes with 2 eggs and slightly less milk. The eggs are separated, the yolks mixed with the flour and liquid, the whites whipped stiffly and added just before frying.

2. The addition of melted butter (cooled and strained) or oil—gives crispness and lightness.

Cakes

3. Use yeast as a lightener, it also gives a crisp finish.

4. Use milk and water rather than all milk for mixing—milk on its own tends to make the batter heavy. Wine, grape or apple juice can sometimes be used for sweet fritters.

Here are some recipes to illustrate these points. The method is evident from the basic method and the above notes.

PANCAKE BATTER

4 oz. 81 per cent extraction flour
Pinch sea salt
1 oz. melted butter or oil
1 egg plus 1 yolk
1 extra white of egg beaten stiffly
A little less than ½ pint of milk or milk and water

FRITTER BATTER

4 oz. 81 per cent extraction flour
Pinch sea salt
A little brown sugar for sweet fritters
¼ oz. fresh yeast
¼ pint (approximate, probably a little less) warm water, cider or apple juice
1 tablespoon oil or melted butter

Dissolve the yeast in the warm liquid and then beat into the sieved flour (with salt and sugar added) with the oil or butter. Leave it to stand in a warm place until the batter has risen slightly (anything from 30 minutes to 1 hour) then fold in the egg-white and use. This is better than recipes which use baking-powder, but it does have to be prepared beforehand.

Fritter batter can be made with more eggs in the same way as pancake batter.

CAKES

In the recipes which follow we use, whenever possible, brown sugar, honey or black treacle and either an 81 per cent extraction

Cakes

flour or a fine wholemeal flour, preferably compost grown. If you cannot obtain these or consider them unimportant, you will find the recipes can be made with white flour and refined sugar. The majority of cakes fall into four main categories, although there are a few which are outside these groups. The headings are:

1. Plain or 'rubbed in' cakes.
2. Rich or 'creamed' cakes.
3. Sponges or 'whisked' cakes.
4. Gingerbread or 'melted' cakes.

If you know the basic recipes and the variations, great fun can be had working out all sorts of different cakes—they may not be quite new because they say there is nothing left to discover in cookery (we wonder!), but they will be your own creation and that is what will matter. It is a good thing to surprise the family occasionally and thus avoid getting into a rut.

Preparation of cake tins

1. Grease with a white fat (having no taste or salt to make the mixture stick). This is sometimes sprinkled with flour, the flour shaken around the tin and then the surplus knocked out.

2. Grease the tin and cut a piece of greaseproof paper to fit the bottom exactly to size, or a piece of shaped greaseproof which runs across the bottom and up both sides of a rectangular tin. Do not forget to grease the greaseproof paper otherwise some of the cake may come off with the paper when it is removed.

3. To line completely with paper, you will need a pair of scissors, a pencil, a piece of string or a tape measure and greaseproof paper. A rectangular tin is lined by cutting the greaseproof paper slightly larger in area than the bottom of the tin plus the sides. Mark out the size of the base of the bottom of the tin in the corner of the paper and then cut from each corner, to the marked corner of the base in the centre. Overlap the corners when placing the greaseproof paper carefully on the bottom. Grease the paper.

To line a circular tin with greaseproof paper, put the tin on the paper and draw round it. Cut out the circle slightly less than the line drawn. Then cut a long strip to go round the sides of the tin —the length should be the circumference of the cake-tin plus

Cakes

3 inches and the height that of the sides plus 1 inch. Measure with the string or tape measure. Fold up about 1 inch all along one side and snip at regular intervals. Put this side-piece in the tin, when the nicked edges should lie flat on the bottom. Cover the bottom of the tin with the circle of paper. The lining should be greased. There should be two layers of greaseproof paper.

Very rich cakes can be lined with brown paper first, then with greaseproof, to assist the long slow cooking. The best way to grease the paper is to use a pastry brush and a tasteless oil or melted fat. If there is a lot of greasing to be done, place a little fat in a small saucepan, melt it and stand it in a warm place for use.

Plain or 'rubbed in' cakes

To 1 lb. flour:

½ level teaspoon sea salt

2–8 level teaspoons baking-powder dependent on the amount of fat and eggs used.

4–8 oz. butter, margarine, vegetable fat or nutter

4–8 oz. brown sugar

1–4 eggs

Milk or milk and water to mix.

ECONOMICAL	RICHEST
½ *lb.* 81 *per cent extraction wholemeal flour*	½ *lb.* 81 *per cent extraction flour (approx.)*
4 *level teaspoons baking-powder (see below)*	2 *level teaspoons baking-powder (see below)*
Pinch sea salt	*Pinch sea salt*
1 *oz. fat*	4 *oz. fat*
1 *oz. brown sugar*	4 *oz. brown sugar*
½–1 *egg*	2 *eggs*
6 *tablespoons milk or milk and water to mix*	*A little milk or milk and water to mix*

The amount of baking-powder needed will vary according to the make, so read the instructions before use. For the most economical recipe self-raising flour can be used: but in the richer recipes,

Cakes

the amount of baking-powder in the self-raising flour would be too much, and cause the cake to rise to excess and then sink in the middle.

Method. Sieve the flour, the salt and the baking-powder together into a bowl. This mixes the ingredients, removes any lumps, cools and aerates them; so please do not be tempted to omit this even if you are in a hurry! Rub in the fat, using only the tips of the fingers and lift the mixture as you work. When all the fat is worked in, give the bowl a shake and crush with your fingers lumps which may come to the surface—if there are still lumps of fat, continue to rub in until they have gone. The mixture will look like fine or coarse breadcrumbs, depending on the amount of fat used. Add the sugar, which should be crushed and any lumps removed. Mix in lightly, lifting the mixture as you do so. Beat the eggs a little in a basin with a fork and add a little milk. Make a hollow in the centre of the mixture and pour in the egg and milk. With a metal spoon, work the mixture together lightly, adding more liquid if necessary. The consistency should be a soft dropping one, i.e. dropping easily from the spoon.

Economical mixtures need to be baked at a higher temperature than the richer creamed mixtures, 400° F. or M5-6. Place in a greased tin, or greased greaseproof paper-lined tin is better, and bake until well risen and brown; these cakes usually crack along the top and are firm to the touch.

There is a definite springy, resilient feeling to a cake when it is cooked; this is learnt by experience. If you are not sure if the cake is cooked, warm a fine knitting-needle or a thin metal skewer and pierce the centre of the cake with it, then withdraw it. There should be no moistness from the cake adhering to the needle or skewer; there might be a few cooked crumbs or a little fat but these merely indicate the cake is cooked. The warmed blade of the cook's knife may also be used but this leaves quite a hole when withdrawn. The time for cooking is generally about 40 minutes–1 hour for a large cake and 15 minutes–20 minutes for a small cake, but this varies with the size and depth of the tin.

This recipe is for an absolutely plain cake, not often made!

Here are some of the flavourings which can be used and how

Cakes

to add them—the quantities are for ½ lb. of flour but the amounts may be varied according to taste.

Coffee and walnut 2 oz. roughly chopped walnuts added with the sugar. 1 dessertspoon powdered coffee dissolved in one tablespoon of boiling water and added with the egg and milk.

Date and walnut 2 oz. chopped walnuts; 2 oz. dates—add both with the sugar.

Sultanas 2–4 oz. added with the sugar.

Currants 2–4 oz. added with the sugar.

Raisins 2–4 oz. added with the sugar.

Lemon Grated rind of lemon added with the sugar.

Vanilla Use vanilla sugar.

Nutmeg
Mixed spice
Cinnamon
Ground ginger } 1–2 level teaspoons sieved with the flour, etc.

Desiccated coconut 1–2 oz. added with the sugar.

Chopped almonds 1–2 oz. added with the sugar.

Ground almonds 1–2 oz. added with the sugar.

Soya flour Lessen the flour by 1 oz. and sieve with the flour, etc.

Raw sugar chocolate 1–2 oz., grated, added with the sugar.

Some of these flavourings can be used together, the spices and the lemon and orange rind combine with any, or with a mixture of the dried fruits, for example. The chocolate cake is much better made with the soya flour.

As these cakes are economical they should be made in small quantities as they become dry if kept for any length of time. They should be stored, like most cakes, in an airtight tin. We use this type of cake mainly for tea breads (made in a loaf-tin, sliced and spread with butter) or rock cakes.

Cakes

Rock Cakes

4 oz. wholemeal self-raising flour (coarse or fine)
Pinch sea salt
½ level teaspoon mixed spice
½ level teaspoon grated or ground nutmeg
1 oz. butter, margarine or white fat
1 oz. brown sugar
1 oz. currants and 1 egg

Heat the oven to 425° F., M6–7. Grease and flour a baking-sheet. Sieve the dry ingredients and rub in the fat. Add the sugar and currants. Bind to a stiff dough with a beaten egg, using a fork to mix. The dough should be stiff enough for the fork to stand upright. If it is too dry add a little water. Place the mixture in rough (rocky) heaps on the baking-sheet with the fork. Bake for 15–20 minutes until brown and firm.

N.B. Egg only is used for mixing so that the mixture does not spread too much. If, however, other liquid is added, allow for the spreading.

Banana-Walnut 'Bread'

8 oz. Scofa scone flour or wholemeal self-raising flour
Pinch sea salt
2 oz. butter, margarine or vegetable fat.
4 oz. brown sugar
1–2 oz. chopped walnuts
1 egg
3 tablespoons yoghourt, cultured cream or milk
2 large or 3 small mashed bananas

Heat the oven to 375° F., M5. Grease a medium–large loaf-tin. Sieve the flour and salt (use a coarse sieve for coarse flours), rub in the fat. Add the sugar and walnuts. Mix the egg, bananas and yoghourt, etc. together and add to the dry ingredients. Mix all well together and bake for 45 minutes–1 hour in the centre or slightly above the centre of the oven.

Cakes

This bread keeps nice and moist for a day or two. It is very good eaten on its own when new or with butter and honey when dry.

RICH OR 'CREAMED' CAKES

To 1 lb. flour:

½–1 lb. butter, margarine or white fat
½–1 lb. brown sugar
4–8 eggs
Up to 2 level teaspoons baking powder (approximate)
Milk to mix if necessary, depends on the amount of fat and eggs used

ECONOMICAL	RICHEST
4 oz. fat	*8 oz. fat*
4 oz. brown sugar	*8 oz. brown sugar*
2 eggs	*4 eggs*
½ lb. 81 per cent extraction flour	*½ lb. 81 per cent extraction flour*
Pinch sea salt	*Pinch sea salt*
Approximately 2 level teaspoons baking-powder	*No baking-powder*
	No extra liquid
4 tablespoons milk	

Method. Leave the fat and sugar in a bowl in a warm place, in an airing cupboard, or on a stove for about half an hour before creaming, or stand the bowl in warm water or leave for a few minutes in the oven. If you are using fat straight from the refrigerator it should be creamed on its own in the bowl until soft, then the sugar added. Cream the fat and sugar until all (or nearly all) the sugar is dissolved in the fat and the mixture is like a pale coffee-coloured whipping cream. If you are not using a mixer, a wooden spoon should be used. Stand the bowl on a damp cloth so that it does not slip about. Mix the fat and sugar together to a soft paste, then beat. The idea is to form an emulsion with the fat and sugar which will hold air; the beating should force air into the emulsion and as you become more practised it will take less time. If you have a mixing machine, follow the makers' instructions. When the fat and sugar are well creamed, break one egg into a cup (to

Cakes

make sure all is well with the egg!) and drop it into the bowl. Mix and then beat well. Continue until all the eggs are beaten in. If you are making the richest mixture you may find that the last egg curdles the mixture; this should not happen if the eggs were at room temperature and each egg has been well beaten in, but we *have* known it to happen even with the most experienced cooks. Either use a wire whisk to beat well (the mixture should be soft enough for this) or throw in an ounce or two of the sieved flour and beat well.

Remove and scrape the wooden spoon. Sieve the dry ingredients over the creamed mixture; gently cut and fold the flour into the creamed mixture with the edge of a metal spoon so that you do not squash out the air beaten in. Continue until well mixed and then bake. These rich mixtures are baked more slowly otherwise they would burn. With large cakes the tins should be lined with greaseproof paper; for small cakes or sandwich cakes the tins are greased and sometimes floured. Small cakes can also be baked in greaseproof paper cases bought from stationers or stores. Small cakes and sandwich cakes are usually baked at 375° F., M5. Rich cakes are placed in the oven at 350° F., M4 and the heat reduced after 30 minutes–1 hour to 325° F., M3 until cooked. If the cake is large the top can be protected by a sheet of greaseproof paper and the oven turned down a little more towards the end of cooking.

Christmas, wedding and large cakes. Start the cooking as above but turn to 300° F., M2, after 2 hours at 325° F.; if the cake is browning too much. These large rich fruit cakes can take 4–5 hours to cook. They become bitter on the outside if baked too quickly. You should know your oven well before attempting one of these.

Flavourings

These are the same as for plain cakes with the exception of the dried fruits; these can be increased from 8 oz. to 3 lb. of fruit per lb. of flour.

These cakes keep better than the plain ones, particularly those which are made from the richest mixture of all. They should be kept in airtight tins and are better for storing a week or so, before eating.

Cakes

Really rich fruit cake should be eaten when fresh or kept 2–6 months to mature. If cut at about one month they are dry and disappointing.

If coarse wholemeal flour and brown sugar are used for these cakes we do find that self-raising flour or half of self-raising flour and half of plain flour gives a lighter result.

Here are some cakes and sandwiches derived from the basic recipe; there are, of course, many more and we hope you will enjoy experimenting for yourself.

We have been careful to call the Victoria sandwich by this name; although it is often called a sponge, it is not a true sponge. These are given in the next section. We often use these cake recipes to make puddings (see first section and Hot and Cold Sweets); many of them can be used with fruit, or steamed, as we do not have a 'tea' meal as such. We also find that those made from the extravagant recipes, though they may seem expensive, keep well and, because they do not need baking-powder, are probably healthier.

SMALL CREAMED CAKES

4 oz. butter, margarine or vegetable fat
4 oz. dark brown sugar
2 eggs, small–medium (if large you can use 5 oz. butter, sugar and flour)
Flavouring as desired
3½ oz. wholemeal 81 per cent extraction flour
½ oz. soya flour
Pinch sea salt

Method. Heat the oven to 375° F., M5. Grease the bun-tins or line with paper cases. Cream the fat and sugar and beat in the eggs. Sieve the dry ingredients and fold in with a metal spoon. Fill each tin or case half to two-thirds and bake until risen and brown, about 15–25 minutes, depending on the size. Cool on a wire rack.

Some suggestions for flavourings and icings

Chocolate Add 1 oz. of finely grated or melted chocolate, beating

Cakes

in the eggs. When cool spread some chocolate butter cream on the top and place a roasted hazel nut or curl of chocolate in the centre.

Cinnamon and orange Flavour with ground cinnamon and a little grated orange rind. Top with orange butter cream.

Fudge Top the plain cakes with fudge icing.

Coffee and walnut Add 1 oz. chopped walnuts to the cake mixture. Ice with coffee butter cream and top with half a walnut.

Lemon and date Add 1 oz. of chopped dates and the grated rind of half a lemon to cake mixture. Top with lemon butter icing with a section of date in the middle.

Fruit Add 1–2 oz. of any dried fruit and spice if liked; usually left plain on the top.

Almond Replace 1 oz. of flour with 1 oz. of ground or finely grated almonds. Ice with butter icing and top with a roasted almond.

The notes on decorating and icings are at the end of the Cake section.

SANDWICH CAKES

These are made in sponge-tins and the following mixture will bake in two 8-inch sponge-tins of about 1–1½ inches high.

      6 oz. fat, butter or margarine
      6 oz. brown sugar
      3 small–medium-sized eggs
      Flavouring
      5 oz. 81 per cent extraction wholemeal flour
      1 oz. soya flour

N.B. If using the coarse wholemeal use half self-raising flour and half plain or add 1–2 level teaspoons baking-powder.

Use the same method as for the small cakes; they will need the same temperature but longer baking—25–40 minutes. The flavourings are the same as for plain or small cakes. Icings and fillings are at the end of the section.

Cakes

WHOLEMEAL DUNDEE CAKE

6 oz. butter, margarine or vegetable fat
6 oz. dark brown sugar (1 oz. can be replaced by 1 tablespoon honey)
3 eggs
Grated rind of 1 orange and 1 lemon
2 oz. chopped nuts (almonds, hazels and Brazils)
10 oz.–1 lb. mixed dried fruits
9 oz. 81 per cent extraction wholemeal flour
Pinch sea salt
1 level teaspoon baking-powder
A little milk to mix
About ½ oz. blanched almonds

Method. Heat the oven to 350° F., M4. Grease and line a cake-
tin. Cream fat and sugar, beat in the eggs. Add fruit, nuts and
grated rinds. Sieve the flour, salt and baking-powder, cut and fold
into the creamed mixture, adding a little milk to make a soft
dropping consistency (should drop slowly from the spoon). Place
in the cake-tin and cover the top with almonds, brush with a little
milk. Bake for 1½–2 hours in the centre of the oven; turn down
the heat a little at the end if the cake is browning too much. Cool
on a wire rack. Keep in an airtight tin for a week or two before
cutting.

The addition of spice to this cake makes a good Simnel cake
mixture.

For very rich fruit cakes use the sandwich mixture with 2–2½ lb.
of dried fruit, some chopped nuts and grated orange and lemon
rind. Replace 2 oz. of brown sugar with black treacle or honey.
Add spice if liked, and for a really luscious result, soak the dried
fruit in about 4–6 tablespoons of sherry, rum or brandy for 3–4
days before making the cake. We put the dried fruits in a screw-
top jar and shake vigorously once or twice a day. These cakes can
be made six months, at least, before being used!

Cakes

SPONGES OR WHISKED CAKES

For each egg take: 1–1½ oz. brown sugar
1 oz. 81 per cent extraction flour

Sponges can be made with 100 per cent wholemeal flour but self-raising flour or a little baking-powder will give a lighter result.

PLAIN SPONGE

4 eggs
5 oz. brown sugar
4 oz. 81 per cent extraction flour
Pinch sea salt

Method. Heat the oven to 350–375° F., M4–5, grease and flour two 8-inch sponge-tins. Break the eggs separately and place in a warm bowl which will fit into the top of a saucepan which contains nearly boiling water. Whisk the eggs lightly and add the warm sugar gradually, having previously crushed or removed any lumps. Continue whisking until the mixture is thick so that, when falling from the whisk to make an initial it will retain the shape for a second. If you are using a balloon or basket whisk this may take 15–30 minutes, depending on your expertise; with a rotary whisk the process is quicker. Keep the water hot but at simmering-point only; it must not reach the base of the bowl otherwise the sponge will be semi-cooked on the bottom of the bowl. Sieve the flour and salt over it and very carefully cut and fold into the mixture. Pour into tins and bake until risen and golden brown. This takes 20–30 minutes. If you lightly 'dance' your fingers across the surface, the finger-marks should disappear. If the light depressions remain, the sponge is not quite cooked. Turn out and cool on a wire rack.

These sponges make a perfect sweet with fresh fruit and whipped cream. The same mixture baked in bun-tins provides sponge cakes for trifles or individual fruit sponges. For a sponge which dries less quickly than the one above, try the following recipe.

Cakes

GENOESE SPONGE

3 large eggs
4 oz. brown sugar
2 oz. cool, melted, strained unsalted butter
3 oz. 81 per cent extraction flour
Pinch sea salt

This sponge is made and cooked in the same way as the plain sponge. The melted butter is either folded in alternately with the sieved flour or when the flour is mixed in. If the mixture is well whisked and the 'folding in' done carefully, this sponge is a success. If you have trouble with it, either practise the plain sponge more or use self-raising flour.

These sponges can be iced and filled as the Victoria sandwiches or form the basis for a pudding.

GINGERBREADS OR MELTED CAKES

Basic recipe

6 oz. black treacle
4 oz. dark brown sugar
3 oz. butter or vegetable fat
½ lb. 100 per cent wholemeal self-raising flour, or
½ lb. 100 per cent wholemeal flour with a level teaspoon
  baking-powder
½ level teaspoon bicarbonate of soda
Pinch sea salt
2 level teaspoons ground ginger
1 egg
¼ pint milk (approximately)

Heat the oven to 325–350° F., M3–4, grease and line a shallow tin 1–2 inches deep. Weigh a saucepan and then measure in the treacle, sugar and fat. Stir over a gentle heat until the fat is melted —do not allow to boil or you will start making toffee and the gingerbread will be heavy—stand on one side to cool. Sieve all the dry ingredients into a bowl and beat the egg in half the milk.

Cakes

Make a well in the centre of the flour and pour in the melted mixture, the egg and half of the milk. Mix together with a wooden spoon, adding sufficient milk to make a thick batter and beat very well until the mixture is smooth. Pour into the tin and bake in the centre of the oven until the centre is firm—1–1½ hours. Turn on to a wire rack and strip off the paper carefully. When cold cut into squares and store in an airtight tin. The flavour improves with keeping.

Variations

1. Add 1–2 teaspoons of cinnamon or mixed spice.
2. Add 1–2 oz. of chopped preserved ginger and use only one level teaspoon of ground ginger.
3. Add 3–4 oz. of sultanas or chopped dates.
4. Replace 1 oz. of flour with 1 oz. of soya flour.
5. Add 2 oz. of ground almonds.
6. Glaze the top with a little beaten egg and decorate with blanched almonds before cooking—this gives a pleasant gilt to the gingerbread.
7. Bake in bun-tins (lessening the cooking time).

Never try to bake gingerbread in a deep tin. It is a very soft mixture and will not stand up, becoming heavy in the middle.

Here is a cake which does not fit into the four groups, but it is a great favourite of ours.

KARI'S NORWEGIAN SPICY CAKE

6½ oz. brown sugar

A good ¼ pint of milk

1 oz. butter

6½ oz. 81 per cent extraction flour, or 100 per cent wholemeal self-raising flour, or plain flour with 3 level teaspoons of baking-powder.

Pinch sea salt

1 teaspoon each ginger, ground cloves and cinnamon

1 oz. ground almonds

1 egg

Cake Icings, Fillings, etc.

Mix the sugar and milk together. Melt the butter and cool. Turn the oven to 375° F., M5. Grease some loaf-tins. Sieve the flour and salt (baking-powder, if used) and spices. Add the ground almonds. Make a well in the centre and break in the egg. Pour in the butter and the milk mixture and beat the mixture until it is smooth. Fill the loaf-tins about two-thirds full. Bake until risen and firm. The top usually cracks. Cool on a wire rack. This cake is excellent served with coffee.

CAKE ICINGS, FILLINGS, ETC.

The decoration of cakes is a rewarding occupation if you have time and patience, particularly cakes for children's parties.

The usual icings will be found in a good general cookery book but here are some food reform ones.

Cake fillings

1. Chop or grate equal quantities of almonds and walnuts and bind with honey and a few drops of lemon juice.

2. Mash 2–3 bananas, add a little lemon juice, honey or brown sugar. Mix in either whipped cream or ground almonds to give a firm mixture.

3. Rum butter. Cream equal quantities of butter and brown sugar, beat in rum to taste.

4. Butter cream fillings (see Icings).

5. Whipped cream with brown vanilla sugar flavouring.

6. Whipped cream with chopped (mashing produces too much liquid) strawberries, raspberries, bananas, peaches, pineapple, etc. Add liqueur to flavour if liked.

7. Any nut cream mashed with banana and some chopped nuts.

Cake icings

FUDGE ICING

2 oz. butter
7 oz. brown sugar
4 teaspoons cream or top of milk
1 teaspoon honey

Cake Icings, Fillings, etc.

Stir together until the sugar is dissolved and then boil, stirring from time to time until a little of the mixture dropped in cold water forms a soft ball. Remove from the heat and stir until thick. Spread as desired and allow to set.

BUTTER CREAM

> 4 oz. unsalted butter
> 4 oz. dark brown sugar
> 1–2 teaspoons boiling water or top of the milk

Cream the fat and sugar until very light and fluffy. Add the boiling liquid drop by drop, beating all the time; this helps to dissolve the sugar and makes the cream lighter.

Additions

1. An egg-yolk beaten in makes it richer.
2. If you have a little carrageen or agar milk jelly left over, whip it well and add it to the cream.
3. Substitute a little honey for brown sugar.
4. Add some whipped cream.

Flavourings

1. Chopped brown nuts, e.g. almonds or hazel nuts.
2. Chopped walnuts.
3. Use very hot strong coffee in place of boiling water.
4. 1–2 oz. of grated or melted chocolate.
5. Grate orange or lemon rind, beat in 1–2 tablespoons of juice also.
6. Use vanilla sugar.

Decorating

1. Sponge cakes can be cut through and filled; one, three or five times.
2. They can be iced on the top and sides. Remember to ice thinly; too much can be sickly.
3. The icing can be finished roughly with a palette-knife or smoothed and piped.
4. Chopped nuts, grated chocolate, pieces or whole fruit can

be used for decoration. If possible the decoration should indicate the type of cake.

N.B. If the sponge cake is iced all over it is usually eaten with a fork.

If fruit or cream is used the cake should be used quickly and kept in a cool place or in a refrigerator until needed.

BISCUITS

Sweet biscuits are much better when home-made, they are a good accompaniment to fruit 'fools', fruit purée or stewed fruit. There are a number of plain wholemeal biscuits on the market so we have not given any recipes for these. In these days when there is not much help in the home, it is useful to have recipes which do not require much rolling!

PLAIN SWEET BISCUITS

4 oz. butter, margarine or vegetable fat
4 oz. brown sugar
1 egg
8 oz. 81 per cent extraction flour
Pinch sea salt

Heat an oven to 350–375° F., M4–5, lightly grease one or two baking-sheets. Cream the fat and sugar, beat in the egg. With a clean hand knead in the sieved flour and salt, very well; it should form a dough which leaves the fingers clean. If too wet, add a little ground almonds or soya flour, if too dry, add a little milk or milk and water. Roll out on a floured board to $\frac{1}{8}$-inch thick and cut into fingers, squares or triangles. This saves kneading scraps and re-rolling and gives a better texture as the first rolling is always the best. Place on the baking-sheet and cook until evenly brown, about 15–20 minutes. Biscuits near the edge of the sheets may have to be taken off before the remainder have finished cooking, a palette-knife does the job well. If you can, leave the biscuits to cool on the baking-sheet as this keeps them crisp.

Biscuits

When cold, store the biscuits in an airtight tin, never with cake or bread or they will become soft.

Variations

1. 1–2 oz. of currants with grated lemon rind
2. 1–2 oz. finely chopped dates with grated orange rind.
3. Orange or lemon rind.
4. 1–2 teaspoons of cinnamon, mixed spice or ginger.
5. Brush the top with egg-white and sprinkle with chopped nuts or brown sugar.
6. Replace 1–2 oz. of flour with ground almonds or soya flour.
7. Replace 1–2 oz. flour with 3 oz. of grated nuts.
8. Use vanilla sugar.

SHORTBREAD

4 oz. butter
2 oz. brown sugar
6 oz. 81 per cent extraction flour
Pinch sea salt

Heat the oven to 350° F., M4. Grease a shallow tin. Cream the fat and sugar until creamy and very soft. Knead in the sieved flour and then the salt, knead very well. Press into the tin so that it is about ½–¾-inch thick. Crimp the edges between thumb and first finger, prick the rest with a fork and bake in the oven until firm and golden brown, about ¾ of an hour. Cut into fingers and allow to cool in the tin. Store in an airtight tin. Shortbread can also be formed into a round and baked on a baking-sheet—it is then cut into wedges.

HONEY BISCUITS

6 oz. 81 per cent extraction flour
Pinch sea salt
2–3 oz. butter, margarine or vegetable fat
Flavouring—lemon or orange rind or ground spice
Enough flowing honey to bind

Heat the oven to 350° F., M4. Grease a baking-sheet. Rub the

Plain Scones

fat into the sieved flour and salt, add the flavouring and mix to a stiff dough with the honey. Roll small balls of even size in the palms of the hands and flatten them with the palm on the baking-sheet. Bake for 15–20 minutes. Cool and place in an airtight tin.

GINGER NUTS

2 oz. butter, margarine or vegetable fat.
4 oz. brown sugar
6 oz. 81 per cent extraction flour
Pinch sea salt
2 level teaspoons ground ginger
1 level teaspoon mixed spice
Black treacle or honey to mix

Heat oven to 350° F., M4. Grease one or two baking-sheets. Cream the fat and sugar and stir in the dry ingredients with enough treacle and/or honey to mix to a stiff dough. Finish as with the honey biscuits above.

PLAIN SCONES

½ lb. 81 per cent extraction or wholemeal flour either self-raising, or add 1 level teaspoon bicarbonate of soda or 2 level teaspoons cream of tartar
Pinch sea salt
1–2 oz. butter, margarine or vegetable fat
Milk, or milk and water, to mix

Heat an oven to 425–450° F., M7–8. Lightly flour a baking-sheet. Sieve the flour, salt and raising agent (if used). Rub in the fat. Mix to a soft, light but easy to handle dough. Turn on to a floured board and cut in two. Form each piece into a round and cut into 4 scones. Place on the baking-sheet near the top of the oven and cook for 10–15 minutes. Cool on a wire rack. Scones should be eaten on the day of making. This scone mixture can be rolled out and cut into rounds with a cutter or it can be divided into sixteen

263

Plain Scones

to make smaller scones. They can also be glazed with beaten egg, or egg and milk.

Variations

Cheese—3–4 oz. grated cheese, season with salt and a little cayenne, paprika or dry mustard.

Sweet—add 2 oz. of brown sugar after the fat is rubbed in.

Fruit—add 2 oz. of currants, sultanas, raisins or chopped dates.

Oatmeal—substitute 2 oz. of fine oatmeal for 2 oz. of flour.

Rich scones—use 2–4 oz. of fat, add 2 oz. sugar and use 1 beaten egg in the milk for mixing. Fruit can be added if liked.

Sour milk scones—these are very good, the sour milk is used for mixing and the amount of cream of tartar is halved.

DROP SCONES

These are cooked on a girdle or the solid hot plate of an electric cooker, failing either of these, a large thick-bottomed frying-pan can be used.

Wipe the girdle (frying-pan or hot plate) with a dry cloth and scour with salt if necessary. Wipe again. Heat evenly until a steady heat can be felt on the back of the hand when it is held one or two inches from the surface of the plate. Take a small knob of butter or vegetable fat and run it lightly over the surface, but do not let the surface run with fat. The girdle is now ready for use. It should be greased after each batch of scones.

8 oz. 81 per cent extraction self-raising flour
Pinch sea salt
1–2 oz. brown sugar
2 eggs
About ½ pint milk or buttermilk

Sieve the flour and salt, add the sugar. Beat the eggs with some of the milk and add to the dry ingredients. Stir well with a metal spoon to remove any lumps. Add more milk to make a thick creamy batter. The consistency of the batter is important; if not correct, scones too thick or too thin will result. With the spoon,

Pastry

drop spoonfuls of the mixture on the hot greased girdle. If the scones are dropped from the side of the spoon they will be oval in shape and if they are dropped from the tip they will be round. After a few minutes bubbles will rise to the surface and burst, the scones can then be turned with a palette-knife and cooked until the other side is golden brown and the sides are firm, this takes about 5–6 minutes. Place in a clean dry cloth on a wire rack and serve with butter or whipped cream and honey.

Dried fruit—1–2 oz. can also be added.

PASTRY

The most common pastry is the shortcrust pastry and its variations, but there are many other kinds. Here are a few:

Shortcrust pastry: Cheese pastry
                       Rich shortcrust or flan pastry
                       Potato pastry
Puff pastry: flaky pastry
              rough puff pastry
Suenut pastry
Wholemeal pastry
Noodle paste
Choux paste

Pastry is usually a mixture of flour, fat and liquid. It is kept as cool as possible before cooking and then cooked quickly in an oven. As a general rule the richer the pastry the hotter should be the oven.

SHORTCRUST PASTRY

    8 oz. 81 per cent extraction flour
    A good pinch of sea salt
    2 oz. butter
    2 oz. vegetable fat
    Cold water to mix

Sieve the flour and salt into a cold basin. The flour is sieved to aerate it, cool it and remove any lumps. This is most important when making pastry. Cut the fat into small pieces with a round-ended knife and add it to the flour, or it can be cut into pieces in the bowl. The fat should be cool, but not too hard or it will be difficult to rub in.

A mixture of butter and vegetable fats gives the best results; the butter gives flavour and the vegetable fat crispness and lightness. To rub in the fat use only the tips of the fingers and thumbs and lift the mixture out of the bowl as you do it. This helps to keep the mixture cool and full of air. When all the lumps of fat seem to have been rubbed in, give the bowl a good shake, any lumps of fat still not rubbed in will come to the surface. Continue until all the fat is rubbed in when the mixture will look like bread-crumbs. Allow the cold tap to run until the water is very cold. Make a well in the centre of the rubbed-in mixture and add a little (2 tablespoonfuls) water. The mixing can be done with two fingers or a round-ended knife, the knife is cooler but beginners usually manage far better with fingers since this way it is so much easier to judge the consistency. Work in circles, gradually drawing in the mixture until a stiff dough is formed; if necessary add more water. The dough should be stiff enough to leave the bowl clean and rub off the fingers quite easily. Turn the dough on to a lightly floured board and knead gently and lightly to remove any cracks. Form into the shape required, i.e. round, square, oval, etc. and roll out. When rolling out, flour the rolling-pin lightly rather than the pastry and work with light, quick strokes. The pastry can be flattened with the rolling-pin before starting to roll out. Start rolling the pastry near to you and work gradually away from yourself right across it. Turn the pastry round, keep the correct shape, and continue to roll until you have the right thickness. Do not be tempted to roll the pastry in any direction other than in a straight line away from yourself, otherwise it will appear uneven in thickness. This may not matter so much with short pastry but it would be disastrous if you are making flaky pastry.

The pastry can be left to stand for 30 minutes–1 hour in a cool place when mixed and/or when it is rolled and shaped. This allows

Pastry

the pastry to relax a little and lose some of the elasticity which has been formed during the mixing, kneading and rolling. The resulting pastry is 'shorter' and lighter.

In order to save time when cooking, the 'rubbed-in' mixture or the mixed pastry, can be stored in a sealed plastic bag in the refrigerator for a day or two. It is preferable to store the former.

Variations—quantities for 8 oz. of flour.

1. Cheese pastry. Add 4–5 oz. of grated dry cheese (Cheddar or Parmesan) to 8 oz. of flour. Add a little cayenne pepper, curry powder, mustard or paprika pepper if desired to bring out the flavour of the cheese. Mix with an egg-yolk and water.

2. Rich shortcrust. This is sometimes referred to as flan pastry, but it can also be used for pie coverings, etc. Use 5–6 oz. of fat and after rubbing this in carefully add 1–2 teaspoons of brown sugar. Mix with an egg-yolk and water. This makes a 'shorter' and lighter pastry.

3. Lining pastry. If you need to make pastry which will keep its shape better than the rich shortcrust, use the whole egg for mixing. This will help it to line the side of a flan-tin better, but the pastry tends to be harder.

4. Potato pastry. Sieve the flour and four level teaspoons of baking-powder together. When the fat is rubbed in, add 8 oz. of dry, sieved potato. Knead to a stiff dough, adding a little water if needed (which is unlikely). This is a very good crust for vegetable pies and savouries and it can be flavoured with grated cheese.

Puff pastries

With these rich pastries a different method of incorporating the fat must be used for when the proportion of fat is slightly more than half fat to flour it becomes very difficult to rub in, so the method known as 'rolling and folding' is used.

There are three kinds of richer pastry:

1. Rough puff.
2. Flaky pastry.
3. Puff pastry.

Pastry

ROUGH PUFF AND
FLAKY PASTRY

PUFF PASTRY

8 oz. 81 per cent extraction flour
Pinch sea salt
4–6 oz. unsalted butter or fat
Squeeze of lemon juice
Cold water to mix

8 oz. 81 per cent extraction flour
Pinch sea salt
8 oz. unsalted butter or fat
Squeeze of lemon juice
Cold water to mix

Each pastry requires a different method. Vegetable fat and margarine can be used successfully for rough puff and flaky pastries and even for puff pastry, but butter gives the best result and flavour. The butter should not contain salt or buttermilk, a good unsalted butter is best.

ROUGH PUFF PASTRY

This is the quickest method, hence it is more often used, but the flakes are not as even or fine as with the other methods and the pastry tends to be heavier.

Cut the fat into ½-inch cubes. It should be firm (not hard) and cool. Toss it in the sieved cold salted flour so that each cube is coated in the flour but still separate. Make a well in the centre and squeeze in about ½–1 teaspoon of lemon juice, add some ice-cold water and start to mix lightly so that the cubes are not broken down. The dough should be rather like a scone dough, light and moist yet not so wet that it is difficult to roll out. Turn out on to a floured board and shape into an oblong with one of the short sides nearest to you. Sprinkle this and a rolling-pin with flour and gently press the oblong into a strip with the rolling-pin. If a piece of fat breaks through the dough, sprinkle with flour and continue rolling. When the pastry has been gently pressed flat, roll into a strip three times as long as it is wide. Fold up one-third from the bottom, press the sides together and then fold the top down over this. Press around sides to trap air. Turn the folded square a half-turn to the left so that it looks like a book, the hinge to the left and the page ready to open on top. This is one of the easiest ways by which to know the pastry is correct for rolling

Pastry

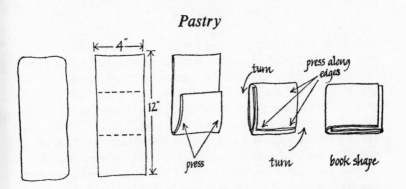

again. Roll the pastry to a strip once more and fold as before. Place on a floured plate and leave in the cool; mark the top with two finger-marks, indicating you have rolled it twice. The pastry is best left in the refrigerator, put in a plastic bag or greaseproof paper to prevent it from forming a skin.

The time it is left depends on whether or not time presses! Half an hour if it is short but 3–4 hours if it is needed for the next day. The pastry is left in the cool to 'relax' or lose some of the elasticity. Roll and fold twice again and leave to 'relax' once more.

As soon as the pastry is ready to handle, take great care to get the corners of the strip really square and the pastry very evenly rolled; this will ensure that the pastry rises evenly and has even flakes. When you finally need the pastry, roll and fold once more, then use. When the pastry is shaped it is good to leave it another ½ hour in the cool so that it is as cool as possible when placed in the oven. The pastry should be put into a really hot oven 450–475° F., M8–9, as one of the secrets of success with rich pastries is to have a sudden rise in temperature from cool to hot at the very beginning. After 5–10 minutes the heat can be reduced to 400–450° F., M6–7, so that the pastry cooks through without burning.

FLAKY PASTRY

Take the cold fat and work it on a cold plate with a round-ended knife until it is mixed well and it is smooth, form into a circle or square and divide this into four. Sieve the flour and salt and rub one part of the fat into it. Mix with cold water and a

269

Pastry

squeeze of lemon juice to a stiff dough (a little firmer than rough puff pastry) and roll out into a strip three times as long as wide. With the round-ended knife take small pieces of one-quarter of the fat and dot them evenly in rows over the top two-thirds of the pastry. Try to make the pieces of fat stand up a little, so that more air will be enclosed during the rolling and folding. Sprinkle the fat very lightly with flour and fold up the bottom one-third, press the sides and fold over the top carefully. Press around the sides. Repeat once more and then leave to 'relax'. Roll out again and use the last portion of fat. Roll and fold once more without any fat. Leave overnight or for 2–3 hours in a cool place. Use as required. Bake as for rough puff pastry.

PUFF PASTRY

Knead the butter in cold running water until it becomes easy to handle. Squeeze and pat it gently on a lightly floured cloth until it is quite dry. Form it into a flat oblong block. Mix the sieved flour and salt with ice-cold water and a squeeze of lemon juice; mix it quickly and lightly until it makes a paste which is firm enough to hold the butter but not so firm that it becomes elastic and difficult to roll. The nearer the consistency of the paste and butter, the easier it is to roll and fold them evenly together. Roll the paste out so that it forms an oblong with one of the longer sides towards you. Place the butter on one half and fold over the pastry to cover it.

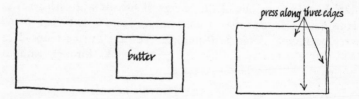

Press around the edges, roll out and then fold. Puff pastry must be left to 'relax' for at least half an hour between each 'roll and fold'. Longer periods are better if you can spare the time. It should be rolled and folded seven times before use and great care

Pastry

must be taken to keep the pastry even and the corners square, especially when bouchées or vol-au-vents are being made. After the last rolling and folding, leave overnight and use the following day. Start baking the pastry in an even hotter oven than for rough puff and flaky pastry, 475–500° F., M9–10, and reduce the heat after 5–10 minutes.

Rolling out scraps

When rolling out scraps of rich pastry do not knead them together as you would shortcrust pastry scraps, but lay them one on top of the other and roll them out. Roll and fold again to the desired shape. The scraps never rise as well as the first rolling.

Glaze for pastry

For savouries, glaze with a lightly beaten egg or egg and milk. For sweet dishes glaze with a lightly beaten egg-white and sprinkle with brown sugar over the surface.

SUENUT PASTRY

This is the vegetarian equivalent of suet pastry—used for baked, steamed or boiled sweet or savoury puddings.

> 8 oz. 81 per cent extraction flour or plain flour with
>   4 level teaspoons baking-powder
> Good pinch of salt
> 3–4 oz. grated suenut
> Cold water to mix

Sieve the flour and salt. Grate in the suenut (take it straight from the refrigerator if you have one). Mix the suenut and flour together, make a well in the centre. Mix with cold water to a consistency similar to a scone dough. Use as required.

For savoury puddings—herbs, grated cheese, seasonings, grated onions, a little oatmeal may be added.

For sweet puddings—a little brown sugar and spices may be added.

WHOLEMEAL PASTRY

Pastry made with 100 per cent wholemeal flour tends to be

Pastry

heavy. To overcome this, choose a finely ground wholemeal flour and use the rich shortcrust recipe, adding 1–2 level teaspoons of baking-powder for every 8 oz. of flour. Because it contains more bran it needs to be mixed a little moister or the pastry will be very dry when cooked, but as it must be rolled out, do not make it too wet. In our opinion the 100 per cent wholemeal flour is not very suitable for the rich flaky type of pastry.

NOODLES

Noodles and ravioli can be bought from shops but we feel that it is much better if freshly made. Not very much time is needed for this.

> 12 oz. 81 per cent extraction flour
> 1 level teaspoon sea salt
> 1–2 eggs and 1 egg-yolk
> 1 tablespoon oil
> A little tepid water.

Sieve the flour and salt. Make a well in the centre and add the eggs and yolk and the oil. Work the ingredients together, adding water as required. The dough should leave the fingers and bowl clean, when finished. Knead well on a lightly floured board for 5–10 minutes, until the pastry is smooth and pliable. Leave to stand for 15 minutes. Roll out very thinly—this is hard work at the beginning but becomes easier as progress is made. Use as required. (See the section on Savouries.)

CHOUX PASTE

> 2 oz. butter or margarine
> ¼ pint of water
> 4 oz. 81 per cent extraction flour
> 3–4 eggs

These quantities may be halved.

Sieve the flour on to a stiff piece of paper and stand in a warm place for an hour or two to warm and dry out a little. Bring the

Pastry

fat and water to the boil in a medium-size saucepan; remove from the heat and add all the flour. Beat well until the mixture comes away from the sides. There is usually enough heat in the water and the pan to cook the flour sufficiently without returning it to the heat. Press the dough lightly with a finger and if the finger comes away clean the dough is cooked enough. Allow the dough to cool a little then beat in the eggs one by one very thoroughly until the mixture is shiny and smooth. It should be soft enough to pipe but firm enough to hold into shape. Use as required.

To line a pudding basin

Form the pastry into a round and roll out into a circle large enough across, to cover the sides and bottom of the pudding basin. Cut out a quarter of the circle and place it on one side. Fit the other part into the pudding basin, using a little water to seal the cut edges together. Knead the small '¼' piece lightly and form into a round and roll out into a circle large enough to cover the top of the pudding basin. Brush around the edges of the lid with cold water, put the filling into the lined basin and put on the lid. Press the lid firmly around the edges. Cover with greased greaseproof paper or a pudding cloth and cook as required.

To line a flan-case

Flans can be baked using a flan-ring on a baking-sheet or in a sandwich-tin. They can also be made in a fire-proof shallow dish of glass or pottery. This has the advantage that the flan can be served in the dish, but remember to stand the dish on a baking-sheet when cooking the pastry otherwise there will not be enough bottom heat to cook the flan-case sufficiently.

To be very correct, savoury flans should be made in a plain flan-ring and sweet ones in a fluted ring. We must admit, though, that we use a heat-proof glass dish and flute the edge for general use. Lightly knead the pastry into a round and roll out evenly to a circle large enough to cover the bottom and sides of the flan-case completely. For a 6-inch flan-case you will need pastry made with 4 oz. of flour (4 oz. of pastry), for 8–9-inch flan-case 6 oz. of pastry. Place the rolling-pin near the edge of the pastry and fold the edge

Pastry

over the top of the pin, roll the pin over the pastry, taking the pastry with it. This is to avoid stretching the pastry; if it is stretched a poor shape results because of shrinkage during cooking. Gently unroll the pastry so that it covers the flan-case, lift the edges inside the flan-ring. Make sure the bottom is covered right into the corners and then work around the edges, lifting the pastry up so that it stands up against the side. Ease the pastry with the fingers so that there are no folds in the side and then flatten the edges of the pastry. If you have a clean cut edge to the ring then roll the rolling-pin across the flan-ring to cut off the scraps, or use a knife to trim evenly around the edge. Pinch the cut edge with the thumb and first finger to flute it or leave it plain. For a fluted flan-ring the pastry must be evenly pressed into the fluting, this is best accomplished with a small knob of pastry, the edge is left plain. Lightly prick the bottom of the flan-case and

 then bake it 'blind' if required. Cut some greaseproof as shown, grease one side and fit it greased side down carefully into the prepared flan-case. Place on the grease proof some beans, rice or macaroni which are kept specially, in a jar, for this purpose. Do not weigh down the

flan-case too much or the pastry will not rise—just use enough 'filling' to keep the sides in place. Bake the flan, remove from the oven when it is nearly cooked and remove the filling and also the flan-ring if used. Return to the oven for five minutes or until the flan-case is crisp and dry.

This baking 'blind' *has* to be done with a flan-ring. We find with our oven-glass flan-case that if the pastry is firmly fluted on the top edge and the bottom well pricked, that we can bake an empty case without using the paper filling.

To line small patty- or bun-tins

To line bun-tins, roll out the pastry and cut into rounds slightly larger than the tins, ease the pastry into each hollow so that the edges are even.

If you have small individual patty- or boat-shaped tins, lay your sheet of pastry over the tins (they should be standing an inch apart) and press the pastry into each tin with a knob of pastry. Roll the rolling-pin across to cut off all the pastry.

To cover a pie dish

Prepare the filling for the pie and damp the flat edge slightly. Roll out the pastry about 1–2 inches larger than the pie dish and roll the pastry on to the rolling-pin. Gently unroll the pin over the pie dish and ease the pastry to the shape of the filling so that the pastry is not stretched. Trim the edges, which should be ½–1 inch in width. Lift up the edges of the pie lid and place the trimmings, cut edge outwards, all the way around the underside of the pie lid. Damp the trimmings and press the lid back into position.

For shortcrust pastry squeeze the edges to make them even and then flute with the finger and thumb.

For rich pastries knock up the edges with the back of a knife; this helps the pastry to flake, then make fluting with the back of the knife and forefinger. Small fluting for sweet pies and larger ones for savoury pies.

Make a small hole in the centre for the steam to escape. A savoury pie can be decorated with leaves and roses in pastry. Glaze (if you like this finish).

To make a covered tart

Line the dish as for a flan-case, but do not trim the edges; leave enough pastry for the lid. Fill the tart and damp the edges of the pastry. Roll out the pastry for the lid and place it over the filling, press the edges firmly together and then trim with a knife. Finish as for a shortcrust pie. If a flaky type of pastry is used, then finish in the appropriate manner.

Covered tarts can also be made on fire-proof plates; the method is the same as above.

YEAST COOKERY

Cooking with yeast is one of the most exciting and wholesome ways of using flour; it seems to satisfy some creative urge within us rather as gardening does. The smell of yeast cookery is sheer

Yeast Cookery

delight—and the home-made produce is so much better than that which is sold over the counter. It is not surprising that there has been a tremendous revival of interest in bread-making and yeast cookery. A large part of the credit for this should be given to Doris Grant, who has ably and courageously written at length on this subject. If you have not already read her books, we recommend you to do so.

When we have been talking about the benefits of making our own bread, most of our friends have agreed but followed up with the remark, 'really one has not the time these days'. If you stay at home for half a day (and who does not do this once or twice a week), bread-making can be fitted in without much trouble. The actual time taken in yeast cookery is very small, say from 10–15 minutes for bread-making, but one has to be about during the rising and cooking. We also prefer rich yeast mixtures to the more conventional cakes. Dough cakes and Danish pastries, croissants and savarins to name only a few; these should be made in small quantities as they become fairly dry quickly, although a 'warm through' in the oven prior to serving works wonders if they are a few days' old. If you have not used yeast before it is better to forget all the rules you may have learnt for the pastry and cake-making. Nearly all the principles of yeast cookery are governed by the fact that yeast is composed of very simple plant-like cells which require three conditions to enable them to grow and raise the dough.

1. *Warmth* Everything used should be as near blood-heat (96–100° F.) as possible; if any ingredients or utensils are a little cooler this means the dough will take longer to rise, but the temperature must not rise much above blood-heat until the baking time arrives, or the yeast will be killed.

2. *Food* Yeast lives and grows on various types of sugars. There is a little sugar present in flour, and the yeast, with the aid of enzymes, breaks down the starch into sugars when it has started growing. The by-products of this are alcohol, which evaporates when cooking and carbon dioxide gas which raises the dough.

Yeast Cookery

3. *Moisture*. This is usually water, but can be eggs or milk.

There are two main types of yeast on the market—the compressed yeast which can be bought from most bakers (particularly if you let them know you want a regular supply) and dried yeast.

The compressed yeast is a grey, putty-looking substance, crumbly (in texture), which will keep in the cool for 2–3 days or 5–6 days if placed in an airtight container in the refrigerator. It has a very pleasant fresh aroma. It should not be brown around the edges, for this would indicate cells which have died for lack of food, and the yeast is stale. In compressed yeast the cells are alive but in a 'resting' state, and when creamed with an equal quantity of sugar they immediately liquify, start feeding on the sugar and multiply.

Dried yeast is in the 'spore' state, i.e. it has formed a wall around the cell and is hibernating until conditions become more favourable. Dried yeast is made by some of the flour-milling companies and directions for use are given on the packet or tin.

There are two main points to remember—$\frac{1}{2}$ oz. of DRIED yeast = 1 oz. of FRESH yeast.

The yeast must be given time to 'wake up' before using it; this takes about 10–15 minutes.

The amount of yeast needed to raise flour does not rise in direct proportion to the amount of flour to be used:

For $\frac{1}{2}$ lb. of flour $\frac{1}{2}$ oz. of fresh yeast is required.

For 1–3 lb. of flour 1 oz. of fresh yeast is required.

For 3–7 lb. of flour $1\frac{1}{2}$ oz. of fresh yeast.

The second point is that the dough must be left in a warm place to rise: we found the airing cupboard an ideal place, until we lagged the tank in the interests of economy! If you have an open fire or a radiator giving off a good heat, stand the covered bowl near but remember to rotate the bowl to ensure even warmth. Some modern cookers have a drawer for heating plates and dishes; this can be used, but please read the cooker instructions as it may become too hot if the oven is in use for very long. If all else fails, stand the bowl over the hot plate and keep a saucepan of water gently steaming underneath it or turn the oven down very low and keep the door open. The bowl must never feel more than comfortably warm to the hand.

Yeast Cookery

BREAD-MAKING

Basic recipe:

> 3 lb. 100 per cent or 81 per cent extraction flour
> 1 teaspoon sea salt
> 1 oz. compressed yeast or ½ oz. of dried yeast
> 1 teaspoon dark brown sugar
> Warm water 96–100° F. approximately 1½–2 pints

Method for 81 per cent extraction or white flour

This is the method generally described in cookery books, but it is not the most suitable for 100 per cent wholemeal flour. We shall describe this method subsequently.

Place the flour and salt into a large warm bowl and put in a warm place until the flour is slightly warm. About 30–45 minutes. If dried yeast is used start liquidizing it according to the instructions, grease and flour the bread-tins (three 1-lb. tins or two larger) and have ready the lukewarm water. If fresh yeast is used grease the tins, etc. first, as fresh yeast liquidizes almost immediately. Place the yeast in a teacup and add the sugar, cream them together with the back of the spoon until they are liquid. Add a little lukewarm water and mix well. Make a well in the middle of the warmed flour, pour in the yeast and two-thirds of the water. With clean hands mix well together, adding more water until a firm, elastic dough is formed which sticks slightly to the bowl and to the hands. The dough is mixed by a process called kneading; the left hand holds the side of the bowl and turns it around slowly whilst the right hand takes an outside portion of the dough and firmly pushed it into the middle and continues doing this all around the outside edge. (Vice versa for left-handed people.)

Alternatively, the dough can be kneaded on a floured board in which case both hands can be used, taking hold of the farthest edge, push it down into the middle, turning the dough a little each time you lift the farthest edge up, and repeat this until the dough is kneaded enough. The kneading mixes the yeast through the dough and takes about 5–10 minutes, by which time the dough becomes less sticky and leaves the board or bowl clean and dry.

Yeast Cookery

Flour the bowl lightly and put in the dough, put a cross on the top to prevent the skin which forms from stopping the dough rising, flour the top and cover with a clean damp tea-towel or similar cloth. Then cover the bowl with a small blanket, put in a warm place until the dough has doubled in size (this is the reason for using a large bowl). This takes about one hour, but have a look earlier in case it rises quickly. When the dough is put to rise, place the greased tins in a warm place too.

When the dough has risen, knead again very gently with a floured hand to distribute the 'gas' evenly, this is known as 'knocking back'. The dough is then formed into whatever shapes are desired, on the floured board (if possible in a warm kitchen). For three loaf-tins, divide the dough evenly into three and knead each piece very lightly into an oval shape. Place the loaves smooth side uppermost in the tins and press the dough gently into the corners. The dough should half fill the tins or a little more. Turn on the oven 425° F., M7. Put the tins in a warm place, cover and leave until the dough rises to the top then place in the hot oven immediately. The fierce heat kills the yeast and sets the dough so that the 'gas' is caught and held. After 10–15 minutes lower the heat to 375° F., M5 and cook for another 30–40 minutes. When they are cooked the loaves will have shrunk away a little from the sides of the tin and will look brown. If a loaf is turned on to a wire cooling-rack and the bottom knocked with the knuckles it should sound hollow and not damp and heavy. Turn the loaves out on to the cooling-rack and leave them until cold before storing in a bread-bin.

Method for wholemeal flour

If it were not for Doris Grant we should still be making our own bread by the above method, but her method is much simpler, quicker and gives a better flavour to wholemeal bread. If you do not mind an uneven texture it is also very good for 81 per cent extraction flour. The recipe is the same.

The flour is warmed, the tins greased, the yeast creamed and the water and yeast mixed in as before. A little water is added to the yeast, this is then poured into a well made in the warm flour and

279

Yeast Cookery

1½ pints of warm water (approximately) added. It is difficult to give the exact amount of liquid because the moisture content of the flour varies and wholemeal flour contains bran (the outside husk of the wheat grain) which absorbs more water. The dough should be wetter than the previous method and slightly slippery, but it should leave the hands and bowl fairly cleanly and 'bind' so that it can be shaped on a floured board to fit the bread-tins. The dough is mixed well for 5 minutes so that the yeast is evenly distributed, as the dough is wetter this is easier and quicker to do. In this method the dough is placed straight into the bread-tins and allowed to rise therein—there is no knocking back.

Shape the dough so that the tins are half full. Put in a warm place and cover. Heat the oven to 400° F., M6. Allow the bread to rise in a warm place to just below the top of the tin, 30–45 minutes, then place in the oven just above the centre to bake. Bake for 40–45 minutes until loaf is brown and sounds hollow when tapped. Cool and store.

Variations

1. Grease some bun-tins or a baking-tin. Take a small piece of dough and shape it into rounds, about ½–1 oz. each for a guide, and place in the bun-tins or on the baking-sheet. Put in a warm place, cover and allow to double in size. Bake at the top of the oven for 15–20 minutes, 400° F., M6. The rolls on the baking-sheet can be flattened with the palm of the hand so that there will

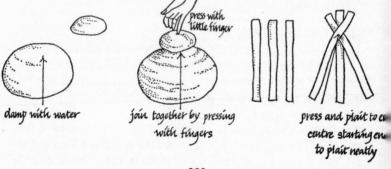

damp with water

press with little finger

join together by pressing with fingers

press and plait to c centre starting en to plait neatly

be more outside crust. If you wish to make something more elaborate for a dinner-party then either shape as small cottage loaves or plaits:

2. Rub 1–4 oz. of butter, margarine or suenut into the flour before mixing with the yeast and water.

3. Use milk and water or all milk for mixing bread.

4. Add 1–4 oz. of crushed whole wheat to the mixture and sprinkle a little on the top of the loaf when it is baking—this is best with the 100 per cent wholemeal bread.

5. Add 2–4 oz. of currants, sultanas, raisins, dates or walnuts to each 1 lb. of flour.

6. For savoury bread: add a little finely chopped garlic to the amount of dough for one loaf and when the dough is ready to go into the oven put a mixture of lightly fried onions and grated cheese on the top. Cover with a greased paper (so that the onions and cheese do not burn) and cook in the usual way. If this is baked flattened in a cake-tin it makes very good bread for picnics, if cut into wedges. It is almost a Pizza, but not quite!

7. For sweet bread: dissolve 1–2 tablespoons of honey or black treacle per 1 lb. of flour in a little hot water and then make the mixture lukewarm by adding sufficient cold water. Use, with more liquid, for mixing with the dough.

8. Add 1–2 teaspoons of cinnamon or mixed spice per lb. of flour—this makes a pleasant tea bread with walnuts and fruit.

9. Malt bread can be made in the same way as sweet bread, using extract of malt instead of honey or treacle. Extract of malt can be bought from a chemist, generally in 1-lb. jars. Fruit and malt loaves are very good.

These various breads can be made in small quantities using 1 lb. of flour and ½ an oz. of fresh yeast or some can be made by taking a piece of ordinary bread dough and kneading in the extra ingredients.

Here is a good recipe for Cheese bread which we sometimes make to serve with salads instead of potatoes:

1 oz. yeast

1 oz. brown sugar

$\frac{1}{4}$ pint tepid water—scant measure, that is, just a little less

1 level teaspoon sea salt

$\frac{1}{2}$ level teaspoon paprika or very small pinch of cayenne pepper

About 1 lb. 81 per cent extraction or 100 per cent flour

6 oz. finely grated cheese

1 egg

Grease and flour two loaf-tins and warm them. Turn on the oven to 375–400° F., M5–6. Cream the yeast with the sugar and add the water. Sieve the flour with the salt and pepper. Beat the egg and cheese together in a large bowl and add the yeast, sugar and water. Mix together, then add enough seasoned flour to make a kneadable dough—knead for 2–3 minutes and form into two loaves, place in the tins which should be half full. Put in a warm place to rise nearly to the top of the tin and bake in the oven for about 45 minutes. Cool and store.

If 100 per cent flour is used make the mixture a little moister so that it is mixed rather than kneaded. If there is any seasoned flour left, use this for thickening savoury sauces, soups or for coating foods to be fried—if the mixture is too moist when all the flour is in add flour until the consistency is correct.

Two interesting variations are: (1) add 1–2 tablespoons of freshly chopped herbs (more if you like), mint is very pleasing, or a mixture of mint, parsley, chives, thyme and a very little sage; (2) chop cheese into small cubes, so that when the bread is baked there are small pockets of melted cheese. This is nicer served hot, for people with good digestions!

DOUGH CAKES

These are really bread with a large proportion of fat, sugar and eggs. They are often mixed with milk.

The easiest way to make them is to reserve from the bread dough sufficient for one loaf (1 lb. of flour), and into this mix:

Yeast Cookery

2–4 oz. creamed or softened butter
2–4 oz. brown sugar
1–2 eggs
4–12 oz. mixed dried fruits
Grated orange or lemon rind, or 1–2 teaspoons of any
    spice or mixture of spices
1–2 oz. chopped or grated nuts if liked

After this mixture has been well beaten together either by hand or with a wooden spoon, half fill two smaller greased, floured and warmed loaf-tins; or the mixture can be baked in a cake-tin prepared as above. Cover and leave in a warm place until the mixture is nearly at the top of the tin then bake in a fairly hot oven 375–400° F., M5–6 until brown and cooked. Cool on a rack and store in a bread-tin. Do not store with cake or it will dry the cakes.

Dough thus enriched takes longer to rise—yeast works quicker with plain flour, but as long as the dough is kept warm it will rise, though it may take 2–3 hours. We have made very rich dough mixtures on a winter evening and left them, covered, on the kitchen table overnight. The only heating was a solid fuel boiler, which took the chill out of the air, but no more and in the morning the dough had risen to the top of the bowl. We planned it so that there would not be too much mess if it overflowed! This recipe can be made with 81 per cent extraction or 100 per cent wholemeal flour. Here is a recipe for Dough Cake if you are starting from 'scratch'.

Make 2 lb. of dough (made with 2 lb. of flour) and put it to rise in a bowl. Grease, flour and warm the tins, turn on the oven to 375° F., M5. When the dough has risen to double its size mix in the following warm ingredients:

$\frac{1}{2}$–$\frac{3}{4}$ lb. butter or margarine
$\frac{1}{2}$–1 lb. brown sugar
4–6 eggs
1–2 lb. mixed dried fruits
1–2 tablespoons spices as preferred } optional 1–2 oz. of
Grated zest of 2 oranges and 2 lemons } any one or two
4–8 oz. chopped nuts

Yeast Cookery

When thoroughly mixed pour into the tins until they are just a little more than half full. Cover and put in a warm place to rise until the dough is nearly at the top. Bake until brown and the mixture has shrunk a little from the sides, or, if in doubt test the centre with a warm thin metal skewer or knitting-needle which should come out clean. The length of time depends on the size of the tin and the depth of the mixture but it will take longer than bread as the cooking is slower.

Dough cakes can be glazed in the following manner:

1. Brush with a little well-beaten, but frothy, egg.
2. Brush with a little well-beaten, but frothy, egg and milk.
3. Warm 1–2 tablespoons of brown sugar in ¼ pint of milk and/or water. When melted, bring to the boil and boil for 3–5 minutes or until slightly syrupy. Brush over the dough cakes when cooked and return them to the oven for 1–2 minutes to dry off.
4. Use the above glaze and sprinkle with chopped or coarsely grated nuts.

Here are two more recipes:

SAFFRON CAKE

This is a Cornish cake which, if new to you, is well worth trying. Saffron is the dried stamens of a variety of crocus, which is much used in the East and the Near East. The Persians and Spaniards still use it to colour and flavour savoury rice. It is very expensive and is obtainable from the chemists by the drachm. Saffron has a deep orange colour and it looks like a mass of fine, tiny pieces of rough cotton. The flavour and colour are extracted by infusing it in hot liquid and leaving the mixture to stand overnight. When needed for use the mixture is strained when the saffron threads should be nearly colourless.

When purchasing ask to have it weighed into these quantities: ¼–½ drachm (15–30 'grains').

> Warm milk or milk and water
> 1 lb. 81 per cent extraction flour (100 per cent wholemeal can be used but the saffron flavour is not so pronounced)

2 oz. brown sugar

Pinch sea salt

4 oz. white vegetable fat

4 oz. butter or margarine

½ oz. fresh yeast

2 oz. currants

2 oz. sultanas

Finely grated zest of orange and lemon (the traditional cake has 2 oz. of candied peel)

The evening prior to making the cake, take ½ a gill of milk and bring it almost to boiling-point, add the saffron, cover and leave to stand overnight. Sieve the warmed flour, add the sugar and salt, rub in the fat and put the bowl in a warm place. Cream the yeast with 1 teaspoonful of brown sugar and add 2–3 tablespoons of warm milk. Leave in a warm place until the yeast has risen. Make a well in the centre of the flour and pour in the yeast mixture, sprinkle with flour until covered and leave in a warm place until the yeast breaks through the crust. (This process is known as 'setting the sponge' and it is done to encourage the yeast to grow quickly—it can be omitted, but the dough will take longer to rise.) Mix to a soft dough with the strained saffron liquid which has been warmed to blood-heat, add more lukewarm liquid if required. Cover and allow to rise in a warm place until double in size. Meanwhile grease and flour a cake-tin and keep warm. Heat the oven to 400–425° F., M6–7. Clean and warm the fruit, grate the orange and lemon. Add the rest of the ingredients, beat well and then put into the cake-tin which should be just half full. Allow the dough to rise to the top and bake it quickly for 5–10 minutes, then reduce the heat to 375° F., M5. It should cook in 40–50 minutes. Cool and store, or use immediately.

Some of the mixture may be used for buns, which should be shaped. You will need to add more flour. These can be cooked in 15–20 minutes, depending on size.

This mixture also makes a very good cake without the saffron if preferred.

Yeast Cookery

SALLY LUNNS

These are a plain spongy dough cake.

> ¾ lb. 81 per cent extraction flour
> Good pinch of sea salt
> ½ oz. fresh yeast
> 1 teaspoon brown sugar
> 1½ gills (7–8 oz. lukewarm milk)
> 1 egg
> 1 oz. melted butter or margarine
> Glaze

Sieve the flour and salt and warm. Grease and flour 2–3 small cake-tins or a baking-sheet and warm these. Cream the yeast and sugar, add the warm milk and well-beaten egg; pour all this into the middle of the warmed flour and knead together lightly, to make a soft light dough. Divide into two or three pieces and shape into rounds; either place in the cake-tins (when they should be half full) or place on the baking-sheet and allow room for some spreading. Turn on the oven to 425° F., M7. Put in a warm place until they are nearly double in size, then bake for 15–20 minutes. Glaze the top.

These are usually served cut through and buttered. The top is then replaced and the Sally Lunns cut into quarters or wedges.

Yorkshire tea cakes are Sally Lunns with the addition of 1–2 oz. of brown sugar and 1–2 oz. of cleaned currants.

SAVARIN

This is a very light rich spongy yeast cake—it is an excellent accompaniment to fruit and cream. It is easy to make but if you have not made yeast mixture before, first gain experience with something plainer.

> ½ lb. 81 per cent extraction flour
> Good pinch of sea salt
> ½ oz. fresh yeast creamed with a little brown sugar
> ¼ pint lukewarm milk
> 4–5 oz. butter or margarine
> 4 eggs or 3 eggs and 2 yolks

Yeast Cookery

Warm the sieved flour and salt and make a well in the middle, cream the yeast and dissolve this in the warm milk, pour the yeast mixture into the well and sprinkle the surface with some of the warm flour. Leave in a warm place for 20–30 minutes; the yeast will then have frothed up and broken through the flour. Melt the butter and cool until just warm, add this with the eggs to the flour and yeast. Beat the mixture very well with the fingers.

Grease a ring mould and add the mixture which should half fill the mould. Cover and put to rise in a warm place until the dough reaches the top of the mould. Heat the oven to 375° F., M5. Bake the savarin for about three-quarters of an hour. Turn out on to a wire rack and allow to cool.

A few ways of using savarin

1. Make a rum syrup and soak the savarin with it—serve with whipped cream. If you make individual savarins and serve as above these are 'babas au rhum'.

2. Make a fresh fruit salad with plenty of juice. Put the savarin in a deep serving-dish and fill it with fruit salad and the juice. Allow to stand for a while then serve with whipped cream or ice cream.

3. Coat the savarin with whipped cream, sprinkle the outside with browned chopped nuts and fill the centre with freshly pre-pared choice fruit, e.g. strawberries, peaches, raspberries, melon and ginger and pineapple. The savarin can be lightly or moder-ately soaked with fruit liqueur or fruit juice beforehand if desired.

Further variety can be obtained by sprinkling the mould with shredded almonds and a few currants before pouring in the savarin dough. The dough can also be flavoured with finely grated orange or lemon zest.

Dough buns

These can be made, like dough cakes, from the bread dough, with various additions and extra flour kneaded in if the mixture is too wet. The mixture is formed into small rounds, allowed to rise, and either baked in bun-tins or on a baking-sheet, the latter is the usual. They take less time (usually 15–25 minutes) to bake, as they are smaller.

Yeast Cookery

Here are some special recipes for buns:

HOT CROSS BUNS

1 lb. 81 per cent extraction flour
Pinch sea salt
1 level teaspoon cinnamon
1 level teaspoon mixed spice
A good ½ oz. fresh yeast
3 oz. brown sugar
4 oz. butter or margarine
4 oz. cleaned dried fruit (usually currants or sultanas)
2 eggs
A little warm milk

Sieve the flour with the salt and spices into a bowl and warm. When the flour is warmed, cream the yeast with a teaspoon of brown sugar. Rub the fat into the flour; add the rest of the sugar and fruit. Make a well in the centre; add the well-beaten eggs, the creamed yeast and enough milk to make a soft dough. Beat with the hand until the dough is not too sticky; this takes about 2–3 minutes of hard beating. Cover and put to rise in a warm place until it is double its size. Grease and flour a baking-sheet. Turn on the oven to 400–425° F., M6–7. Turn the dough on to a well-floured board and after kneading lightly, cut the dough into 12 or 16 pieces of even size. Shape into buns and place on the baking-sheet. Mark each with a cross, with a floured knife. Allow the buns to rise again until nearly double the size and then bake in the oven for 15–25 minutes. Glaze and cool on a rack.

The crosses may be marked with thin strips of shortcrust pastry which are removed after baking but before glazing.

Without the spice and the cross these are ordinary 'penny' or currant buns.

CHELSEA BUNS

1 lb. 81 per cent extraction flour
Good pinch of sea salt
1 level teaspoon mixed spice (may be omitted)

2 oz. butter or margarine

2 oz. brown sugar

3 eggs

Little lukewarm milk

A good ½ oz. fresh yeast creamed with a teaspoon of brown sugar

For the filling:

1-2 oz. butter or vegetable fat

1-2 oz. brown sugar

3-4 oz. cleaned currants

Glaze

Make the dough as for hot cross buns (there is no fruit to be added); when it has risen, knead lightly to an oblong on a floured board, and roll out a ¼ or ½ inch in thickness, keeping the oblong shape. Place the longest side across the floured pastry-board and spread on the softened or melted fat. Sprinkle over with the fruit and sugar and roll it up like a Swiss roll. Cut into slices with a sharp knife, about 1½ inches across and place these pieces, cut side down, in a greased gingerbread-tin or similar tin with 1-2-inch straight sides. Leave a little room between each bun. Turn on the oven to 400-425° F., M6-7. Allow the buns to rise (in this case it is extension really as they rise mostly sideways!) and when they are nearly double in size and almost touching each other, bake in the oven for 15-25 minutes or until cooked, then turn out of the tin on to a wire rack. Do not separate the buns until they are cool.

SWEDISH RING

Filling:

2 oz. butter

2 oz. brown sugar or 1 oz. honey, 1 oz. sugar

4 oz. finely grated almonds or finely grated nuts

Make the dough as for Chelsea buns, without the spice. The quantity of fats may be increased. Continue with the method until the oblong piece of dough is ready to be spread. To make the filling, cream the butter and sugar (or sugar and honey) and stir in the nuts. Spread this over the dough right up to the edges, leaving a strip at the long end to dampen so that when it is rolled up this makes a good join. Place the roll on a warmed, greased and floured baking-sheet with the join underneath. Heat the oven to 375° F., M5. Turn the ends to join together so that a circle is formed. With the kitchen scissors make cuts from the outside edge nearly through to the centre edge. Allow 1–1½ inches between each cut. Take each cut piece and twist it so that the Swiss roll effect shows:

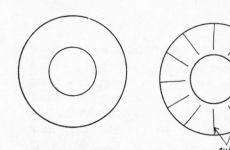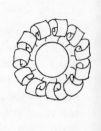

Put in a warm place to rise and bake for about 40–50 minutes in the oven. Glaze and sprinkle with chopped nuts; if you have used almonds in the filling, sprinkle with chopped almonds also with other varieties of fillings. Return to the oven until the nuts are brown. Lift off the tin with two palette-knives and cool on a wire rack.

DOUGHNUTS

These are fried buns and we make them for special occasions.

> ½ lb. 81 per cent extraction flour
> Pinch sea salt
> 2 oz. butter or margarine
> 1 oz. brown sugar
> ½ oz. fresh yeast creamed with a teaspoon of brown sugar
> About ⅛ pint warm milk
> 1 egg or 2 yolks

Yeast Cookery

Warm the sieved flour and salt. Rub in the fat and add the sugar. Add the beaten egg and warmed milk to the creamed yeast. Mix all this well with flour and allow to rise in a warm place until double in size. Shape into 12 balls and leave to rise again until nearly double in size. Have ready the deep-fat pan, without the basket, heated to the point when a croûton of bread dropped in the fat just sizzles gently, but not so that the fat is hazing. Add the doughnuts and fry until browned on one side, then turn to cook the other side. The doughnuts must cook for 8–10 minutes at least, otherwise the centre will not be cooked. If they appear to be browning too quickly, remove the pan from the heat, and allow the doughnuts to continue cooking in the heat of the oil alone. It is better to achieve the correct temperature at the beginning in order to avoid this. Toss the doughnuts in caster sugar or caster sugar and cinnamon. The doughnuts can be filled with apple or fruit purée and have whipped cream piped over them. They should then be served immediately.

If they are to be eaten as pastries, allow them to cool on a rack.

There are two yeast recipes in which the dough is treated rather like flaky pastry and we find them both useful. One is a rich but plain roll called 'croissants' and the other recipe is for Danish pastries, which are quite popular now.

CROISSANTS

> 1 lb. 81 per cent extraction flour
> Good pinch of sea salt
> Good ½ oz. fresh yeast creamed with a teaspoon of brown
>   sugar
> Approximately ½ pint milk or water
> 3–4 oz. butter or margarine to roll into the dough

Sieve the warmed flour and salt; add the creamed yeast and sufficient liquid to make a soft bread dough. Knead and leave to rise in a warm place until double in size. Cream the butter and divide into three or four portions. Knead the dough on a floured board and roll out into a strip as for flaky pastry. Continue thus until all the butter is used up. Either shape immediately or leave over-

291

night in the refrigerator. To shape: roll out until $\frac{1}{4}$-inch thick and cut into 5-inch squares. Cut the squares into triangles, turn the triangles over and lightly brush with water. Roll up from the base of the triangle and seal the tip on to the roll. Pull the ends around to form a crescent, horseshoe shape. Heat the oven to 425–450° F., M7–8. Allow to rise for 15–20 minutes and bake in the oven for 10–15 minutes until they are brown and sound hollow when tapped. Glaze with egg and milk, dry the glaze in the oven for a minute or two, then cool on a wire rack.

These are lovely when fresh but after a day or two they should be warmed through before being eaten. They are very pleasant served with soup or salads.

DANISH PASTRY

2 lb. 81 per cent extraction flour

1 level teaspoon sea salt

5 oz. brown sugar

A good 1 oz. fresh yeast creamed with a teaspoon of brown sugar

Approximately 1 pint of warm milk

12 oz.–1 lb. butter.

Fillings:

2 oz. butter

2–3 oz. brown sugar

4 oz. grated nuts

Stiff apple purée flavoured with lemon and 1–2 egg-yolks beaten in

mincemeat made with suenut

2 oz. butter

4 oz. finely grated almonds

2 oz. cleaned currants

Glaze and flaked or chopped nuts

Sieve the warmed flour and salt into a warm bowl and add the sugar. Cream the yeast and add a little of the warmed milk. Pour into the flour and mix with the warmed milk to make a firm dough (like bread). Knead until smooth and roll out thinly on a floured board into a square. Dot evenly with small knobs of butter over the whole area and sprinkle lightly with flour. Fold as shown in the diagrams:

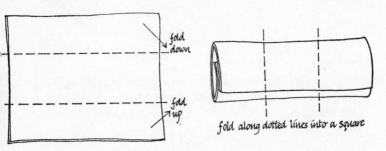

fold along dotted lines into a square

Roll out again into a square and repeat this operation 3–4 times. If the pastry should become so elastic that it is difficult to roll, leave it in a cool place, or covered (in a plastic bag or with grease-proof) in the refrigerator for an hour or two, then continue the rolling and folding until it is completed. Leave the pastry in a cool place or in the refrigerator for at least an hour, overnight is better. If you do leave it in the refrigerator overnight, remember to bring it out of the refrigerator an hour before you want to use it, otherwise it may be too stiff to handle or roll. Roll the dough out to about a ¼-inch thick.

The pastries can be shaped in the following ways:

1. Cut the dough into two equal pieces. Spread one piece with a filling and cover with the other piece as with a sandwich. Cut into strips 1–1½ inches in width and twist the strips. Cut these into 3–4-inch lengths. These measurements are only a guide and can be smaller or larger as desired.

2. Prepare the pastry and filling as above but cut into narrow strips ¾-inch wide. Plait the strips in threes. These are usually cut after baking.

Yeast Cookery

3. Cut the dough into squares of 4–5 inches and spread each square with filling. Take each corner to the centre and press firmly down.

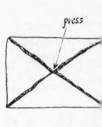

press

4. Cut into squares as above and spread with filling. Make cuts from the corners with a knife almost to the centre and then fold the outside corners to the centre—rather like a child's windmill toy.

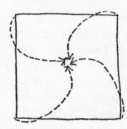

Place the shaped pastries on a warmed, greased, floured baking-sheet and put in a warm place to allow them to rise. Heat the oven to 400–450° F., M6–7. Bake the pastries for 25–35 minutes. Glaze and sprinkle with nuts. Return to the oven to dry the glaze and to lightly brown the nuts.

11

Endings

FRESH FRUIT

After a cooked meal, or after any meal in summer, one of the nicest conclusions is some choice fruit served 'au naturel', provided always that the meal has not started with melon or grapefruit. The fruit may either be piled artistically in a wooden bowl or small basket from which people can help themselves, or it may be arranged on separate plates. A few green leaves picked from the garden make a good background for say, a perfect peach, a small bunch of grapes with a pear and so on. If the meal is a formal affair, finger-bowls should be provided.

THE CHEESE BOARD

Many people like to leave the table with a savoury rather than a sweet taste in their mouths; in which case some of the many interesting cheeses from abroad, our own farmhouses cheeses (if you can get them!) or home-made cottage and cream cheeses, may be served. They are served with light crisp biscuits and ice-cold butter, shaped in rolls or pats.

There should always be a choice of cheese when possible. A cream cheese (home-made petit suisse, etc.), a hard cheese (Gruyère, Cheddar) and one which is flavoured or interesting (Camembert, blue-veined cheeses, smoked cheeses, raisin de tomeau, etc.). The cheese should be as fresh as possible; any dry parts should be removed before being served.

Endings

FRUIT SWEETS, HOT OR COLD

First, some general methods used for cooking and preparing fruit sweets, then an alphabetical list of fruits with ideas for each fruit on serving.

MUESLI

This is a complete meal in itself and makes a wonderful breakfast. For each person use:

> 1 level tablespoon oats soaked in 3 tablespoons of water for 12 hours
> 1–2 eating apples
> Juice of ½ a lemon
> 2 tablespoons cream
> Brown sugar or honey to taste
> 1 tablespoon finely grated nuts

Mix the oats, lemon juice, sugar or honey together. Wash the apples and remove any bruises and the stalk. Grate the whole apple into the oat mixture and stir together immediately to prevent discoloration of the apple. Stir in the cream. Pour the mixture into a bowl and top with grated nuts.

DRIED FRUITS

Wash well and scald with boiling water. Cover again with boiling water and leave in a warm place for 12–24 hours, add more liquid if required, grape or apple juice may be added. For tender fruit this is generally enough, but if the fruit is still hard, cook very gently, either on top of the stove, or better still in the oven, until the fruit is tender. Dried fruit does not usually need sweetening, but a little honey or brown sugar may be added if desired. A strip of lemon peel or a piece of stick cinnamon and a piece of bay leaf may be added to the syrup to give flavour. Remove these flavouring agents before serving!

FRUIT SALADS

These are a mixture of two or more fresh fruits, prepared and

Endings

cut into small to medium-size pieces. They can be prepared immediately before serving, in which case the fruit should be tossed to mix it together. For convenience the fruit salad is usually prepared about ½–1 hour before it is eaten. To prevent pears, apples, bananas and other fruit becoming discoloured, use either a syrup, or an acid fruit juice (lemon, orange, pineapple, etc.). When the fruits are cut into pieces toss them in the juice or syrup and cover; put in the refrigerator, or a cool place until needed.

Syrups or Juices for Mixing

1. Fresh orange juice with a little honey or brown sugar. Eau-de-Cologne mint or crushed scented geranium leaves may be added if desired.

2. Lemon or pineapple juice as above. Grapefruit juice may be used but be sure the flavour does not clash with that of the other ingredients.

3. Boil apple and grape juice with a little honey for 2–3 minutes. Cool and slice the fruit into it. A strip of lemon peel, piece of cinnamon stick or a piece of bay leaf all give a good flavour to the syrup.

4. Fruit syrup left from the stewed fruits may be used: if it is rather strong and sweet, dilute with apple or lemon juice.

Be careful not to use too much syrup or juice because it is rather like the salad dressings; it should do its job of preventing discoloration, flavouring and sweetening, but the fruit should not be swimming in it. When estimating the volume of juice likely to be required, bear in mind that a certain amount comes from the cut fruits themselves after they have been standing a while.

Fruit salad should be composed with an eye to colour and flavour. Here are some of our favourite combinations:
1. Green and black grapes with bananas and oranges.
2. Melon, peach and raspberries or strawberries.
3. Apricot, apple (with red skins if possible) and pear.
4. Apricot and green grapes.
5. Pineapple and cherries.
6. Grapefruit, orange, apple and date.

Endings

7. A little of all the fresh fruits available.

A mixture of dried fruits is usually called a compôte and is usually very gently cooked with the flavourings mentioned in the Dried Fruit section. If some of the dried fruit take longer to cook than the other fruits, e.g. pears, cook them alone first of all then add the other fruits. A handful of soaked raisins or sultanas may be added or a little strained cold tea or a little sherry.

Fruit salads may be served on their own or accompanied by nut cream, fresh cream, cup custard, ice cream or crisp home-made biscuits.

Fruit Fools

Made by sieving fresh or stewed fruit, mixed with an equal quantity of whipped cream. Up to half the cream may be replaced with a cold egg custard or a sweet white sauce.

Sprinkle the fool with toasted oatmeal or toasted grated nuts or grated, raw sugar chocolate and serve with crisp finger biscuits.

Fruit Ice Cream

Fruit fools are very good when frozen in the ice-cube trays of the refrigerator. Everything should be cold. Use the ice from the ice-cube trays which come from the refrigerator to cool the mixture and turn the refrigerator to the highest mark to freeze the mixture. When the mixture is half set turn into a cold bowl and beat well—return the trays to the refrigerator. This may be repeated several times during freezing as it helps to prevent ice crystals forming. The addition of a beaten egg-white or two also helps to make the mixture smooth, light and to prevent the formation of ice crystals.

Fruit ice lollies can be made by freezing pure fruit juices in special moulds. The moulds can be bought from kitchen supply shops. These particular lollies are much better for children than the artificially flavoured and coloured lollies generally offered for sale.

Fruit Mousse or Soufflés

A mousse is made by adding 1–2 beaten egg-whites to the fruit fool mixture; 1 level teaspoon of agar-agar per ½ pint of mixture

Endings

will set it if desired for a mould. The agar-agar should be completely dissolved in a little boiling water and added to the mixture.

A cold fruit soufflé is made by adding egg-yolks to a fruit and cream mixture, then the stiffly beaten egg-whites and lastly agar-agar, as above, to set. Orange and lemon soufflés are very good.

The soufflés can be served in individual dishes or glasses or they can be made in a soufflé case.

A band of greaseproof paper is tied around the soufflé dish and the mixture poured into a level higher than the top of the case. When set the paper is gently eased away and the edge of the soufflé decorated with chopped nuts or grated chocolate.

STEWING FRUIT

We have found that if cooked fruit is desired it is far better to cook ripe dessert fruit in a very small amount of fruit juice, so that it almost steams. In this way very little sugar or honey is needed to sweeten.

If the fruit is to be puréed then wash it, cut out any bruised portions and remove any stalks or stones. Heat a little grape juice or fruit juice in the saucepan and add the fruit cut into pieces; simmer very gently until tender and then put through the 'moulin légumes', or a sieve.

The fruit can also be cooked in the oven.

Juicy fruits such as apricots and plums make so much juice that a little may have to be poured off before sieving or the purée will be too thin. This spare juice can be used for fruit soups, fruit cocktails or stewing more fruit.

If the fruit is to be served as 'stewed fruit', cut it into larger pieces of even size. Take care the fruit does not break up during the cooking process (it must be cooked very slowly), then leave to cool in the syrup or juice.

Serve cold with a little juice or warm gently before serving. The whole stewed fruit can be used in flans, etc.

Stewed fruits or fruit purée may be served with cream, nut creams, ice cream, egg custard (baked, or as a sauce) or a sweet white sauce. The cream and white sauce can be flavoured in a complementary fashion, e.g. if stewed apples, flavour the sauce with cinnamon.

EVE'S PUDDING

Half cook some fruit in a little syrup in a large covered fire-proof dish in the oven—the fruit should come half-way up the dish. While the fruit is cooking make a Victoria sponge mixture, an average amount is 4 oz. of fat, sugar, egg and flour. Flavour it as desired and place the mixture on the top of the fruit. Return to the oven at 375° F., M5 and cook until the cake is cooked and the fruit tender.

This has many variations. An excellent one results from re-placing half the flour with very finely grated nuts. Our favourite is apricots topped with chocolate-almond sponge.

UPSIDE DOWN CAKE

This is another variety of Eve's pudding. The fruit may be any one of the various types, e.g. sliced pineapple, apricots, plums, etc. Place the fruit in a mixture of 2 oz. of melted butter and 2 oz. of brown sugar.

Top this with a cake mixture and bake in an oven at 375° F., M5 until cooked. Turn out and serve either hot or cold.

Fruit with pastry

FRUIT PIES

These may be made with either short or flaky-type pastry. The method of using the pastry is given in the Pastry section.

FRUIT FLANS

These can be made from flan pastry, flaky pastry or a sponge mixture. The pastry or sponge flan is often baked beforehand. The flan is filled with pieces of cooked or raw cold fruit. It is then glazed with a little fruit syrup or a little jellied juice (can be poured on) and allowed to set. Finally decorate with whipped cream. The artistic cook has plenty of scope here as anyone who has seen French fruit pastries will realize. These are very good made in individual dishes as tartlets or pastry boats.

Endings

STEAMED FRUIT PUDDINGS

The pudding basin is lined thinly with a sweet suenut crust and filled with sliced, raw fruit sprinkled with a little sugar. The lid is put on and the pudding boiled in the usual manner. Serve hot with a sweet white sauce or egg custard sauce.

FRUIT FRITTERS
(see also page 243)

Choose the fruits to make into fritters; apples and bananas are usually chosen but pineapple may also be used. Marinade the fruits and dip in a batter. Deep-fat fry the coated fruits and serve either hot or cold. A sauce may accompany the fritters, preferably a clear sauce—syrup, lemon, orange, etc.

FRUIT GATEAUX

These are made from the sponge mixture. Bake two sponges and split each cake in two, sandwich with mashed fruit (adding a little cream if liked, but fruit should predominate). Cover the sides and top with whipped cream, garnish with the fruit, unless it is a fruit that discolours, e.g. banana.

The gateaux should be put together just before the meal is served so that the fruit juices soak into the sponge before they are served. If the cake has to be kept for a time before being served, place it in the refrigerator. Liqueurs, sherry, brandy, etc. may be used with the fruit if desired. Any of the following fruits may be used:

apricots	bananas	blackcurrants
goldenberries	cherries	gooseberries
loganberries	nectarine	peach
pineapple	raspberries	strawberries

Apple purée, usually flavoured with orange or lemon or mixed with another fruit such as blackberries.

Any of the tangerine family.

Greengage or dessert plums.

Fruit gateaux are also attractive when made in individual cases.

301

Endings

The gateaux may also be made using a flaky type of pastry or a rich, sweet shortcrust pastry with milled nuts in place of the sponge.

Ice cream may also be used in place of some or all of the cream.

FRUIT CONDÉS

This is a creamy mixture of brown rice cooked in a double saucepan with milk; 2–3 oz. of rice per 1 pint of milk and sweetened with either brown sugar, honey or dried fruit. When cold the mixture is mixed with whipped cream and flavoured if preferred. It is served with stewed or fresh fruit. The consistency of the rice can be altered by adding more milk if a soft mixture is required. If a rice mould is required, dissolve some agar-agar in a little boiling water and add this to the warm mixture. Pour into a mould and leave to set. Turn out carefully and serve with the fruit.

APPLE

COMPLEMENTARY FLAVOURS
spices, cloves, nutmeg, orange and lemon, chocolate,
quince, apricot, blackberries

Apples are to fruit what the potato is to vegetables, in that they can be served and will mix well with practically any flavouring or other fruits or make a good fruit dish entirely on their own. They can be served as a dessert or fruit baked, fried, puréed, and made into flans or puddings.

DANISH APPLE PUDDING

Fry some wholemeal breadcrumbs in butter until they are crisp or brown, stir in a little brown sugar and put in layers with apple purée in a serving-dish. Chill and top with cream and grated chocolate.

APRICOTS

COMPLEMENTARY FLAVOURS
almonds, chocolate

A wonderful fruit, as anybody who has read about the Hunza

valley will readily appreciate—very good eaten raw at the end of a meal, and excellent in fruit salads, too.

Apricot tartlets and 'fools' are good.

BANANA

COMPLEMENTARY FLAVOURS
ginger, walnuts, chocolate, lemon or orange

These should be ripe before use. They are a starchy fruit. They make excellent fritters or baked in the oven with butter, brown sugar and orange juice. Bananas discolour when exposed to air, so chop into syrup or juice.

BLACKBERRIES

COMPLEMENTARY FLAVOURS
apple, quince, rose geranium leaves

The wild ripe ones are sweeter than the cultivated type. They are good served with cream and brown sugar. If the pips are disliked, sieve them and stir the juice with whipped cream. When cooked they are almost always used to flavour cooked apple. The mixture may be used for puddings and pies.

BLACKCURRANT

COMPLEMENTARY FLAVOURS
cinnamon, lemon

Another very valuable fruit which is sour unless picked when fully ripe. The ripe berries can be washed and eaten as dessert. Otherwise they may be cooked and made into flans and tartlets or creams.

RED AND WHITE CURRANTS

Can be treated in the same way as blackcurrants (but beware of the large pips!). Red currants are often mixed with raspberries and strawberries.

Endings

CHERRIES

If really ripe, serve raw as dessert. They lose some of their flavour when cooked. Morello cherries require sugar whether raw or cooked. They are very good served with a sweetened cream cheese or they can be made into pies and flans. (If there is time Morellos are better stoned beforehand.)

DAMSONS

Small black plums with a sharp decided taste. If they are to be eaten as dessert they should be washed and one of them tasted to see if sweet enough. Use also for pies, puddings and stewing, or puréed with cream.

DATES

Have an excellent natural sweetness which assists with rhubarb, plum and other acid fruits requiring added sweetness. They are also good in dried fruit salads or fresh fruit salads and combine well with grapefruit. They can be chopped and added to salads, or soaked and cooked a little.

FIGS

Are one of the best dessert fruits; there are two kinds, green and purple. They should be grown under glass in this country, although they can be grown outside, but usually with poor results. They are imported during the summer and autumn. Cut up and mixed with whipped cream, they make a good sweet. Dried figs may be eaten with dessert fruit or soaked and stewed.

GOLDENBERRIES

These are the fruits of the Cape gooseberry which, when ripened, are canned in South Africa. They make an unusual addition to a fruit salad.

Endings

GOOSEBERRIES

Mostly marketed when they are, alas, under-ripe. They should be picked, even for cooking, when soft and ready to eat. There are some excellent dessert varieties (notably 'Golden Drops')— worth all the pricks inseparable from picking! Gooseberries make a good 'fool', also pies and tartlets. They are good when served with browned oatmeal or flapjack finger biscuits.

GRAPES

Come from different countries and they vary considerably; there are green and black and a reddish brown—Californian. Also the small sweet seedless grapes from Cyprus which are very good in fruit salads.

Grapes should be washed well, so that the skins can be left on, but whether or not the pips are removed is a matter of taste.

GRAPEFRUIT

COMPLEMENTARY FLAVOURS
mint, dates, orange and lemon

This fruit has a clean decided but pleasant and refreshing flavour of its own and needs to be used sparingly with other fruits. It makes a good breakfast fruit or beginning to a meal.

GREENGAGE

When this fruit is ripe it is considered to be one of the best dessert plums, but it can also be cooked and used as other plums.

LEMON

COMPLEMENTARY FLAVOURS
melon, apples, plums, rhubarb and mint

This is a fruit without which we would almost be lost. It has so many uses both in sweet and savoury cookery. Its cousin, the lime, is imported during the summer/autumn and can be used in much the same way for flavouring, but it has a stronger flavour so it should be used carefully.

LOGANBERRY

A cross between a blackberry and a raspberry.

LYCHEES

Available either tinned or fresh. The white flesh is sweet and almost scented.

MELON

There are many varieties of melon, but charentais are said to be the best. The honeydew melon is popular. It has a white skin with a green flesh or a dark green skin. The water melon is very refreshing, without much taste, but has a lovely dark pink colour in the centre in which are lots of pips. The cantaloup is segmented with a greenish crusty skin and an orange, sweet-tasting flesh. All melons should be eaten when ripe. To test for ripeness press with the thumb top and bottom. A slight yielding indicates that the melon is ready to eat. It should not resist pressure entirely, nor should the thumb sink in easily.

NECTARINES

A smaller type of peach, tasting a little of apricots. Better eaten raw.

ORANGES

COMPLEMENTARY FLAVOURS
cranberries, apples, plums and rhubarb

They are a good source of vitamin C and available all the year round. Generally eaten raw as a dessert fruit or squeezed for fruit juice or in fruit salads. They are also good for making an 'upside down' cake.

Endings

PEACHES

A good dessert fruit; they need careful washing if it is desired to eat the skin. The two chief varieties are the white-fleshed and the orange-fleshed.

If prices are low on account of a glut, it becomes economic to cook them very carefully and serve with ice cream (peach melba) or in flans. Either makes an excellent sweet.

PEARS

COMPLEMENTARY FLAVOURS
chocolate, coffee, ginger or spices, quince and walnuts

Imports enable this fruit to be available all the year round. They are best eaten raw, but they can be stewed carefully. They also make an excellent sweet with chocolate or coffee ice cream.

PINEAPPLE

Available most of the year and best served alone but it will mix well with other fruits (better than does grapefruit) and is valuable in fruit salad as it prevents bananas, etc. from discolouring. Pineapple may be served in rings, or diced. The flesh may be prepared and the hollowed-out skin filled with pineapple and various fruits.

PLUMS

We find it is best to use sweet, eating fruit for all purposes. They are pleasant served raw but they can also be used in puddings and flans.

They are imported from South Africa during the winter months.

POMEGRANATES

These have a sweet, but not strong, flavour. Cut in half across the centre and eat the red pulp with the seeds. If the seeds are hard, scoop out the flesh and sieve, mix with whipped cream, return to the skin and chill.

Endings

PRUNES

COMPLEMENTARY FLAVOURS
orange, lemon, cinnamon and soft cheeses

These are a special variety of plums which have been dried. If you can, try to obtain the sun-dried, non-sulphured fruit—which, though not so attractive, is far more wholesome. Like all dried fruits, prunes must be washed and soaked. They can be stewed gently if necessary. Stoned and stuffed with a creamy cottage cheese mixture, they are very nice.

QUINCE

This is a pear-shaped rather furry-skinned fruit which has to be cooked. It is used to flavour cooked apples or pears. It also combines well with orange and lemons.

RASPBERRIES

COMPLEMENTARY FLAVOURS
peaches, strawberries, cinnamon

One of the loveliest flavoured summer fruits and, like strawberries, their season is all too short. As their flavour is so wonderful, they should whenever possible, be used fresh. The only time we cook them is when they are being bottled. They can be used for flans, ices, as a dessert for gateaux in muesli, etc.

RHUBARB

COMPLEMENTARY FLAVOURS
lemon and orange

This is a stem, not really a fruit. When forced early in the year, the flavour is delicate, unlike the garden rhubarb available later. Rhubarb is usually cooked, but it is very acid in flavour (it all contains oxalic acid; this is one of the reasons it should not be served too frequently) and so needs more sweetening than most fruits. Dates and honey are good sweeteners and combine well with rhubarb which can be stewed or made into 'fools' or puddings.

STRAWBERRIES

These are a valuable source of vitamin C and when ripe one of the finest fruits. They are picked unripe for market and thus they travel better. The best, therefore, are home grown. They may be served for dessert with cream or with ice cream, gateaux, flans, etc.

TANGERINES

Are small oranges with a sweet flavour. The zest has a quite distinctive flavour and is good for flavouring cakes, puddings and sauces. The best of the small orange family is the 'Clementine' which is imported just before Christmas. Mandarins have not quite the same delicate flavour and tangerines usually have many pips! Any of them can be used instead of oranges if preferred.

ENDINGS TO A MEAL WHICH DO NOT CONTAIN FRUIT

BAKED EGG CUSTARDS

2–4 eggs (or 2 eggs and 1–4 yolks)
1 pint of milk (some of this can be cream)
Vanilla or nutmeg flavouring

Heat the milk until it is hot but NOT boiling (or the eggs will curdle), pour on to the eggs previously beaten up with the sweetening. Strain the warm mixture into a greased fire-proof dish and grate nutmeg over the top. Stand the fire-proof dish in a tin containing warm water (this makes a 'water jacket' so that the custard will not cook too quickly) and bake in a slow oven 300–325° F., M2–3 until the custard is set in the centre. If you are not sure whether the custard is cooked, pierce the centre with a sharp-pointed knife; if any liquid wells through the cut the custard is not cooked.

Endings

Variations

1. Bread and butter pudding: add 2–3 thin slices of wholemeal bread and butter and some washed sultanas and raisins. Leave the pudding to stand a little while before baking.

2. Flavour the milk with vanilla pods, lemon or orange zest, instant coffee or grated raw sugar chocolate.

3. Instead of bread and butter, use fruit or plain cake to make a richer pudding.

4. Make some caramel by boiling brown sugar and water until the mixture becomes toffee-like. Place this in the bottom of the fire-proof dish and pour the custard on to it.

This custard mixture can be made in a double saucepan (it is better to use only yolks of egg if you have plenty) for a custard sauce, or it can be steamed and turned out (in which case more than 2 eggs per pint of liquid must be used).

Ice Cream

Nearly all ice cream nowadays is mass-produced commercially. It is over-sweetened with refined sugar, artificially flavoured and coloured and very often not vegetarian, although the animal by-product is very, very small.

Home-made ice cream can be a revelation, particularly so if you are fortunate enough to own a bucket freezer. These are wooden buckets which hold a metal canister in the middle of a freezing mixture (ice and salt); across the top of the bucket is a handle which turns two paddles inside the canister. This produces a perfect ice cream as it is mixed whilst freezing, so that a creamy consistency is obtained and no ice crystals form. Most of us have to use the ice-cube trays in the refrigerator; the best method here is to make sure: (1) that the recipe is suitable, (2) that the refrigerator is at its coldest, also have the mixture as cold as possible before placing it in the refrigerator; (3) that the mixture is turned out into an ice-cold bowl and beaten well with a fork several times during the freezing process.

The mixture should have an egg custard sauce or sweet white sauce base and an equal quantity of lightly whipped cream folded in just before freezing. If the sweet white sauce is used, a stiffly

Endings

beaten egg-white added to each ½ pint of mixture helps to prevent the formation of ice crystals. The richer the mixture the softer and creamier it will freeze.

Flavourings

1. *Vanilla* use a piece of vanilla stick in the milk when making the sauce. Remove the stick when the sauce is cold, or sooner, if less flavouring is desired. Wipe the vanilla stick and store in an airtight container for further use.

2. *Chocolate* use cocoa or melted raw sugar chocolate to flavour the sauce to your own taste.

3. *Coffee* use strong black coffee to flavour.

4. *Caramel* cook 2–3 oz. of brown sugar slowly in a little butter for 3–5 minutes until it smells of toffee. Dissolve this in the warm unsweetened egg custard or white sauce and continue as above.

5. *Nuts* add brown and chopped nuts to the mixture before freezing.

6. *Dried fruits* add a little chopped dried fruit and freeze. This is particularly good with fruits and nuts mixed.

7. *Peppermint* add a few drops of oil of peppermint.

Sweetenings

Use dark brown sugar, which must be added after the sauce has thickened as it will curdle unthickened milk; or a mixture of dark brown sugar and honey. The sauce should be just pleasantly sweet.

To serve

Serve in cold glasses, either alone or accompanied by fruit, home-made biscuits or a sauce.

It should be mentioned here that ice cream should be eaten slowly; each mouthful being completely melted in the mouth before it is swallowed. The reasons for this are: (1) so that the stomach lining is not chilled; (2) so that it can be tasted. As the ice cream melts the flavour becomes apparent because the taste-buds in the tongue do not function when cold. It is because people eat ice cream too quickly that the manufacturers make it over-sweet and over-flavoured!

CAKE PUDDINGS

These are made from the creamed cake mixtures; they can be either baked or steamed (usually the latter means placing the basin on a stand in the saucepan with boiling water reaching nearly to the top of the basin). They can be flavoured in the same way as the cakes and should be served with a complementary sauce or with cooked fruit.

YOGHOURT

Milk is really a food for calves; ideally, if milk is to be taken by humans, it should be eaten as a food, and as an intestinal bactericide, in the form of soured fresh (not pasteurized!) milk, e.g. yoghourt, etc.

There seem to be many ways of making soured milk preparations and everyone swears by his or her own particular recipe and is convinced that, produced in this way, it is a more health-giving product! For those of you who have no particular recipe, let us introduce you to the following which we have found very satisfactory.

Yoghourt: this needs conditions rather similar to those for bread-making, i.e. a warm even temperature just slightly above blood-heat. In this case too, the airing cupboard is an ideal place, but failing this, a contraption rather like a hay-box, placed in a warm room makes good yoghourt.

Yoghourt should be firm but creamy, so that it will cut with a spoon. When made with fresh bacillus it will have a fairly sweet flavour. (Sour yoghourt is made from old bacillus; if you start with a sour yoghourt it will take a little while, a week or so, for the yoghourt to sweeten.) If lumpiness occurs it is generally through using too much 'starter'.

The yoghourt is greatly improved by the addition of a little cream. It can also be made entirely from thin cream.

312

Endings

1 pint fresh unpasteurized milk

½ teaspoon yoghourt from a previous batch or from a bought yoghourt

Method. Prepare the containers; we use four wide-necked jars which contain about ¼ of a pint each. These should be quite clean and warm. Find a biscuit-tin, cardboard or wooden box which will hold the four jars with plenty of room to spare. Line the sides and bottom with hay or other insulator (glass fibre, cellulose wadding, etc.); make four 'nests' into which the jars will fit. The heat-retaining material should be packed tightly around the jars and a layer of the packing prepared to place over the top of the jars.

The box and jars should be warm before the yoghourt is poured into the jars. We find filling the jars with boiling water an hour or so before using them, then placing them in the container helps to retain the required heat. This has the advantage of keeping the jars warm for receiving the yoghourt.

To make the yoghourt. Bring the milk to the boil and boil for 1 minute. Allow to cool until comfortably warm, 100–108° F., take out a little of the warm milk (about ½ a teacupful) and mix this with the 'starter'. Divide the remainder of the milk evenly between the four jars and pour an equal volume of 'starter' into each jar. Place them in the box and cover with a clean folded cloth. Replace the lid with the padding and leave undisturbed for about 8 hours or overnight. Remove the lid and packing and allow the yoghourt to cool in the 'nests' for an hour or so, or it can be eaten immediately.

In really hot weather, a rare circumstance (!), yoghourt can be converted into a most refreshing drink.

Whisk it well until bubbles form on the surface and add half its volume of iced water with chopped or whole mint leaves to taste. Whisk all well together and serve in tall glasses. Many people feel that as the milk for yoghourt is boiled and the mixture is not aerated, it does not make the best sour-milk preparation.

A very pleasant but not solid, sour milk can be obtained by standing a covered bowl of fresh milk in a warm place and whisking well every hour or so. If you already have some sour milk, cream or yoghourt, a teaspoon of either makes a good 'starter' to this method. If the place is warm enough and a 'starter' is used, the milk should be ready for use in 24 hours. Yoghourt prepared in this way is probably better.

Sweet Soufflés

These are made in exactly the same way as savoury soufflés (see Egg and Cheese); they are usually baked though they may be steamed.

For each $\frac{1}{4}$ pint of milk allow $\frac{1}{2}$–1 oz. of brown sugar or brown sugar and honey.

Flavourings

1. *Chocolate* melt $1\frac{1}{2}$ oz. of raw sugar chocolate in the milk before making the thick sauce (panada); more sweetening is not usually required.

2. *Coffee* use half milk and coffee for making the panada.

3. *Lemon or orange* flavour the panada with finely shredded zest and use the juice to make an accompanying sauce.

4. *Pineapple* add 1–2 oz. of chopped and well-drained pineapple to the mixture. Serve with pineapple juice and mint sauce.

Sweet omelettes

These are generally soufflé omelettes (see Egg section) which are filled with a warm fruit purée or stewed fruit. A little sugar may be added to the eggs in place of the seasoning.

Suggestions:

Omelette flavoured with lemon rind and filled with apple purée.

Plain omelette filled with stewed cherries.

Omelette flavoured with orange rind and filled with warm mashed banana.

Milk Puddings

Use brown rice, whole barley flakes or a similar unrefined

314

Endings

cereal. Allow 1½–2 oz. of cereal or more, to 1 pint of milk; this depends entirely on whether milk puddings are preferred thick or thin. Honey, brown sugar or dried fruit may be used to sweeten the pudding.

There are two methods of cooking:

1. Baking in the oven. Wash the rice and place with the sweetener in the bottom of a greased fire-proof dish. Pour on the milk and grate some nutmeg on the top. A few pieces of butter may be added if desired. Place in a slow oven 300–325° F., M2–3, and bake for 2–3 hours or until the rice is cooked. If the rice is left to soak in the milk for ½–1 hour before cooking, this lessens the cooking time. During the first 1–1½ hours, stir the pudding 2–3 times.

2. Steaming in a double saucepan. Place the rice, milk and sweetener in a double saucepan (warming the milk beforehand shortens the cooking time) and cook. Stir occasionally until the rice is cooked and the mixture is creamy. This takes about 2 hours.

Flavourings and variations

1. Add beaten eggs or whipped cream towards the end of the cooking time to enrich the pudding. If these are added sooner the mixture will tend to curdle and for this reason eggs and whipped cream are usually added to the *steamed* rice puddings.

2. Serve hot or cold with stewed or puréed fruits. The rice may be packed into a lightly oiled ring-mould and then turned out. The rice mixture must be stiff and a little agar-agar dissolved in the mixture may help it to keep its shape.

3. Grated nutmeg is traditionally used with baked puddings but other spices such as cinnamon or powdered clove make a pleasant change.

4. Add 1–2 oz. of raw sugar chocolate to the warm milk and dissolve it gradually before adding it to the rice. The few shreds of butter on top will not be required as there is quite enough natural fat in the chocolate.

CARRAGEEN AND GELAZONE

Carrageen is also known as Irish moss. It is a seaweed which grows along the sea-shores and is gathered, washed and dried. Like all sea products it is particularly valuable for the trace minerals it contains. Carrageen may be obtained in its natural state or as a dry powder known as 'Gelazone' from health food stores. In each case the manufacturers supply recipes and methods for use.

It is generally used in place of rennet to make a solid milk sweet, e.g. blancmange, but it can also be used to thicken ice creams, fruit mousses and even soups. If carrageen or 'Gelazone' is used to make a blancmange-type of sweet, this is improved by beating with a fork or balloon whisk when cold and set. Whipped cream or stiffly beaten egg-whites may be added if desired.

Flavourings for 'Irish moss' blancmanges

1. Vanilla. Place a piece of vanilla pod in the cold milk and remove when the sweet is cooked.
2. Sweeten the pudding with brown sugar, black treacle or honey after the milk and Irish moss have been boiled together.
3. Chocolate. Add 1–2 oz. raw sugar chocolate to the milk.
4. Coffee. Use $\frac{1}{2}$ milk and $\frac{1}{2}$ black coffee to make the pudding.
5. Pare the zest from oranges or lemons or a mixture of both and place in the cold milk; remove after cooking.
6. Stir in some grated brown nuts and chopped dried fruits when beating the blancmange after it is cold.
7. Beat in some chopped ginger when the sweet is cold.

Serve the sweet in glasses topped with whipped cream, garnish with fruits or grated nuts.

AGAR-AGAR

This is also of seaweed origin. It has the same advantages and is used in the same simple way as Irish moss. It can be bought from health food stores, in packets in which directions for use are printed. Agar-agar is especially used for making fruit juice jellies. It makes a clearer jelly, and can be dissolved in a little hot or boiling liquid, then added to the fruit juices. As these are not heated they retain their nutritional and purifying value.

Endings

A good fruit jelly should be cloudy, and it is interesting to note that even the orthodox makers are now making a cloudy jelly and claiming it has a 'full fruit flavour' and that it is made from 'real fruit juice'. This makes us wonder what they used before! Many attractive jellies can be made by setting fruit in them—in fact jellied fruit salad is a summertime favourite, especially with children.

Index

318

Index

Index

321

Index

Index

watercress, 92; sauce, 217
whipping process, 46
white: currants, 303; sauce, 224; wine sauce, 217
wholemeal: flour, 21, 22, 246; stuffed rolls, 211
working space, 16

yeast, 23
yeast cookery, 275; bread, 278–82; Chelsea buns, 288; crois-sants, 291; Danish pastry, 292; dough cakes, 282; dough-nuts, 290; saffron cake, 284; Sally Lunns, 286; savarins, 286; Swedish ring, 289
yoghourt, 312
Yorkshire: pudding, 240; tea cakes, 286

zest, 47
zucchini, 168